I0813447

SWEET LECHERY

REVIEWS, ESSAYS & PROFILES

sweet LECHERY

REVIEWS, ESSAYS & PROFILES

THE PORCUPINE'S QUILL

2014

Library and Archives Canada Cataloguing in Publication

Heer, Jeet, author
Sweet lechery : reviews, essays, & profiles / Jeet Heer.

ISBN: 978-0-88984-378-3 (pbk)

1. Literature and society. I. Title.

PN51.H43 2014 C814'.6 C2014-906256-7

1 2 3 4 • 16 15 14

Published by The Porcupine's Quill, 68 Main Street, PO Box 160, Erin, Ontario NOB 1TO. http://porcupinesquill.ca

Readied for the press by Carmine Starnino.

Represented in Canada by Canadian Manda.
Trade orders are available from University of Toronto Press.

We acknowledge the support of the Ontario Arts Council and the Canada Council for the Arts for our publishing program. The financial support of the Government of Canada through the Canada Book Fund and the Government of Ontario through the Ontario Media Development Corporation is also gratefully acknowledged.

Canada Council for the Arts Conseil des Arts du Canada

To the memory of Mohan Singh Heer

CONTENTS

Introduction 9

CULTURE AT LARGE

Philip Roth as Ghost Writer 15
John Maynard Keynes and the Sexuality of Economics 17
Forging Van Gogh 23
Oedipus Updike 27
Updike: Portrait of the Artist as a Young Fan 32
Guy Davenport, Cartoonist 40
Guy Davenport, RIP 49
Gail Singer's *Watching Movies* 54
Elizabeth Kolbert's *Sixth Extinction* 57
Jesus and Recycling 60

CANADIAN CULTURE

Alice Munro as a Literary Entrepreneur 65
Clark Blaise's *Southern Stories* 69
Leon Rooke's *Last Shot* 72
John Metcalf's Literary Wars 76
Atwood's *MaddAddam* Trilogy 82
Shoah Business: Yann Martel's Holocaust Novel 86
Lisa Moore's *Caught* 93
Annabel Lyon's *Sweet Girl* 96
Zsuzsi Gartner, The Anti-Munro 99
Cannibalistic CanLit 102
Vegetable Sex 107
Smut and Literature 110
The Messiah Is the Message: McLuhan's Religion 117
Hugh Kenner, RIP 124

RIGHT-WING POLITICS

The Philosopher: Leo Strauss 133
Addendum to Strauss: The Classics and the Closet 139
Hilton Kramer: A Dissenting Obituary 141
Joseph Epstein: Nostalgia for Empire and the Closet 146
Tory Stories: Neo-Con Novels 154
Rob Ford and Rexdale 161

SCIENCE FICTION

Robert Heinlein: Abandoning the Future 167
Philip K. Dick versus the Literary Critics 181
Stanislaw Lem's Communication Failure 189

COMICS

Little Nemo 194
Françoise Mouly at *The New Yorker* 213
Ben Katchor's Urban Poetry 220
Chris Ware's *Building Stories* 223
Seth's Imaginary Library 227

INTRODUCTION

Books are work, essays are play. I realize that this is a generalization even the most incompetent hunter could shoot full of holes. The world, after all, is filled with playful books (everything from *Tristram Shandy* to *Pale Fire*) as well as sombrely serious essays (written by the likes of Samuel Johnson and Susan Sontag). Yet if my adage fails as a universal law, it rings true as a personal credo. I don't see essays as having the deadly finality of scholarly monographs, where hefty authority can smother the subject. Rather, the job of an essay is to survey a topic and return with a quick and entertaining report.

The essays in this book deal with a wide array of topics. They include the economics of John Maynard Keynes (and its relationship to his sexuality), the political philosophy of Leo Strauss, the cartooning of John Updike, the entrepreneurial acumen of Alice Munro, and Philip K. Dick's attempt to become an FBI informant.

What unites the essays is my approach: to open up new lines of attack, to paint familiar scenes from hitherto unused perspectives, to find connective links previously unseen. In sum, to keep the spirit of intellectual play alive during the course of an investigation.

My title is taken from the first story in Guy Davenport's debut story collection *Tatlin!*: 'We must shatter the glass wall that Socrates and Aristotle placed between nature and the sweet lechery of an inquiring mind.' Davenport, that playful polymath, is a presiding spirit in these essays. To claim him as a model is presumptuous, yet his ebullience and free-spiritedness can perhaps be emulated.

To be playful is not the same as being frivolous, nor does playfulness deny the reality of suffering. While these essays take up weighty political and social issues—the legacies of war and oppression, the damage done by bigotry, our responsibility to the natural world—my hope is freshness of voice might allow me to confront realities we otherwise shut our ears to.

To give order to this fugitive round-up, I've gathered together the essays in some rough and ready categories: culture at large, Canadian culture, right-wing politics, science fiction and comics. These groupings are approximate. Many essays could easily overstep the boundaries I've set. Margaret Atwood shows up as a Canadian writer but the essay on her could be moved to the section on science fiction. Hugh Kenner is also carded as a Canadian, although he wouldn't be out of place with conservative intellectuals like Leo Strauss and Hilton Kramer. Guy Davenport and John Updike are placed with the general cultural essays although both could fit snugly into the company of cartoonists.

One of the most significant events of my life was a border crossing. As a child I immigrated to Canada with my family, from India. Perhaps that's why I'm fascinated by intellectual borders, the closely guarded zones where competing values are staked out. I keep returning to the contested territory where politics and culture meet. For me, culture always has political implications just as politics always has a cultural resonance.

To be completely apolitical and only live for culture is to risk becoming a dandy. To disdain culture and care only for politics is to become mired in soulless earnestness. Balancing the claims of culture and politics is a difficult task but a necessary one, in order to make culture properly grounded in social awareness and politics rightly respectful of aesthetic values.

As a social democrat living in a conservative era, I've tried to understand the ideas of those I most disagree with. In exploring right-wing thinkers such as Leo Strauss, Hugh Kenner and Hilton Kramer, I've had to deal with another type of balance: the equipoise and empathy required to understand an alien worldview while criticizing it.

Another kind of empathy is summoned in the essays on Canadian culture, which are very much the notes of a non-native son. I'm a proud citizen of this country but not a nationalist. While Canada is my home, having the dual consciousness of an immigrant makes me look at many of the standard national myths with the bemused eyes of an outsider.

One border that has thankfully collapsed in recent years is the divide between high and low culture. A playful attitude is not amiss when writing about science fiction or comics. The essays on comics selected here are only a sample of my writing about this form. A fuller gathering might be in order in the future, but for now I wanted to register the importance comics have for me as a vital contemporary art form.

These essays were written for many venues over the course of more than a decade. In giving them a more permanent form, I've made gentle revisions here and there.

It's the job of the readers to find whatever coherence they can in these various pieces. One clue might be helpful: the title *Sweet Lechery* has an erotic overtone and one recurring concern in these sundry essays is the role of sex as the spark for creativity.

The display type, initials and dingbats used throughout this book are based on calligraphic letterforms developed by the Canadian cartoonist Seth.

CULTURE AT LARGE

PHILIP ROTH AS GHOST WRITER

It's virtually impossible to write good fiction if you don't believe in ghosts. Philip Roth is a stone-cold materialist, a scoffer at superstition and magical thinking. Yet Roth has been known to visit the grave of his one-time lover Janet Hobhouse and hold conversations with her. 'I tell her things I don't tell anyone,' explained Roth to fellow novelist Richard G. Stern. 'I ask her advice. And get it.'

Roth's graveside conversations should not be dismissed as evidence of loopiness but rather as a natural outgrowth of his vocation. The fiction writer's brain is wired towards the hypothetical mode, to thinking of people in 'what if' situations. The dead, for the novelist, are never fully vanished, but only awaiting reanimation by being pondered and turned into stories. On some primordial level, the very act of narration is a form of conjuring, a summoning forth of unseen presences.

Just because you don't believe in God doesn't mean you can't believe in ghosts. Philip Roth is an unwavering atheist and perhaps the most sternly this-worldly of all the great writers. Not only does Roth not believe in God, his novels are so steadfastly focused on the physical, bodily dimensions of human life (sex and disease) as to be completely free of the sort of residual religiosity that writers like John Updike or Cynthia Ozick possess, with their muted echoes of liturgical music and flickering spiritual hopes. Roth's whole attitude towards religion is curtly summed up by this description of the anonymous hero of the 2006 novel *Everyman*: 'Religion was a lie that he had recognized early in life, and he found all religions offensive, considered their superstitious folderol meaningless, childish, couldn't stand the complete unadultness—the baby talk and the righteousness and the sheep, the avid believers. No hocus-pocus about death and God or obsolete fantasies of heaven for him. There was only our bodies, born to live and die on terms decided by the bodies that had lived and died before us.'

Yet Roth is also, unexpectedly but markedly, a ghost-haunted man. His enduring strength as a writer is his memory, his almost extrasensory ability to conjure up the sights and sounds of his youth, the unexpectedly rich soil of mid-20th century Newark which has season after season yielded literary fruit for Roth. 'You must not forget anything,' is Roth's credo. With his potent power of recall, Roth can't let the past go. For him the dead—an ever-growing list and litany which now includes his parents, his first wife and many friends—don't stay buried. They live on inside his mind, always ready to be summoned and interrogated.

Has anyone ever looked at Philip Roth as a writer of ghost stories, an heir to Edgar Allan Poe and Nathaniel Hawthorne, equally obsessed as they with how the mouldering past lingers among the living? The evidence is all there in his titles: *The Ghost Writer*: the first proper Zuckerman book. *Exit Ghost*: the last in the series. The way Roth characters keep returning to cemeteries (in the Zuckerman books, in *Sabbath's Theater*, in *Everyman*). The way Roth called up the spirits of his parents to serve as characters in *The Plot Against America*. In *Exit Ghost*, the former mistress of E. I. Lonoff spends decades carrying on posthumous conversations with her long gone lover. In one chapter of *The Counterlife*, one of the many incarnations of Nathan Zuckerman dies, but then has a conversation with his widow. 'I know now what a ghost is,' the widow says. 'It is the person you talk to. That's a ghost. Someone who's still so alive that you talk to them and talk to them and never stop. A ghost is the ghost of a ghost.'

In general, Roth's impulse is to blur the seemingly firm line between life and death, as he does between fact and fiction. Long before his parents died, he imagined their funerals in various novels; and then when the actuality occurred he gave it the non-fictional treatment.

These are of course not the ghosts of horror stories: they are not unearthly beings from another realm. They are very much material ghosts, created by the brain after living with flesh-and-blood creatures at close quarters. Still, they are no less ghosts for all that, evidence of how human presences have an afterlife.

Sans Everything, December 21, 2007

JOHN MAYNARD KEYNES AND THE SEXUALITY OF ECONOMICS

John Maynard Keynes was the sexiest economist who ever lived. This might seem like half-hearted praise since in our mind's eye the typical financial expert appears as a dowdy and almost always balding man, full of prudential advice about thrift and the miracle of compound interest. Keynes, with his caterpillar moustache and mesmerizing bedroom eyes, cut a more dashing figure.

He had many lovers of both genders, and was married to one of the great beauties of the age, the ballerina Lydia Lopokova. His genius at playing the stock market allowed him to enjoy the life of a bon vivant, socializing with the writers and artists of the Bloomsbury group such as Virginia Woolf and E.M. Forster rather than dull beancounters he knew at Cambridge and in the British Treasury. While other economists focused on maximizing economic growth, Keynes wanted to go further and maximize the pleasures of life.

Given all this, it's perhaps not surprising that a much-publicized recent attack on the Keynesian policy of using government deficits to overcome economic recession resorted to homophobia to discredit it. In early May of 2013, in a question and answer session following his lecture, Harvard historian Niall Ferguson startled his audience at the Altegris Strategic Investment Conference in California by calling Keynes a childless gay man who couldn't give his wife conjugal satisfaction and had no concern for the impact of deficits on posterity.

A storm of criticism followed, and in an effort to salvage his reputation, Ferguson—a vocal critic of both President Obama's mild stimulus policies and the more ambitious Keynesianism of economists like Paul Krugman—quickly and comprehensively apologized, saying his original remarks were as 'stupid as they were insensitive' and 'disagreements with Keynes's economic philosophy have never had anything to do with his sexual orientation.'

Ferguson's repudiation of his original homophobic comments should be commended. But Ferguson has a history of making jibes about Keynes's sexuality. University of Michigan economist Justin Wolfers called attention to the fact that in Ferguson's 1999 book *The Pity of War*, Keynes is described as being depressed by World War I, in part, because 'the boys he liked to pick up in London all joined up.' Later in the same book, Ferguson toys with the idea that Keynes may have been influenced to become a harsh critic of the Treaty of Versailles by an attraction to the German negotiator Carl Melchior. (It's embarrassing to have to refute arrant nonsense with facts and logic, but Keynes was likely depressed by the war because he didn't like pointless mass slaughter, while his Treaty of Versailles critique was vindicated by the post-war political and economic chaos he predicted.)

But there is something deeper and weirder going on here. Homophobic slurs against Keynes, it turns out, have a long pedigree. As both Berkeley economist Brad DeLong and the *Washington Monthly*'s Kathleen Geier have documented, the attempt to dismiss Keynes as someone heedless about the future because he was a childless gay man has been a staple of conservative thought for nearly seven decades.

The accusation was early made by the towering Harvard economist Joseph Schumpeter, who in a 1946 obituary complained that Keynes 'was childless and his philosophy of life was essentially a short-run philosophy.' The words of Schumpeter—still remembered for his contention that capitalism rests on 'creative destruction', and a conservative who thought intellectuals such as Keynes were undermining the moral foundation of the free market—have been echoed by many other thinkers, including George Will, Gertrude Himmelfarb, Greg Mankiw, Mark Steyn and V.S. Naipaul. Himmelfarb argues that Keynes's famous statement—'In the long run we are all dead'—has 'an obvious connection with his homosexuality', while Mark Steyn described the economist as a 'childless homosexual' and 'libertine'. Harvard economist Greg Mankiw also used the word 'childless' to describe Keynes, raising the question: what's wrong with Harvard?

The Schumpeter claim has had a surprisingly robust life despite the fact that it is both biographically wrong and logically absurd. Keynes was not childless by choice. He and Lydia Lopokova wanted to have a larger family, but failed due to a heart-breaking miscarriage. Moreover, childless people of any sexual orientation are more than capable of caring about the future of the species. Would we want to dismiss such famous non-parents as Immanuel Kant, Jane Austen, Emily Dickinson and Beethoven, not to mention Christ, for being exclusively focused on the present moment? Keynes's heart-felt concern for posterity is evident in his 1930 essay 'Economic Possibilities for Our Grandchildren'.

Still, the best response to Schumpeter and Ferguson may be to rethink—and re-argue—the link between sex and economics. We can reject the homophobia but take up the question they raise: What is the connection between Keynes the great lover and Keynes the great economist? To answer it, we have to acknowledge that economics is not a morally neutral science but rather is intimately connected with questions about what we want from life, including the type of sex we want to have.

Historically, attempts to prohibit sodomy (defined broadly as non-procreative sex) have had an economic dimension as well as a moral one. Economics, for the ancient Greeks, was household management (*oikonomia* being the Greek counterpart to our word 'husbandry'). While the pre-Christian Greeks didn't have any notion that homosexuality was sinful, they did develop the idea that there was a tension between sodomy and the procreative goal that they saw governing proper household management.

By remembering how the Greeks saw economics, we can make sense of the curious argument made by Aristotle—that usury was similar to unnatural sex, a case of money being generated by interaction with an outside party rather than the growth of a household through the fruitful union of husband and wife. In the *Politics*, Aristotle argues:

> There are two sorts of wealth-getting, as I have said; one is a part of household management, the other is retail trade: the former necessary and honourable, while that which consists in exchange is justly censured; for it is unnatural, and a mode by which men gain from one another. The most hated sort, and with the greatest reason, is usury, which makes a gain out of money itself, and not from the natural object of it. For money was intended to be used in exchange, but not to increase at interest. And this term interest, which means the birth of money from money, is applied to the breeding of money because the offspring resembles the parent. Wherefore of any modes of getting wealth this is the most unnatural.

Aristotle's linkage of non-procreative sex with usury profoundly influenced Christian thinkers. Thomas Aquinas, whose *Summa Theologica* codified the fusion of Aristotle with Christianity, argued that sodomy and usury were both 'sins against nature, in which the very order of nature is violated, an injury done to God himself, who sets nature in order.' Echoing Aquinas, Dante placed sodomites and usurers in the same circle of Hell in *The Divine Comedy*. In his 1935 tract 'Social Credit,' Ezra Pound, whose obsession with crackpot economics took him down many historical byways, argued that 'usury and sodomy, the Church condemned as a pair, to one hell, the same for one reason, namely that they are both against natural increase.'

There is a flipside to this tradition of seeing sodomy as the enemy of the natural economy of the household: the counter-tradition of liberal economics founded by Adam Smith challenged the household model by seeing economics as rooted in the free trade of goods between households and nations. Precisely because Smith was more receptive to previously condemned or taboo economic activities like trade and manufacturing, he was also more open to sexual liberalism.

Smith's friend Alexander Dalrymple is now thought to have written an anonymous tract, *Thoughts of an Old Man* (1800), recalling that the founder of modern economics believed that 'sodomy was a thing in itself indifferent'—a radical thing to say even in private at a time when sodomy was a capital offence, condemned by church and state. Interestingly, Smith was more reluctant to challenge the traditional prejudice against usury, although his students would conclude that the normalization of usury was the rational outcome of Smithian economics.

Smith's new and somewhat inchoate ideas were pushed further by Jeremy Bentham, who in an unpublished essay observed that sodomy 'produces no pain in anyone' but 'on the contrary it produces pleasure.' Pain and pleasure were key categories for Bentham as he developed the philosophy of utilitarianism, which argued a new goal for society: 'It is the greatest happiness of the greatest number that is the measure of right and wrong.'

It's no accident that in 1787 Bentham wrote *A Defence of Usury*, which tried to convince Adam Smith to take a more benevolent view of the hitherto morally sanctioned economic activity. On the subject of both usury and sodomy, Bentham's inclination was to take Smith's liberal impulses to their logical end. Bentham was in favour of consensual adult acts (be they sexual or economic) that led to greater happiness, whether they violated pre-existing taboos or not.

Although Keynes would revise the classical liberal tradition in many ways, he shared Bentham's aversion to unnecessary pain. In his essay 'My Early Beliefs', Keynes put forward his core creed: 'The appropriate subjects of passionate contemplation and communion were a beloved person, beauty and truth, and one's prime objects in life were love, the creation and enjoyment of aesthetic experience and the pursuit of knowledge. Of these, love came a long way first.'

The primacy Keynes gave to love is the key to understanding his greatness as an economist and moral figure. Valuing love as he did, Keynes was willing to ignore or overturn traditional creeds that, to his mind, inflicted unnecessary suffering whether it be the prohibition against homosexuality or the use of austerity as a solution to economic crises.

Keynes was neither a libertine nor a libertarian. Just as he thought sex existed in the service of love, he also believed that the goals of economics should be subordinated to the larger social good. He was even willing to support mild usury laws, not out of sense that predatory lending was immoral but because it was socially destructive.

If Keynes's economic vision is intertwined with his larger views on sex and love, meanwhile, the same is surely true of the many strands of pro-austerity thinking that oppose Keynesianism. Schumpeter was fundamentally a nostalgist who longed for a return to the heroic days of bourgeois family capitalism, a world he knew was irrevocably lost. No wonder Schumpeter was so unsettled by Keynes, a man at home with both modern economics and modern sexuality. Gertrude Himmelfarb's denunciation of the 'higher sodomy' of Keynes and his social circle is part and parcel with her calls to return to 'Victorian values' both morally and economically.

As Mark Blyth has shown in his new book, *Austerity: The History of a Dangerous Idea*, the power of arguments for austerity comes from the fact that they invoke the traditional moral system of the West, a way of thinking that is rarely questioned because it seems like common sense. Implicit in austerity are all sorts of moral adages: no pain, no gain; suffering builds character; thrift is virtue.

Keynes was able to see through the fallacy of austerity because he didn't think traditional moral strictures should be uncritically accepted. Rather, he wanted to test these strictures by their consequences. If we follow Keynes's example, we can use the same critical intelligence that has overturned the prejudice against homosexuality and start challenging the orthodoxy of austerity. No wonder Keynes remains a threatening figure for conservative economists and moralists alike.

The American Prospect, May 7, 2013

FORGING VAN GOGH

Prudent parents who worry about their children taking up artistic careers should avoid reading biographies of Vincent Van Gogh, which will only serve to tie knots in their stomachs. Although the 19th-century Dutch post-Impressionist immeasurably widened the range of human perception with his vibrantly otherworldly colours and quivering thickly hewn brush strokes, only one of Van Gogh's paintings found a buyer in his lifetime. Van Gogh's often shaky handle on reality was rattled by his destitution and neglect, which contributed to his suicide at age 37 in 1890. Yet today only the world's wealthiest people can afford to buy a Van Gogh. In 1990, *Portrait of Dr Gachet*, painted in the last year of the artist's life, sold to a Japanese businessman for US $82.5 million (or more than $144 million in current terms).

The chasm separating Van Gogh's earthly penury from the posthumous valuation of his work has led more than one painter to conclude that the one sure way to make money is to forge the work of a deceased master. Wyndham Lewis, the formidable modernist painter and writer, pursued this idea in his 1937 novel *The Revenge for Love*, which tells the story of an impoverished artist who is reduced to earning money by producing fake Van Goghs.

The painter discovers that 'the trick' of mimicking the Dutch genius involves learning a few 'formulas', including painting the pupils of the eyes 'as a nest of concentric wedges of greens, reds, blues and yellows, with their apex turned inwards.' Interestingly, *The Revenge for Love* connects forged paintings to political concerns, finding parallels between the rise of antidemocratic ideologies in the 1930s, particularly those on the left, and the dishonesty in the art world.

Strangely enough, Modris Eksteins does not discuss *The Revenge for Love* in his new book, *Solar Dance: Genius, Forgery and the Crisis of Truth in the Modern Age*. This is an odd omission because Eksteins's deeply researched historical study tells the story of the Van Gogh forgeries that flooded the German art market in the 1920s and the way that the counterfeiting of masterpieces was part and parcel of a larger cultural breakdown that destroyed German democracy, all themes that can be usefully linked to the Lewis novel. The pertinence of *The Revenge for Love* is tragically ironic because of Lewis's own sorry record as a fascist sympathizer, something he would later regret and apologize for.

The neglect of Lewis is all the more surprising because Eksteins is among the most erudite and perspicacious of scholars. In explaining the forgeries of the 1920s, he gives us an eye-opening and wide-ranging history of the Van Gogh cult, finding unexpected evidence of the painter's spectral influence in everything from a novel written by Joseph Goebbels to the childhood of the scientist J. Robert Oppenheimer to the fall of the Berlin Wall.

Although Eksteins's encyclopedic cultural knowledge allows him to roam through many continents and decades, *Solar Dance* is anchored by the story of Otto Wacker, a shadowy art dealer who amazed collectors and curators of Weimar Germany by bringing to the market a stockpile of previously unknown Van Goghs. Questioned about the provenance of his mysterious Van Gogh booty, Wacker spun out a colourful yarn about a Russian exile and an oath of secrecy.

A prototypical young man from the provinces in the pattern of Julien Sorel or Jay Gatsby, Wacker was a slippery character with no official background in art and a checkered history as a dancer and habitué of Berlin's sexual and social underworld. An offspring of a resourceful working-class family that made its money on the outskirts of polite society, Wacker managed through sheer brazen guile to get some of the world's top Van Gogh experts to certify the authenticity of his collection. Even when the grand poohbahs of the gallery scene started questioning how so many Van Goghs could suddenly have appeared out of nowhere, Wacker still had his defenders even as he stood trial for his alleged fraud.

The story of Wacker's unlikely rise and equally quick unravelling makes for compulsive reading. A crackerjack archival researcher, Eksteins brings to life not just Wacker but the world that created him and allowed him to briefly thrive. It's that larger world of early-20th-century European culture, racked as it was by war and the rise of totalitarianism, that is Eksteins's real concern. For him, both the lionization of Van Gogh and the forgeries that flourished in the art market are symptomatic of a larger cultural sickness, one that has serious implications for both the past and present.

Eksteins is a major historian and *Solar Dance*, like everything he writes, deserves a wide and attentive readership. Having said that, I have serious reservations about some of the lessons Eksteins draws from the tale he has so expertly reconstructed, so I want to record a few respectful demurrals and provisos.

Eksteins has an associative mind, one that is happy to make connections but that doesn't always bother to prove causation. In his memoir *Walking Since Daybreak*, he admits to having 'doubts about causality and continuity in history'. What this means is that he finds it fruitful not to say that X caused Y but rather that X and Y have deep affinities with each other.

The many parallels Eksteins draws are often suggestive but also sometimes strain credibility, as when he compares the film director Fritz Lang to Adolf Hitler: 'Fritz Lang's and Adolf Hitler's first love was painting. Lang personally sold painted postcards in Paris before the war; Hitler did the same in Vienna and Munich. Both became decorated war heroes. After the war, both turned to film. The difference was that Lang stood behind, and Hitler in front of, the camera.' This type of facile comparison can be made about any two disparate figures. What would we say if someone wrote, 'Queen Victoria and Jack the Ripper both knew how to get attention and dominate the headlines. They shared a hatred of prostitution. Queen Victoria opposed sex workers by upholding the laws of her nation while Jack the Ripper took the route of killing them.'

A cultural conservative in the European tradition, Eksteins takes a dim view of modern art, seeing it as emblematic of disorder, madness, despair, an idolatry that replaces religion with the cult of the artist, sensationalism and the loss of faith in older and more humane traditions. This dingy view of modernism is reinforced by the fact that Eksteins sees Berlin, not Paris, as the centre of 20th-century culture. The son of a Baptist minister, Eksteins has retained some of the severe skepticism many low church Christians have to aesthetic experiences.

Frowning on modernism, Eksteins over-emphasizes the parallels between the art world and noxious political movements like Nazism. There is a smidgen of truth to Eksteins's perspective: some of the great modernists did flirt with the darker forces of European politics, Wyndham Lewis being a prime example. But it's also the case that the Nazis viewed modernism as 'degenerate' art and celebrated nostalgic kitsch, very different in spirit and form from the abrasive and challenging works of the great moderns.

Modernism shouldn't be caricatured simply as art that wallows in doom and gloom. Many of the great modernists, Van Gogh being chief among them, brought joy to the world by creating works of unprecedented daring, colour, innovation and vitality. Our humanity is enlivened and deepened by Van Gogh's work, a fact that you can only get a glimmer of in Eksteins's too often doleful book.

National Post, February 3, 2012

OEDIPUS UPDIKE

When it came to fathers and sons, Sigmund Freud only knew the half of it, perhaps even less than that. It is undeniably true that on their path to maturity sons have to murder their fathers (only a symbolic butchery in the best case scenarios). But the full gamut of filial emotions is much wider than the Oedipus complex. Our fathers appear to us first as gods, then in various successive guises as heroes, mentors, friends, clowns, rivals, victims, and, perhaps finally, as remorseful memories. Mourning the slain father is also part of the Oedipus story.

John Updike was one of the towering and inescapable patriarchs of American literature, a writer so dauntingly skilled and so impossibly prolific that subsequent generations can only look back at him with resentful awe. When he was alive, the range of responses to Updike ran from knee-bending reverence to knife-wielding rage. While women writers felt free to either admire Updike's stellar prose or dismiss him as a sexist old coot, male writers tended to have a more visceral reaction. For Ian McEwan, Updike was one of his 'father figures'. Nicholson Baker's *U and I* (1991), a deliciously creepy memoir of his obsession with Updike, is puckishly written but also frank in its sexual emulation. Baker saluted Updike's erotic explicitness, hailing him as the first writer 'to take the penile sensorium under the wing of elaborate metaphorical prose'.

The late and now-sainted David Foster Wallace was more brutally Oedipal. In a notorious and opinion-shaping 1997 review of Updike's *Toward the End of Time*, Wallace railed against the elderly writer as a 'phallocrat', a 'narcissist', a 'solipsist' and quoted the devastating judgment of a friend who memorably summed up Updike as 'a penis with a thesaurus'. As with Baker, paternal sexuality is the key to Wallace's response. Updike was the bard of suburban adultery, the definitive chronicler of bed-hopping among the barbecue set.

Wallace looked at Updike with the disenchanted eyes of a son pondering his old man's feckless skirt-chasing. 'The children of the same impassioned infidelities and divorces Mr Updike wrote about so beautifully,' Wallace complained, 'got to watch all this brave new individualism and self-expression and sexual freedom deteriorate into the joyless and anomic self-indulgence of the Me Generation.'

Baker and Wallace should be seen as two vantage points of the same monument, both obsessed with Updike's formidable generative member. 'What a big dick Updike has!' Baker marvelled. 'What a big dick Updike is!' Wallace replied.

Adam Begley's hefty new biography of Updike belongs to this history of conflicted sonly emotions, an attempt to thread a middle path between Baker's abject worship and Wallace's adolescent rebellion. As it happens, Begley, as an editor at the *New York Observer*, commissioned Wallace's review, and in this book the biographer tries to make amends by complicating (although not wholly eradicating) the image of Updike as a self-absorbed sex addict.

Beyond the Wallace connection, Begley has a long history with Updike, one that predates the biographer's birth: the man writing Updike's life is as close to being Updike's son as one can get without being able to pass a paternity test. Begley's father, the lawyer-turned-novelist Louis Begley, was born a year after Updike and studied with Updike at Harvard in the early 1950s. In 1953, Updike married Mary Pennington; in 1956, Louis Begley married a woman with a name comically similar to Mary Pennington: Sally Higginson. Adam Begley was born in 1959, the same year as Updike's second son, Michael. As a family friend, Updike would drop by to entertain Louis Begley's clan. According to family lore, Updike's juggling provoked the first burst of laughter to fly from the lips of the baby Adam. The film *About Schmidt*, based on a Louis Begley novel, borrowed a central narrative device from 'Dear Alexandros', an obscure 1959 Updike short story.

Louis Begley and Sally divorced in 1970, prefiguring the separation of Updike and Mary in 1974 (and their divorce in 1976). For ample reasons, the impact of family breakup on children is a major concern in Begley's biography.

Begley repeatedly hammers at the point that Updike was an 'autobiographical writer'. This is a half-truth or perhaps a quarter-truth. Updike had two major modes, the domestic and the exotic. As a domestic writer, he imagined hypothetical alter egos who owed much to his own experiences. The Updike who crafted fun-house mirrors of his own life is dominant in novels like *The Centaur* (1963) and *Couples* (1968), not to mention the stories set in Olinger, Penn., or tracing the rocky marriage of Richard and Joan Maple. But Updike also had an adventurous side which took him to the imaginary African nation Kush, to Brazil, to medieval Denmark, and to the post-American future, among other far-flung locales.

Even dealing with familiar territory, Updike consistently imagined characters who decidedly were not him. Harry Angstrom, the protagonist of the Rabbit novels, is like his creator a native of Pennsylvania but the fictional character has only slightly over half of Updike's IQ points and a completely different life trajectory. Yet Angstrom is as wholly plausible as any character in American fiction. To see Updike as primarily an 'autobiographical writer' is to miss the crafty witchery that he put into even the fiction that was closest to his experiences.

Begley deftly recapitulates a story familiar to readers of Updike's memoir *Self-Consciousness* as well as novels like *The Centaur*: the swaddled childhood in small-town and rural Pennsylvania; the strong-willed mother with her own literary ambitions; the self-sacrificing father; the brightness and talent that opened the doors to Harvard and *The New Yorker*; the 1953 marriage, while still an undergraduate, to Mary; the four children (two sons and two daughters); the adulteries that both Mary and Updike indulged in as part of the swinging crowd of Ipswich, Mass.; the tormented love affair with Joyce Harrington that almost tore apart the marriage in 1962; the crazy sexual adventurism in the aftermath of that affair when Updike seems to have slept with nearly every housewife in Ipswich; the bestselling fame; the final dissolution of the marriage in the mid-1970s; the remarriage to his now-divorced former mistress Martha Bernhard; the lingering guilt over the impact of all this on his kids and stepkids (three sons from Martha's first marriage).

Begley's account of Updike's life is often shrewd but it is also severely damaged by misinterpretations and partisanship, a byproduct of who Begley talked to. He interviewed Updike's first wife, Mary, and their four kids but not the second wife, Martha, and the three stepsons from that relationship. As a result, Mary is presented as nurturing, maternal, shy, serene and artistic as well as tolerant of Updike's creative and personal foibles. By contrast, Martha is depicted as an evil stepmother worthy of a fairytale rather than a biography.

Although Begley provides a few softening caveats and provisos, the dominant narrative is that Martha was a predatory home-wrecker who had designs on Updike. Once Updike and Martha married, she allegedly became a controlling wife who isolated him in a remote mansion and sharply regulated his access to the children and grandchildren produced by his first marriage. Martha, Begley claims, 'was perfectly willing to bully [Updike] for his own good'. Begley strongly hints that the wife in *Toward the End of Time* (who he describes as a 'fearsome nag' as well as 'shrewish') is a likeness of Martha. The dubious gender politics of this account should be obvious.

Begley's sinister portrait of Martha is simplistic and rings false. Could it be that the biographer resents the second wife for not co-operating with his project? Begley's account almost completely erases Martha's sons (Updike's stepsons). In the book *Updike in Cincinnati* (2007), James Schiff has a small anecdote about how John Bernhard, Updike's stepson, made a visit to a literary reading and was greeted by the novelist with 'a smile and a kiss'. This throwaway remark in a book commemorating a small Updike conference is a more humanizing portrait of John Bernhard than he receives in Begley's massive biography.

Is Begley right in his claim that Updike was cut off from the lives of the grandchildren from his marriage to Mary? Three of those grandchildren are mixed-race (a daughter and a son from the first marriage both married black Africans). Updike's increasing sensitivity to issues of race and the special experience of mixed-race families, evident in novels like *Brazil* (1994) and *Terrorist* (2006), was surely connected to his grandfatherly interest in the non-white branch of his family tree. Updike had a long-standing and tangled history with race which Begley only sketchily covers and the experience of having dark-skinned grandkids changed the novelist in ways this biography doesn't contemplate.

Begley notes that 'Oedipal struggle' is a recurring theme in the Rabbit books. Not just Oedipal struggle but unresolved anger towards an imperfect father figure is the major motive behind this flawed biography. The father can't be quite forgiven nor totally blamed for leaving the family, so the stepmother becomes the scapegoat.

We're never really finished with our parents, not even after their deaths. Begley's imperfect book is one attempt to wrestle with Updike's ghost, but there will be many more. One hopes those future biographies will deal more fairly not just with Martha Updike but also the rich and complex patrimony Updike has bequeathed us.

The Globe and Mail, April 4, 2014

UPDIKE: PORTRAIT OF THE ARTIST AS A YOUNG FAN

I can't remember the moment when I fell in love with cartoons, I was so young,' John Updike once recalled in *Hogan's Alley* magazine. 'I still have a *Donald Duck* book, on oilclothy paper in big-print format, and remember a smaller, cardboard-covered book based on the animated cartoon *Three Little Pigs*. It was the intense stylization of those images, with their finely brushed outlines and their rounded and buttony furniture and their faces so curiously amalgamated of human and animal elements, that drew me in, into a world where I, child though I was, loomed as a king, and where my parents and other grownups were strangers.'

This is one of many autobiographical passages where Updike talks about his childhood love of comics, a theme that recurs not just in essays but also in poems and short stories. What deserves attention in this passage is not just what Updike is saying but the textured and sensual language he's using when he recalls the 'oilclothy paper' and the 'buttony furniture'. Updike's tingling prose, where every idea and emotion is rooted in sensory experience, owes much to such modern masters as Joyce, Proust and Nabokov, but it was also sparked by the cartoon images he saw in childhood, which trained his eyes to see visual forms as aesthetically pleasing. Indeed the comparison with Nabokov is instructive since the Russian-born author of *Lolita* was also a cartoon fan. The critic Clarence Brown has coined the term 'bedesque' (rough translation: comic strip–influenced) to describe the cartoony quality of Nabokov's fiction, including its antic loopiness, its quicksilver movement from scene to scene and its visual intensity. Following Brown, I want to suggest that one reason Updike felt an affinity for Nabokov is that they both wrote bedesque prose.

The origin of creativity is a riddle that can never be solved, yet if we love an artist it is hard not to look for clues as to the secret source of his or her gifts. Literary biography—an enterprise that Updike regarded with some skepticism—is largely a hunt for such deeply buried evidence. As an aid to future biographers and anyone else interested in pursuing the mystery of Updike's prodigious talent, I'd like to suggest the value of paying attention to his lifelong love affair with cartooning, a passion which burned hottest when he was young but remained warm until his dying days, when he ceased to draw but still repeatedly referred to the comics he loved in childhood.

The outlines of the story are clear enough. Before he could read, Updike was enamoured of the anthropomorphic kingdom of talking rodents and fowls presided over by Walt Disney, enjoying both the moving Mickey Mouse seen on the silver screen and the still Mickey found in Big Little Books and the newspaper funnies. This passion for all things Disney fed early ambitions of being an animator. Updike's interest in cartooning soon spread to all the other characters found in the newspaper funnies section, and he was regularly following strips like *Barney Google, Captain Easy, Terry and the Pirates, Alley Oop, Little Orphan Annie, Li'l Abner* and many others.

Branching out from comic strips and animation, the young Updike also developed a taste for comic books, a new form of pop culture ephemera which mushroomed in popularity in the 1930s and that initially reprinted old strips but soon offered vibrant four-colour fantasies featuring masked vigilantes and superbeings like Batman, Wonder Woman and Superman. Updike's taste ran towards the more humorous of the superheroes rather than the more earnest examples of the genre. He enjoyed C.C. Beck's Captain Marvel, Jack Cole's impossibly stretchy Plastic Man and Will Eisner's masked avenger The Spirit. All of these were superheroes that the artists themselves never took too seriously; they were always aware of the absurdity latent in the genre.

On the cusp of adolescence, Updike intensified his cartooning fervour when he became fascinated by the single panel gag cartoons found in magazines like *Collier's* and the *Saturday Evening Post*. When he was twelve his aunt Mary bought his family a subscription to *The New Yorker*, which quickly became the most important magazine of all for Updike as he yearned to appear in its sophisticated pages. Although Updike would go on to become the pre-eminent *New Yorker* writer, he was at first far more interested in the drawings of Thurber and Steinberg than in the magazine's acres of prose.

The teenage Updike mailed off a steady stream of cartoons in the hopes of breaking into the visual humour market. He would continue cartooning as an undergraduate at Harvard, where he sprinkled the pages of the *Harvard Lampoon* with his drawings. But Updike's undergraduate years also marked the end of his cartooning career and his transformation into a writer. Updike simply felt that the other artists at the *Lampoon* were much more talented than he was, and also discovered his facility for light verse and narrative prose. It could be that Updike was too harsh on his early cartoons. The sample cartoons reprinted in Updike's collection *More Matter* (1999) display a memorably jagged bluntness that calls to mind Virgil Partch (1916–1984), who was on the cutting edge of the stylistic revolution of the 1940s and 1950s that opened up cartooning to energetically angular, poking shapes.

Yet Updike's past as wannabe cartoonist has left many residual traces on his work, like little flecks of ink that get caught in an illustrator's fingernail. 'One can continue to cartoon, in a way, with words,' he noted. 'For whatever crispness and animation my writing has I give some credit to the cartoonist manqué.'

The connection between Updike's drawing and his writing is evidenced not only by the cartoons he mailed off for publication but also by other pieces of epistolary testimony: the letters that he sent off to newspapers and cartoonists. When Updike was nine or ten, the local newspaper stopped carrying the *Mickey Mouse* comic strip, provoking the future novelist to write an indignant protest letter. That missive was the first in a long string of comics-inspired correspondence. The adolescent Updike wasn't satisfied with just printed cartoons. He hungered for original art and thus started writing cartoonists beseeching inquiries. 'Our acquaintance was slight but long,' Updike recalled of his affection for Steinberg in an essay for *The New York Review of Books*. 'In 1945 I wrote him from my small town in Pennsylvania asking that he send me, for no reason except that I wanted it, the original of a drawing I had seen in *The New Yorker*, of one man tipping his hat and another tipping back his hat with his head still in it. At this time:

> I was an avariciously hopeful would-be cartoonist of 12 or 13 and Steinberg a 31-year-old Romanian Jew whose long American sojourn had begun but four years before. Perhaps he thought that his new citizenship entailed responding to the importunities from unknown American adolescents. He sent me not the original but

> a duplicate he had considerately made, with his unhesitant pen, and inscribed it, in impeccable New World Fashion, 'To John Updike with best wishes'.

As did Nabokov, from the 1950s onward, Steinberg, in the 1940s and later, provided Updike with an unexpected kindred spirit, someone who taught the American-born writer to see his native land with foreign eyes. Steinberg, when Updike wrote to him, was in the midst of instigating a stylistic revolution at *The New Yorker*. While other artists such as Otto Soglow and James Thurber had already expanded the stylistic range of magazine cartooning by bringing in starkly simple and expressive drawings, Steinberg took this new-found liberty a step further by doing cartoons that avoided easily understood gags based on social humour and instead offered elliptical comments on the American visual landscape. In Steinberg's cartoons, the line between words and pictures disappeared as he drew glyphs and signs that carried human passions.

Appropriating images from advertising and popular entertainment while giving them a satirical tweak, Steinberg in the 1940s anticipated everything from the paintings of Andy Warhol to the experimental fiction of Donald Barthelme. Steinberg also prefigured, I would suggest, the future attempts of his fan John Updike to do poems and stories that mashed up words and images, as in 'Mid-Point' or 'The Invention of the Horse Collar'.

Aside from the Steinberg drawing, Updike solicited 'treasures' from other artists. In a letter to me, Updike mentioned that his letters to cartoonists earned him 'an Otto Soglow Little King, and a Thurber dog he drew for me when he was all but blind. Also I have a Barnaby strip with the pasted-on lettering falling off, and half of a "Sunday Mickey Finn." I must have had 20 or more in my prime.' Luckily enough, at least two of the letters the adolescent Updike wrote still survive. They are worth quoting briefly because they actually let us see up close the exquisite writer emerging from his cartooning cocoon.

On September 6, 1947, Updike wrote to Milton Caniff, then among the most famous cartoonists in America because of his two major strips, *Terry and the Pirates* and *Steve Canyon*. *Terry and the Pirates* was one of the great comic strips of the 1930s and 1940s: it had action, lovely ink-rich noir art, a winsome young hero who matures during the course of his adventures, an exciting Asian backdrop (which in the late 1930s became timely and even urgent), and sexy femme fatales (most prominently the famed Dragon Lady). In 1946, Caniff left *Terry* and started a new strip, *Steve Canyon*, a move that caught the attention of comic strip fans all over the nation. John Updike, then fifteen years old and living in his mother's ancestral farm in Plowville, was one such Caniff follower and used the fact that the comic strip artist was in the news in order to entice him to send some original art.

Updike began his letter: 'For a long time, I was under the impression that Terry and the Pirates was the best comic strip in the United States. Imagine my dismay, then, when I heard that its creator, its mastermind, was going to desert Terry, leave it in the lurch, and wander off to some new interest, called Steve Canyon. Apprehensively I subscribed to the paper that carried Steve Canyon and waited for the results. It didn't take me long to discover that Steve Canyon was now the best comic strip in the United States. Obvious conclusion: Milton Caniff is the best cartoonist in the world.' The charm of this letter is inseparable from the exuberantly adolescent longings that course through it. Already a fluid writer, Updike manages to be brassy even as he lays on the flattery in an obviously obsequious manner. Part of the manner of the letter owes something to the very cartoonist that Updike was praising, since Caniff's dialogue tended towards wise-guy knowingness. (The original of this letter can be found in the Caniff papers held at Ohio State University's Billy Ireland Cartoon Library & Museum.)

Updike never forgot Caniff. In Updike's last novel, *The Widows of Eastwick*, a trip to China includes a description of the country's history in the early 20th century that shows the author was still mindful of *Terry and the Pirates*. China in Updike's novel is remembered as a land of 'Pearl Buck peasants, dragon ladies, rickshaws, and comic-strip pirates'. What started as a fannish passion became part of Updike's mental furniture till the end of his life.

A few months after writing to Caniff, Updike sent some equally enthusiastic fan mail to Harold Gray, creator of *Little Orphan Annie*. A Dickensian melodrama about a poor orphan named Annie who struggles against an oppressive society while being intermittently aided by her guardian, 'Daddy' Warbucks, Gray's strip was notable for its strident right-wing politics. In Gray's universe, the bad guys were invariably do-gooding reformers, union bosses, pointy-headed academics and other liberal types, while the heroes were he-man entrepreneurs. Updike having grown up in a household that cherished Franklin Roosevelt's New Deal, my guess is that he would have had little use for Gray's politics but his love of cartooning transcended any ideological litmus test.

Dated January 2nd, 1948, Updike's letter to Gray contains a marvellously confident and crisp account of Little Orphan Annie's blustery melodramatic universe. 'Your villains are completely black and Annie and crew are perfect, which is as it should be,' he wrote. 'One of my happiest moments was spent in gloating over some hideous child (I forget his name) who had been annoying Annie toppled into the wet cement of a dam being constructed.' This is an extremely astute bit of criticism. As in traditional melodrama, part of the joy of Gray's strip orchestrated his audience's indignation by showing the heroine constantly suffering at the hands of self-satisfied brutes. The moments when these villains get their comeuppance is always a highlight in *Little Orphan Annie.* While much has been written about the strip by both journalists and academics, few have gotten to the emotional core of the strip with as much insight as the teenage Updike.

Updike's future career as a part-time art critic can also be seen in the authoritative way he described Gray's art. 'Your draughtmanship is beyond reproach,' Updike wrote. 'The facial features, the big, blunt fingered hands, the way you handle light and shadows are all excellently done. Even the talk balloons are good, the lettering small and clean, the margins wide, and the connection between the speaker and his remark wiggles a little, all of which, to my eye, is as artistic as you can get.' Updike's attention to things like Gray's portrayal of hands or his distinct lettering style bespeaks the eyes of a fellow craftsman. The cartoonist Chester Brown, author of such bestselling graphic novels as *Louis Riel* and *Paying for It,* once told me he loved Gray's expressive use of hands. He was surprised when I told him that John Updike also took note of the same aspect of Gray's art. (The original of this letter is found in the Harold Gray papers at Boston University.)

There is much to be said about the remarkable letters Updike sent to Caniff and Gray. First, Updike's standard letter-writing gambit seems to have been to start with extreme flattery. He claimed that both Caniff and Gray were his favourite. Like a Casanova of comic-strip fans, Updike was willing to say anything to complete a successful seduction. The ability to woo with words is a trait that the adult Updike would prize, since it won him both readers and lovers. The origins of his skill at using language as a persuasive tool are to be found in these letters. Updike's letters are also very atypical in their verbal dexterity, especially considering the age of the author. Further down in his letter to Gray, Updike mentions that 'I need a picture to alleviate the blankness of one of my bedroom walls.' The unexpected use of the word 'alleviate' in this context is both startling and apt.

Updike was still in the middle of high school when he wrote these letters. The critic Sanford Schwartz once observed in *The New York Review of Books* that 'Updike found his assured voice, as a critic and fiction writer, when he was fairly young' and was 'writing with an eerily developed authority and fluency when he was still in his 20s.' One could argue he had achieved this 'eerily developed authority' even earlier, while still an adolescent. According to Schwartz, Updike has never quite grown up: his early effortless verbal fluidity made the author a perennial boy wonder.

But we can turn Schwartz's critical remarks on their head by seeing Updike's perpetual boyishness as part of his strength. Like most children, Updike was amazed by the world he found himself born into but unlike most adults he never lost his youthful sense of wonder. There is much else that could be said about Updike and cartooning. His poems, short stories, and novels are rich in cartooning allusions. His sensual prose—which was arguably nonpareil in its responsiveness to the visual world—owed something to the long hours he spent poring over cartoons and learning to draw.

What did Updike mean when he wrote that 'one can continue to cartoon, in a way, with words'? I've often talked about Updike with my friend Chris Ware, the cartoonist best known for his graphic novel *Jimmy Corrigan*. Like me, Chris is an Updike addict. He once told me that he felt Updike's attempts to cartoon with words can be most effectively seen in the Maple stories and the Bech stories. Although both these story cycles deal with very adult subjects—notably adultery and divorce—they are often written in a bright, chipper, affectionate tone that evokes classic cartooning. Again, Clarence Brown's invented term 'bedesque' captures some of this quality.

The critic William H. Pritchard notes that the first Bech book was written with a 'comic lightness and brio' that distinguished it from some of Updike's weightier fiction of the 1960s. Pritchard takes note of a sentence from the story 'Bech Panics' where the hero goes to a hotel for an unsuccessful assignation with a lover: 'But the overflowing meal at the boorish roadside restaurant, and their furtive decelerated glide through the crackling gravel courtyard of the motel (where a Kiwanis banquet was in progress, and had hogged all the parking spaces), and his fumbly rush to open the tricky aluminoid lock-knob of his door and to stuff his illicit guest out of sight, and the macabre interior of oak-imitating wallboard and framed big-pastels that embowered them proved in sum withering to Bech's potency.'

Pritchard rightly sees Nabokov as a source for the adjectival mirth of this passage ('boorish' and 'aluminoid') but behind the Russian master there is also Updike's love of cartooning with words. It's no accident that the covers of the Bech books all contain caricatures of the hero done by one of Updike's favourite cartoonists, Arnold Roth. Nor is it surprising that in 'Bech Noir' the writer takes on a superhero identity, becoming a kind of literary Batman avenging writers who have been mistreated by critics. Bech as Batman even has a sidekick named Robin, an eventual lover and spouse.

A full inventory of the impact of cartooning on Updike's writing would require a much longer essay. It would include a discussion of a poem that features Al Capp (creator of *Li'l Abner*), Harry 'Rabbit' Angstrom's resentful affection for the girlie comic strip *Apartment 3-G*, the superhero references in the later Rabbit books, the story 'Intermission', which features a young writer of comic strips, the novel *Marry Me*, which features a character who works in advertising animation and the essays Updike devoted to cartoonists such as Ralph Barton, James Thurber and Charles Schulz. Such a discussion would also look more deeply at the visual potency of Updike's prose and his habit of limning vividly grotesque secondary characters (think for example of the story 'The Madman'), a fictional practice that owes as much to the tradition of caricature as to the model of Dickens.

John Updike stopped cartooning while he was an undergraduate at Harvard. This is a factually true statement, but it ignores a larger reality. While Updike might have ceased cartooning, the visual language of comics was never far from his mind. Cartooning was an inextricable strand in his creative DNA.

Previously unpublished

GUY DAVENPORT, CARTOONIST

Perhaps this is too confident a statement and needs a more tentative punctuation. 'Guy Davenport: Cartoonist?' After all, Davenport wasn't mainly known as a cartoonist, and the world of comics has only a peripheral awareness of his existence. Aside from comic book artist Gil Kane's stated fondness for Davenport's essay collection *The Geography of the Imagination* (1981) and a stray allusion that Carter Scholz once made in *The Comics Journal*, Davenport's name is rarely bandied about in cartooning circles.

When Davenport died in early 2005, many obituaries and memorial notices paid tribute to him as a man of letters of intimidating range and versatility. Aside from penning many brilliant short stories, Davenport was a premier translator of many ancient writers and sages (Sappho, Herakleitos, Diogenes, Jesus), an immensely erudite literary critic who could expertly explicate difficult modernists like Wallace Stevens and Ezra Pound and a pioneering iconologist who illuminated the symbolic vocabulary of painters like Grant Wood and Balthus. Lost among all the eulogies for Davenport the writer were his achievements as a visual artist: tucked away in a busy lifetime was an almost secret career as a painter, illustrator and, yes, cartoonist.

I first encountered Davenport as a cartoonist before I became acquainted with his other accomplishments: he did the satirical illustrations that accompany two eccentric books of literary criticism that Hugh Kenner wrote in the 1960s. Charmed by these drawings, I looked up Davenport's writings, but even as I grew to appreciate his literary achievement I never forgot that he drew. It was easy to keep this in mind, since the dust jackets of many of his books came from his hands, along with frequent illustration that accompanied his stories. More profoundly, Davenport was always a very visual writer, so much so that I think any just appreciation of his work has to appraise the tight bond between his words and pictures.

To look at Davenport as a cartoonist is not to take a sidelong glance at the moonlighting a writer did at the fringes of his more important work.

Rather, it brings us close to the heart of this fully rounded creator, a genuine exemplar of the Renaissance Man ideal.

Born to indulgent middle-class parents in Anderson, S.C., in 1927, Davenport drew and painted long before he started reading and writing. By his own account, his formal schooling was late blooming and less important than what he learned in playtime, cultivating his rich inner world during ample hours spent alone. At age 12, he started a neighbourhood newspaper, recording family jaunts, local gossip, the comings and goings of cats and dogs. Davenport was both the chief reporter and staff cartoonist for this little journal. Only a few years later, the teenage Davenport was providing pen-and-ink sketches for the town newspaper.

Despite all his extracurricular activities and late literacy, Davenport also found he could glide through school with ease. He developed a lifelong habit of winning big academic prizes, which carried him from Duke University to Oxford to Harvard. He had the rare (perhaps unique) distinction of being a Rhodes Scholar as a young man and a MacArthur Fellow in his maturity.

The Rhodes Scholarship took him to Oxford in the late 1940s, where he wrote an early thesis on Joyce. Returning stateside, he served in the army during the Korean War and then did a Harvard thesis on Ezra Pound.

All throughout these years of intense study, he never gave up on drawing and painting. *Archive*, an undergraduate journal at Duke University, is a rich storehouse of his early short stories, drawings and literary essays. In 1958, he painted the cover for Clay Fisher's *The Crossing*, a Western set during the Civil War. Eschewing the homey and rough-hewn conventions of Western art, Davenport's cover is a stark and linear image of a horse-riding Confederate soldier, the profile of his face facing sternly rightward, one hand keeping a tight leash on his horse while the other brandishes a rifle, displayed with the solemnity of a flag.

As with so many other Davenport paintings, this scene cunningly plays off representation and abstraction. In the foreground, the soldier is tense, intent, mindful of the present. But the background has a timeless, ornamental quality, almost like a Persian carpet. As we shift our focus away from the main figure, we realize that everything in the background is a variation on the triangle: four teepees, the angular landscape of the plains, even the accidental triangle created by the crook of the elbow on the rifle-bearing arm. While the solider is caught at the cusp of a moment of action, the West persists in its pastoral idyll. (The cover also contains a hint of male sexual beauty, a theme that Davenport would often return to in his fiction and drawings.)

In its crisp sense of design, the cover is indebted to the vernacular modernism popularized by such 1950s clean-line masters as Gene Deitch, Jim Flora and Milton Glaser. The cover is all the more impressive since it was most likely done as a lark. *The Crossing* was published by Houghton Mifflin, whose offices were a stone's throw away from Harvard, so Davenport probably executed the painting as a break from his graduate studies.

As a young English professor at Haverford College in the early 1960s, Davenport sat in on the life-studies classes of the painter Fritz Janschka. Deferring to the demure wishes of his students, Janschka allowed the model to wear a bathing suit while modelling. Davenport shocked the class when he brought in a model who was willing to pose *au naturel*. When he made the University of Kentucky his final academic home in 1963, he built a studio in his backyard. His neighbours called it Guy's tree house.

Through his interest in Joyce, Pound and the other great modernists, Davenport developed a literary friendship in the late 1950s with Hugh Kenner, the Canadian-born scholar whose studies of 20th-century literature were revolutionizing academia. The two men had much in common: they were both passionate partisans of Pound and other recondite poets, both prolific and vivid writers ill at ease with the pedantry of traditional scholarship, both public intellectuals who were as comfortable writing for *National Review* and *Harper*'s as for intellectual quarterlies.

Like Davenport, Kenner had an off-kilter sensibility, a restless desire to examine familiar subjects from a new angle. It was natural, therefore, that reading the manuscripts of two of Kenner's books inspired some marvellous Davenport cartooning.

The Kenner books were *The Stoic Comedians: Flaubert, Joyce and Beckett* (1964) and *The Counterfeiters: An Historical Comedy* (1968). (Both these books have recently been reissued by the Dalkey Archive Press.) As their titles indicate, comedy is the unifying theme, but it's a quirky view of comedy. In a nutshell, Kenner argues that modern literature is deeply shaped by the rise of technology since the 17th century, but the upshot hasn't been a deadening of feeling, but rather an efflorescence of satire. Mechanical culture can be seen not just in nuts and bolts but more subtly in language being reduced to uniform parts on the printed page, our erotic imagination fired by images of air-brushed and interchangeable models, our education expended on mastering standardized tests, our health reduced to actuarial statistics by insurance companies and doctors.

Some writers have reacted to the rise of the machines with prophetic rage: the response of William Blake, John Ruskin, D.H. Lawrence. But Kenner is more interested in the sly souls who in effect co-opted the machine: writing books that use the very properties of technological language to register the mechanization of humanity. This, Kenner, demonstrates, was the tactic of Alexander Pope, Jonathan Swift, Gustave Flaubert, James Joyce, Samuel Beckett. They all belong to the tradition of the stoic comedian.

The thrust of Kenner's argument can be gleaned from his discussion of Joyce. 'Joyce chose to raise Flaubert to a higher power, generating a fictional machine of such echoing and reentrant complexity as Flaubert never dreamed up,' Kenner observes. 'For he glimpsed the paradoxical possibility of the novel, as it grew more highly mechanized, growing gayer, not with the grim necessitarian futility of Flaubert's irony, but with the comedy of utterly inevitable coincidence, as when the chair moves just as the fat man sits. Joyce's is like the comedy of the silent films, in which the flicker of the medium itself reduces men to comically accelerated machines, contending with other machines—cars, revolving doors, ice cream dispensers; and we know that however often the film is shown it will always go the same way.'

Silent films were an important touchstone for Kenner. Buster Keaton, whose stone face remained unwavering even as out-of-whack machines put his body through the wringer, is surely the very physical embodiment of stoic comedy.

In illustrating Kenner's two books on these themes, it was natural for Davenport to turn to the silent films as inspiration. The drawings in *The Stoic Comedians* are a bit stiff compared to Davenport's best work, but they remain intensely funny because of how he exploited the Keatonian principle of showing men in ridiculous poses maintaining the gravity of classical statues. One drawing has Leopold Bloom, the hero of *Ulysses*, furtively glancing into a porn novel while being studied by the cagey Joyce. Another drawing shows Flaubert pondering the *mot juste*, wielding a cigar in one hand with a top hat in the other, looking like a high bourgeois counterpart to Oliver Hardy.

In *The Counterfeiters*, Kenner returned to the themes of *The Stoic Comedians* but told the story in a much wilder tempo, like Scott Joplin doing a riff on a traditional melody. Bringing the full range of his astonishing learning to bear, Kenner linked modernism with such disparate phenomena as 18th-century clockwork dolls, Charles Babbage's Victorian-era attempts to build a calculating machine, Noam Chomsky's linguistic theories, Andy Warhol's pop art and even the history of bad poetry. There is no other book of literary criticism that is quite like *The Counterfeiters* in bringing together an unlikely array of subjects and demonstrating that they are all interconnected. It is telling that the novelist William Gaddis had thought about doing a book on many of these same themes, but gave up when he realized that Kenner had beaten him to the punch.

Perhaps liberated by the exuberant energy of Kenner's text, Davenport did his best cartooning for *The Counterfeiters*. In one scene, Karl Marx and Charles Babbage cross paths in a red-brick London street, with Sherlock Holmes looking on. In another drawing Lemuel Gulliver is humbly talking to two noble horses, high-minded Houyhnhnms who are warily inspecting this unusual yahoo. Meekly holding his three-corner hat, his feet demurely turned inward, his head pointed towards the ground with his eyes peering upward in supplication, Gulliver is clearly admitting the inferiority of irrational man to the rational horse.

In a 1976 essay in the literary journal *Vort*, Kenner noted that Davenport's literary cartoons belong to the tradition of Max Beerbohm. Both Davenport and Beerbohm specialized in comic scenes of unlikely meetings and unusual juxtapositions. 'There are Davenport drawings in that manner too, with a Cocteau base under the draughtsmanship,' Kenner noted. 'Twenty of them finished like steel engravings, illustrate two published books of mine, and I cherish a folder of unpublished improvisations. (One caption: 'Mr Pound and Mr T.E. Shaw of Arabia, in the latter's rooms at All Souls College, Oxford, are interrupted in their discussion of Gunnar in the *Pit of Vipers* by the arrival of Mrs Lindsay, on a trip around the world, and her son Vachel, the troubadour.' The Vachel Lindsay figure is early George Price. Lawrence of Arabia looks like Stan Laurel.)'

Kenner rightly linked Davenport not just with Beerbohm but also Jean Cocteau. Davenport once quoted Cocteau as saying that his drawings were writing untied and 'knotted up again in a different way.' Like the French master, Davenport's best drawings have anatomical weight and solidity: his characters, no matter how absurd the scene, are drawn as if they have sturdy skeletons under their flesh.

George Herriman was another cartoonist Davenport frequently alluded to. In an essay on E.E. Cummings, Davenport noted that we can appreciate this poet by 'remembering that at any moment in any of his poems he is likely to be ventriloquizing the elate Krazy.' In his utopian story 'Apples and Pears', Davenport imagined a colony of artists who had access to 'all of Piet Mondriaan, all of George Herriman'. (In his recently published correspondence with James Laughlin, Davenport praised three cartoonists: Herriman, Fontaine Fox and Bill Watterson.)

Davenport stopped writing fiction when he was an undergraduate. In 1970, at age 43, he returned to imaginative writing and also in the process started a new phase of his career as a visual artist. Of his eight short-story collections, four are illustrated: *Tatlin!* (1974), *Da Vinci's Bicycle* (1979), *Eclogues* (1981), and *Apples and Pears* (1984). In *Eclogues*, the drawings are by Roy R. Behrens; in the other three books, Davenport illustrated his own stories (except for two pages taken from Henri Gaudier-Brzeska).

In all these books, the drawings are not mere ornamentation. Rather, they are tightly woven in with the texts, words and pictures providing mutual reinforcement. In a deep sense, the words and pictures come from the same hand working for the same purpose.

'The prime use of words is for imagery,' Davenport once told an interviewer. 'My writing is drawing.' On another occasion he observed that 'Writing and drawing, distinct as they are, must converge in their root-system in the brain.'

This can be seen clearly in Davenport's early story, 'Tatlin!' which is the opening and title story of his first collection, setting the stage for his career. The story is based on a historical figure: the Russian painter and designer Vladimir Tatlin, who briefly flourished after the Bolshevik revolution in the great flowering of the 1920s, before being crushed, spiritually and aesthetically, by Stalinism. Tatlin is paradigmatic of Russian art in the 20th century, both its great promise and long suffocation.

The story opens in 1932, with a Moscow showing of Tatlin's newest invention, a glider. 'Tatlin, the ironic Tatlin, is exhibiting Constructivist works at the People's Museum of Decorative Arts. Lenin's face from posters beside every entrance. Lenin's face is among the exhibits inside.' This early stage setting announces the theme of art and politics. Because

Lenin is first seen as a poster, we're reminded that not only does politics dominate art, sometimes politics becomes art.

Then we're given an early glimpse of Tatlin's glider. 'From the ceiling hangs a flying machine. It looks like nothing so much as the fossil skeleton of a pterodactyl. To those who have seen Leonardo's sepia designs for a Tuscan ornithopter, that is what it looks like.' Although a piece of technology, the glider is made to seem welcoming and humane because it grows out of the biological universe. Early machines are often like that. We're told about Clemont Ader's Avion, which lifted 'shaking like a dragonfly above a French meadow in the wild wet spring when Tatlin was twelve.' Equally organic is Tatlin's design for the glider: 'There are interesting drawings of sinuous parallel lines which part from each other around diagrams of the glider, like the grain of wood around a knot. These are air currents. There are arrows to indicate the direction of flow.'

We're in the third page of the story now, and, if we're at all attentive to language, we realize that Davenport has a rare gift for visual description: his words plant images in our mind. But on the opposite page of these word-pictures is an actual drawing: Tatlin sitting down with one of his Constructivist assemblages behind him. Looking sharp and thoughtful, with high cheekbones and deep-set eyes, Tatlin is an artist enjoying his show. There are eleven more pictures in the story, tied to other moments in time.

The second picture, on page 4, is a close-up of Lenin, with a hammer and sickle in the background. On page 16, the same picture of Lenin. Then there is a series of close-ups of Tatlin's art, mostly collages: these are on pages 20, 23, 25, 27, 29. Lenin returns on page 32. The last three pictures are identical images of Stalin: an agitprop image of the dictator facing leftward, peering into the future, wearing full military regalia. These images are on pages 39, 45, 50.

Both the content and sequence of these pictures repays close attention. In progression they tell the story of the move from Lenin to Stalin, from early revolutionary enthusiasm to the deadening hand of state propaganda. Whereas Lenin and Tatlin are both wearing suits, Stalin is in uniform.

With the symmetry that is everywhere present in his work, Davenport balanced six Tatlin images with six Lenin/Stalin ones. But the quality of the pictures is very different, as well. No two images of Tatlin's are replicated, whereas Lenin and Stalin seem as mass-produced as Campbell's soup cans. Moreover the political drawings are crisp, having the false clarity of ideology; the images of Tatlin's art are more fragile and blurred.

As Davenport explained to an interviewer from *The Paris Review*, 'With "Tatlin!" I had to reconstruct, from fuzzy Benday-dot photographs, actual works of art that had been destroyed. There were no sources for Vladimir Tatlin's paintings or his constructs at that time, and I like the idea of working with something that almost isn't there.'

Like 'Tatlin!' all of Davenport's illustrated stories are inventions. The pictures never serve simply to replicate what is in the words but rather add new information or a fresh perspective. These illustrated stories paralleled and anticipated some of the experiments of writers like Donald Barthelme and W. G. Sebald (kissing cousins in Davenport's literary universe).

'It was my intention, when I began writing fiction several years ago, to construct texts that were both written and drawn,' Davenport noted in the introduction to his 1996 book *Fifty Drawings*, a gathering of his fugitive pen-and-ink work. 'In my first work of fiction, *Tatlin* (1974) I drew careful replicas of works by Vladimir Tatlin that exist only as poor reproductions. These were meant to be as much a part of the story as my narrative and required more time to do than the writing. No critic has commented on them, as seeing and reading are now alienated.'

The alienation of reading and seeing eventually led Davenport to become disillusioned with this technique, largely because he felt that readers didn't understand what he was up to. 'I continued this method right through *Apples and Pears*, in which I constructed images that a Dutch philosopher had pasted in his "philosophical sketchbook". The designer understood these collages to be gratuitous illustrations having nothing to do with anything, reduced them all to burnt toast, framed them with nonsensical lines, and sabotaged my whole enterprise. I took this as a final defeat and have not tried to combine drawing and writing in any later work of fiction.'

This is not exactly true, since Davenport did a few limited-edition books where the designers carefully integrated his text and drawings. Now fetching princely prices on the rare-book market, titles like *The Bowmen of Shu* (1984) and *August* (1992) are perhaps the finest embodiment of Davenport's fusion of drawing and writing.

Although he stopped illustrating his own stories, Davenport kept drawing and painting, largely for his private pleasure. Despite the fact that they were never offered for sale, his artworks acquired enough of a word-of-mouth reputation that they inspired a thoughtful and richly illustrated book, *A Balance of Quinces: The Paintings and Drawings of Guy Davenport* (1996) by Erik Anderson Reece. Full of smart observations about Davenport's worldview and close examinations of his art, this book vindicates Davenport's half-hidden career as a artist.

In reading Reece's fine monograph and returning to Davenport's books, I'm struck by how much an artist he remains even in his most prosaic moments. In his famous essay 'The Geography of the Imagination' (found in the essay collection of the same name), Davenport invites us to take a closer look at a painting that might seem in no need of explication, since we've seen it reproduced and parodied so often: Grant Wood's *American Gothic*.

Although the work is considered an American classic, Davenport wanted to trace the roots of Wood's painting deep into the European and African past. 'She is product of the ages, this modest Iowa farm wife: she has the hair-do of a medieval Madonna, a Reformation collar, a Greek cameo, a nineteenth century pinafore,' Davenport noted. 'Martin Luther put her a step behind her husband; John Knox squared her shoulders; the stock-market crash of 1929 put that look in her eyes.'

The very pose of the couple has a history. 'Grant Wood's Iowans stand, as we might guess, in a pose dictated by the Brownie box camera, close together in front of their house, the farmer looking at the lens with solemn honesty, his wife with modestly averted eyes. But that will not account for the pitchfork held as assertively as a minuteman's rifle. The pose is rather of the Egyptian prince Rahotep, holding the flail of Osiris, beside his wife Nufrit—strict with pious rectitude, poised in absolute dignity, mediators between heaven and earth, givers of grain, obedient to the gods.'

In looking at *American Gothic* so closely, Davenport has given us a virtually new painting. His analysis is a magnificent piece of writing, but wouldn't have been possible if he didn't have the eyes of an artist himself. As so often in his work, we find here that Davenport has perfectly integrated a painter's skilled eye with high literacy.

The Comics Journal, No. 278, October 2006

GUY DAVENPORT, RIP

In both his short stories and essays, Guy Davenport often called attention to philosophers who co-existed on easy terms with animals. One of Davenport's heroes was Charles Fourier, the 19th century utopian whose crowded apartment was a haven for alley cats. Another Davenport touchstone was Diogenes, a sage of ancient Athens who was called a 'cynic' (doglike) because he tried to live as simply as a dog. 'He was, to tell the truth, the leader of a pack of dogs, mongrel strays the lot of them,' we are told about Diogenes in a Davenport story. The tale ends with the philosopher's death: 'He was buried under the pines beside the road into the city. We could not know then how terribly the dogs would howl.'

Guy Davenport, who died of cancer at age 77 in January of 2005, was a man of many distinctions: a beloved teacher, a sure-footed literary critic, a keen-eyed analyst of the visual arts, a translator of texts from many languages, an illustrator often called upon to adorn the books of his friends, and a short story writer whose revolutionary innovations have been celebrated all over the world. But like Fourier and Diogenes, he was also a thinker who felt akin to animals, and it is perhaps this part of his personality that offers the easiest key to his character and achievement.

When still a child, Davenport started up a small newspaper to report local news; one of his first articles was an obituary notice for a neighbourhood cat. While doing a doctorate in English at Harvard in the late 1950s, Davenport was shocked at how lab rats were treated. Psychologists, wanting to test the importance of social life to animals, raised rodents in total isolation, carefully recording how they slowly went mad from loneliness. 'They had never snuggled against their mothers or another rat,' Davenport remembered in *Harper's Magazine*. 'When the room was momentarily empty, I took a rat out of its cage, cuddled it, and may even have kissed it. The rat seemed overjoyed, eagerly sniffing graduate-student sweat and grime. Hearing footsteps, I returned it to its solitary confinement. When my sins and kindnesses are weighed by Osiris, I hope to see a white rat on the scales.'

In Lexington, Kentucky, where Davenport spent most of his adult life teaching English at the local university, all sorts of animal life could be seen milling about his house. 'Guy Davenport has ants and bugs in his kitchen,' the very young daughter of a friend once noted with astonishment. In response he confessed that he 'kept a saucer of water for the wasps, hornets and ants that I liked to see in the house.'

Cats were especially also welcome in Davenport's world. One of Davenport's books was dedicated to his cat Humphrey; another tomcat, Max, became a character in a short story, transformed in fiction into a fidgety and willful travel guide. (A feline of literary distinction, Max also made it into a poem by Louis Zukofsky.) As with Diogenes, Davenport's death will be mourned by humans and animals alike. 'He was the kindest, most thoughtful, most considerate person I ever have known,' his former student Charles Ralston noted. 'The informed writers and poets of our time in due course will write encomia about Guy Davenport and critical essays about his work. But, the cats living in Lexington's Bell Court today will have to find another curious professor with whom to share their thoughts.'

The distinction between humans and animals is one of the many binary divisions that our civilization has created over the centuries, in its compulsive desire to divide the world into twos. Other dualisms include the division between art and science, emotion and reason, body and soul, men and women, gays and heterosexuals.

A deeply civilized and learned man, Davenport was aware of the long construction of these foundational divisions, going back at least as far as Plato. Without wanting to overturn civilization, he questioned how viable these divisions were; his lifework can be seen as a persistent exploration of how categories that are seen as separate and distinct, like humans and animals, are actually overlapping, complementary and mutually reinforcing. Humans are also animals; more paradoxically, we can become even more human by carefully attending to our animal companions and the animal within us. Balance and harmony, so valued by archaic Greek thinkers, were also Davenport's watchwords.

The factual resumé of Davenport's life is easy enough to record: born in South Carolina in 1927, the son of a Railway Express agent; trained initially to be an artist, and then more extensively educated in literature at Duke, Oxford and Harvard; military service in the XVIII Airborne Corps from 1952 to 1955; a professor at the University of Kentucky from 1963 until his retirement in 1990. He had the habit throughout his life of picking up awards: he was a Rhodes Scholar in his youth, a MacArthur 'genius' Fellow in his old age. He is survived by Bonnie Jean Cox, his travel-mate and companion of nearly forty years, as well as his younger sister Gloria Williamson.

As a young writer he fell under the sway of the first modernist generation, writing pioneering scholarly theses on James Joyce and Ezra Pound. Like these writers, Davenport saw an affinity between the very old and the very new: to cite one example of many, the way Picasso's art was nourished on the vitality of freshly discovered cave paintings from prehistoric times. Wanting to trace the roots of modern literature, Davenport learned ancient Greek so he could read Homer in the original. In the process he became a masterful translator who, like Pound, could make classic texts sparkle like a coin fresh from the mint.

Davenport's fiction, starting with the volume *Tatlin!* in 1974, was another outgrowth of modernism. As a painter turned storyteller, he chafed at the way drawing and writing were kept in separate compartments (another overly sharp dichotomy). Taking inspiration from the painter-novelist Wyndham Lewis, he developed a highly visual prose. In some of his earlier books, Davenport mixed drawings and text together, prefiguring the experimentation of W.G. Sebald. Here is a scene set in a swimming pool: 'The blue-eyed man dove, piercing the water as adroitly as a key slips into a lock. His green body slid in a comet of foam underwater, rose with a scissor kick, and burst to the surface in a grand spray of fiery light.' Like a skilled artist, Davenport uses prose to help guide our eyes and sharpen our vision. Although often elliptical and demanding, his fiction is filled with writing of a great lyrical beauty, especially in his descriptions of the natural world.

Never a bestseller, Davenport was nonetheless much admired by fellow writers, indeed envied for his deep fund of erudition, his unfailing verbal inventiveness, his panache. This distinguished fan club included Carol Shields, Anne Carson, George Steiner, Samuel Delany and Alexander Theroux.

His stories can be divided into two broad camps, historical and utopian. The historical recreations work like time machines, magically taking us back to remote eras: the Athens of Diogenes, the Jerusalem of Jesus, the Copenhagen of Kierkegaard, the Prague of Kafka.

From one of these stories, here is an unexpected view of Socrates, seen with a downward gaze. 'Socrates' feet, we heard, were enormous, bony, unshod, knuckly of hallux, hairy, with oxbone ankles. The man's mind was all there, its strength and endurance.' From another story, here is a pen-portrait of Jonah, a prophet fleeing from the mission assigned to him by the Almighty: 'He had a fine black beard, round as a basket. Though his carpetbags were neatly strapped and his clothes showed he was an experienced traveller, there was a furtiveness in his eyes, as if there might be someone about he did not care to meet.'

In both these passages, we see one of the signature touches of Davenport's prose, his intense visualness. But there is an oral dimension to Davenport's writing as well. A child of the South, Davenport possessed the alertness to vernacular found in writers from that region. His books are spiced up with quirky words ('mumpery') and charmingly idiomatic turns of phrases ('he's a caution'). Speaking of Davenport, his sister told a reporter, 'money didn't mean a doodle to him'. We can hear the family lilt in her use of the word 'doodle'.

A glimmer of Davenport's sensibility can be seen in some of the unusual words that he often returned to: trill, chirr, macadam, and caisson. He liked to contrast rooted Anglo-Saxon words with foreign implants. The fabric of English weaves together strands taken from many languages. With great care, Davenport unravelled this haphazard embroidery and re-knit it to form a more consciously created pattern.

Always toying with language, Davenport fashioned a prose that was in constant motion: it kept evolving and morphing not just from book to book but from story to story. But a few general trends can be noticed about the arc of his evolution. In the early stories collected in *Tatlin!*, Davenport was still an essayist trying his hand at fiction. The prose in these stories is glittering and rich, but perhaps too much so: we're dazzled by Davenport's leaping erudition but this keeps us distant from what actually happens. The stories gleam with a hard, enamel surface.

As Davenport grew more experienced and confident, the thick writing of *Tatlin!* has given way to a more agile and limber prose. Unlike the over-powering voice of the early essay-fictions, the tone of the later stories is gentle, tentative, and evocative. His voice became more internal and intimate. It almost seems indecent to comment on some of the later stories, so personal are they in their exploration of a rich inner life.

Davenport's utopian fiction, much influenced by Fourier, tends to be set in an imaginary Scandinavia where sex was freed from social constraints. Criticized by some as prurient and obsessive, these utopian tales are part of Davenport's larger project of returning to the archaic roots of creativity. All of his work grows from a single, harmonic vision.

His best essays can be found in *The Geography of the Imagination* (1981); his most accessible fiction is in *Da Vinci's Bicycle* (1979). But in fact everything he wrote is worth reading. His stature will only grow with time.

National Post, January 13, 2005

GAIL SINGER'S 'WATCHING MOVIES'

Movie-going is rarely a solitary act, nor should it be. Most of us start seeing movies from an early age and when we think back on them we remember not just what we saw on the screen but also the surrounding ambience: what theatre we were at and with whom. Sociability is part of movie going, and contributes to the hold film has over us.

Rereading the reviews of Pauline Kael recently, I was struck by how often she dwelled on the social aspect of film-going, especially the friendships that are kindled in the heat of discussions about movies. Many of Kael's reviews record not only her reactions but also interesting observations made by friends who saw the movie with her. 'Being able to talk about movies with someone—to share the giddy high excitement you feel—is enough for a friendship,' Kael wrote in a short note looking back on her decades as movie reviewer.

Movie-going not only helps cement friendship. The more intimate bonds of romantic love are also forged under the shared flicker of the screen. For nearly a century now film-going has been intertwined with courtship and coupledom. For spooning teenagers and hand-squeezing seniors alike, movie-going is one of the rituals of love.

Every so often a filmmaker will decide to turn the camera lens on the audience and examine the impact that movies have on those who watch them. Giuseppe Tornatore's *Cinema Paradiso* (1989) is perhaps the best-loved of the movies about movie-going, but Woody Allen has also essayed the topic several times, from *Play it Again, Sam* (1972) to *The Purple Rose of Cairo* (1985).

Now Gail Singer tackles the same rich subject in her delightful documentary *Watching Movies*. 'What do we know about this mysterious urge to secrete ourselves away in the half-light?' Singer asks. 'What is the magic that keeps us spellbound at the movies?' To answer these questions, Singer has assembled an array of chatterboxes who share her own passion for movie talk, ranging from the renowned (director Atom Egoyan) to ordinary film-goers with strong and articulate opinions (notably high school student William DiNovi, who has very detailed theories about how to select a proper seat). Especially engaging is the political scientist Nelson Wiseman, who can barely contain his jumped-up delight at Jackie Chan movies.

Singer's motley cast offer zestful thoughts on all the common experience that make up movie-going but rarely get analyzed: Is it better to show up early to do some people-watching or come in late just to catch a flick? Do you want to sit up front to be immersed in the filmic universe or sit in the back so you can enjoy analytical distance? Does popcorn provide us with a soothing comfort or is it any annoyance to those around us? (One fact is clear: you shouldn't munch on popcorn anywhere near Atom Egoyan, or his face will scrunch up in pain.)

This is an artful documentary where Singer slyly juxtaposes conflicting voices and visual cues. Thus we hear earnest experts talk about the correct posture for sitting and the nutritional content of snack food. These overly sober ideas are wryly parodied in accompanying cartoons. These cartoons also save the film from the visual boredom that usually afflicts talking-heads documentaries.

The same skill at mix-and-matching film editing can be seen in the contrast between two movie-going couples. Retired academics Margaret and Colin Visser are almost regal in their shared opinions: Margaret, with her brisk Zimbabwe English accent, holds forth confidently while Colin nods in agreement, only once piping in a few words. The journalists Johanna Schneller and Ian Brown are completely different: like the bickering couples in a screwball comedy, their relationship is built on conniption fits and barbed disagreement. By including clips from both couples at well-timed intervals, Singer illustrates the different ways that movie-going duos interact.

Despite these different personal styles, everyone in Singer's movie acknowledges the social aspect of film-going. 'I think there is a collective emotional energy that floats above the people who are watching movies,' Schneller notes. 'There is no question that watching a film with an audience that is intent, drawn into it, and has a certain level of understanding enormously enhances the film,' Margaret Visser agrees. 'It's nothing like seeing it on your own.'

Although it moves along at a breezy pace, *Watching Movies* is extremely thought-provoking. After seeing it, it is hard to take the darkling glamour of the movie theatre for granted.

National Post, December 11, 2003

ELIZABETH KOLBERT'S 'SIXTH EXTINCTION'

To look into the eyes of a frog is to travel back in time. The earliest amphibians hoisted themselves out of the water some 370 million years ago, long before there were any birds in flight, mammals scurrying around, or even dinosaurs stomping the earth. A full chronicle of amphibian history would start prior to the existence of the seven continents, when the only landmass on our planet was a sprawling expanse scientists have labelled Pangaea, not yet splintered by tectonic plates.

Squishy and soft though they may be, amphibians are in fact hardy survivors. Since life appeared on earth 3.5 billion years ago, there have been five major extinction events, traumatic changes in climate and environment that have felled many, and sometimes most, species existing at a particular moment. With their mournful, limpid eyes, amphibians have witnessed four of these five extinction events, the most spectacular and notorious being the asteroid that wiped out the dinosaurs and many other species 65 million years ago.

The unsettling news of Elizabeth Kolbert's powerful book *The Sixth Extinction* is that we are witnessing a wide-scale dying off of species comparable to the earlier extinction events. An early and startling symptom of the Sixth Extinction is the sudden and global collapse of countless varieties of frogs, the very animal whose ancestors were so adept at surviving. The culprit behind this extinction is no asteroid but a single species, humanity. In countless ways, we are rendering the earth uninhabitable to many of our fellow earth-dwellers.

Summing up the scientific consensus, Kolbert notes that 'it is estimated that one-third of all reef-building corals, a third of all fresh-water molluscs, a third of sharks and rays, a quarter of all mammals, a fifth of all reptiles, and a sixth of all birds are headed toward oblivion.'

Why is our planet once again turning into a spherical graveyard? Climate change is a major cause. It is darkly ironic that the very dinosaurs wiped out by that fateful asteroid are now the fossil fuels igniting another extinction event. But beyond climate change, the full impact of which we only have a small glimmer of, many of the traits that make humanity so successful as a species are also lethal to other life forms. Our versatility and cleverness have allowed us to expand into virtually every corner of the globe, bringing into fragile ecosystems invasive new species that eliminate all the local competition.

Humanity has so thoroughly transformed the planet that we may be the first life form that deserves to have a geological epoch named after us, the Anthropocene (the term is gaining popularity in scientific circles although hasn't been formally accepted yet by the International Commission on Stratigraphy). Before the Anthropocene is over, much of what we now call zoology will become a branch of palaeontology. Those animals that survive won't live in the wild but will be domesticated or be confined to prisons we call reserves and zoos. In order to insure the reproduction of the survivors, the most intimate relations of these animals will be carefully monitored by the species that brought them to the abyss of non-existence.

Mass extinction is a grim topic yet Kolbert's book is an exhilarating read. A staff writer for *The New Yorker*, Kolbert has wisely marshalled her arguments into the form of an intellectual adventure. She notes in passing that one of the scientists she meets 'decided to become a paleontologist when he was seven, after reading a Tintin adventure about a dig.' Perhaps taking a cue, Kolbert has cast herself as Tintin, a globe-trotting reporter joining field researchers all over the world as they try to solve the ultimate murder mystery: Why are so many animals dying and how can we stop it?

The Sixth Extinction is a book that cannot be recommended highly enough. It deals with the most important possible topic, the fate of life on earth, in a responsible, entertaining, and mind-expanding way. It is profound without being ponderous, edifying without being hectoring.

An important book is by necessity one that provokes serious disagreement as well as thought. It's a tribute to Kolbert's achievement that I also ended up having some serious philosophical reservations about her ultimate argument.

Kolbert wants to avoid blaming the Sixth Extinction merely on industrial modernity and instead asks us to think of it as an outgrowth of humanity's supposedly inherent alienation from nature. 'Though it might be nice to imagine there once was a time when man lived in harmony with nature,' she argues, 'it's not clear that he ever really did.'

As sober as she is, Kolbert ends up adopting a position of misanthropy (or as she says, 'sounding antihuman'). Kolbert's misanthropy is bemused rather than scornful but still the burden of her argument is that right from the start humanity was always bad news, a position she finds support for in mankinds' possible role in extinguishing sibling species such as the Neanderthal and the Denisovan. One problem with this line of argument is that it is too speculative (anything we surmise about the Neanderthals is shaky and provisional). Secondly, this is also a depoliticized argument that blames human nature rather than social systems created by humans. Rather than pondering the uncertain demise of the Neanderthal, she would have been better off reading environmental historians such as Alfred Crosby's *Ecological Imperialism: The Biological Expansion of Europe, 900–1900* (1986), whose accounts of extinction give room for human agency.

More deeply, to say humanity is the enemy of nature is to fall into a pre-Darwinian dualism that sees humans as being separate and apart from nature. But as Darwin taught us, humans are animals. When you look into a mirror, you are seeing nature.

Kolbert should have pondered the words she quotes in the epigram of her book from the great naturalist E.O. Wilson, who notes the irony that 'in the instant of achieving self-understanding through the mind of man, life has doomed its most beautiful creations.' If humanity is nature come to self-consciousness, then our intelligence can become a tool whereby nature learns to save herself.

The ecological crisis we face is so severe that we can't afford the luxury of misanthropy. Throughout the book Kolbert is too dismissive of efforts at conservation, which are surely inadequate but worth supporting. Rather than browbeating ourselves about the inherent wickedness of our species, we need to use one of the greatest gifts of nature, our intelligence, to learn how to live at peace with our fellow creatures.

The violence that humans have done to the planet will not heal easily, and countless species have already died or are doomed. But thinking of humans as being anything other than an animal is a false path that takes us away from real solutions.

National Post, February 14, 2014

JESUS AND RECYCLING

Jesus thought a great deal about garbage. He had been raised in a tradition that made a fundamental distinction between purity and impurity, kosher and *treif*, the sacred and the profane. These seem like very strict and absolute binary divisions but Hebrew scripture also contained an ambiguity. The sacred texts abound in narratives that contradict the absolute division between the clean and the dirty by celebrating people who were closest to the grimy ground, the rejected and the dejected. Prototypically, there were slaves of Egypt who became the chosen people (slaves being those who do the dirty work of society); there is also Ruth gathering gleanings (i.e., picking up food not worth the farmer's time); and also the many unkempt prophets who were closer to God than all the Rabbis. Consider Jonah: a man of God swallowed by a whale and then extruded, the prophet as vomit or excrement, yet fulfilling his divine mission even in his humiliation. (The story of Jonah is one that seems to have been particularly dear to Jesus.)

'The stone that the builders rejected has become the cornerstone,' Psalm 118: 22 (echoed by Jesus in the Synoptic gospels).

Again and again, Jesus talked about waste and refuse, about the stone the builder rejected, about old wine sacks and garments needing patching, about the appropriateness of eating unclean food. There are some limits to recycling: as a practical matter new wine shouldn't be put in old sacks, lest they burst (although even this injunction comes with a reminder that it's better to drink old wine than new). There is a kind of linguistic recycling as well in the way Jesus often preferred to reuse the words of the Hebrew scripture rather than come up with anything new.

Jesus kept company with those who were condemned as 'dirty': prostitutes, lepers, fishermen, debt collectors, Samaritans. (The Samaritans apparently had the same social position in ancient Palestine that the untouchables have in India.) The Scottish preacher George McLeod once took note of the fact that the crucifixion seems to have taken place near the town garbage heap.

The Jesus movement can be seen as a reclamation project: an attempt to redeem what the world rejects as 'garbage', to take trash and make it useful again. The critique of 'purity' lies at the heart of the project: we can't be pure just by separating ourselves from garbage.

One way to think about God is to see him as wholly other, completely outside of humanity and nature, a pure being. But Jesus had the intuition that this was wrong; that God was not so far away; that God was inside of him (and inside everyone else); that being pure meant not just keeping one's exterior clean (obeying the law) but also being clean inside, in thought and spirit. This is of course a spiritualizing of the law, but it also has an interesting side effect in making it possible to see that the material world is not unclean, nothing is unclean except that we make it so through our bad purposes.

'Nothing outside a man can make him "unclean" by going into him. Rather, it is what comes out of a man that makes him "unclean".' Mark 7:15.

Part of our ecological problem comes from the way we think about garbage, or more exactly the way we don't think about garbage. Our material abundance is such that we can put garbage totally out of our mind (something not possible for Jesus, living as he did among the poor in the ancient world). There is always someone else to attend to our waste; our affluence saves us from worrying about effluence. The assumption we live by is that our resources are endless, that everything we consume can be disposed of without thought and perpetually replaced. This is not true, and we need to think more seriously about garbage. Those who call themselves Christians might want to attend to how Jesus himself dealt with trash.

Sans Everything, January 23, 2008

CANADIAN CULTURE

ALICE MUNRO AS A LITERARY ENTREPRENEUR

Writers, like almost everyone else, have to make money to survive. But serious literary writers, unlike most people, have to be very careful about how they earn that money. An accountant may, without guilt, take on any client she wants, short of a mobster or the Enron Corporation.

An author, in contrast, has to avoid not just the taint of criminality but also the more subtle dangers of commercialism. A high-brow prose-smith who simply writes on demand for the highest bidder will soon earn the reputation of being a 'hack'.

For a woman of Alice Munro's generation, the economic dilemmas of writing fiction posed even greater problems. Munro, the subject of a new book titled *Reading In: Alice Munro's Archives*, started writing in the early '50s, but she did not make a decent living from writing short stories until the late '70s, when she cracked the U.S. market by becoming a fixture in *The New Yorker*.

During her quarter-century apprenticeship, Munro had to juggle her roles as wife and mother with her furtive literary aspirations, writing during stolen moments away from her family. Earning only a sporadic income from her writing, for many years Munro doubted whether she would ever become a real, professional writer. In a story entitled 'The Office', the narrator expresses, with Munro's characteristic sensitivity to social embarrassment, the insecurities of a housewife/writer. 'But here comes the disclosure which is not easy for me: I am a writer. That does not sound right. Too presumptuous; phony, or at least unconvincing. Try again. I write. Is that better?... It doesn't matter. However I put it, the words create their space of silence, the delicate moment of exposure.' (We know that this would-be writer has great potential because this unexpected burst of eloquence—'the delicate moment of exposure'—takes flight after the halting attempts at self-definition.)

With the help of unpublished biographical material, JoAnn McCaig's *Reading In: Alice Munro's Archives* is an attempt to map out some of the issues raised by stories such as 'The Office'. Using Munro's career as a case study, McCaig sets out to illustrate the difficulty of being, specifically, a female Canadian short-story writer in a literary marketplace where each of those adjectives represents a barrier to success.

McCaig's somewhat single-minded focus is on the business end of Munro's career, rather than on her writing. None of Munro's many excellent stories gets discussed in any detail. Instead, we hear about the pressures the writer faced 'to make money, crack the American market, write novels'.

Through McCaig's economic lens, Munro emerges, surprisingly, as a successful entrepreneur whose rags-to-riches story one might have expected to read in the pages of *Fortune* or *Forbes*. Despite starting with meagre cultural capital, Munro adroitly negotiated with editors and agents to develop one of the most lucrative brand names in CanLit.

McCaig's book has an interesting backstory that sheds light on taboos in the literary world surrounding money. After an earlier excerpt from the book was published in *Essays in Canadian Writing* in 1999 and publicized in the *National Post*, Alice Munro wrote to this paper saying that McCaig's article was 'riddled with bizarre assumptions and written with blatant disregard for fact'.

In the aftermath, Munro and some of her literary friends and associates denied McCaig the right to quote from their unpublished writings. Since almost all of McCaig's arguments rely on private letters found only in archives, Munro's restriction seriously impedes the ability of readers to judge either side's arguments.

Munro's hostility to McCaig is interesting since McCaig, an academic, is not at all an intrusive biographer looking for salacious details. Fixated on economics, McCaig mentions Munro's two marriages and her family life only in passing. Yet, for Munro, as for many other people, it seems money may be the more touchy personal issue. As Norman Podhoretz once argued, in our society, it is money, not sex, that is the dirty secret everyone is reluctant to talk about in public.

That said, even if one wishes Munro had taken a more tolerant attitude toward the use of quotations from her letters, there are aspects of the book that do suggest McCaig's analysis may not be that reliable. As is characteristic of an academic novice, McCaig seems eager to twist every shred of evidence toward supporting her thesis, not realizing that the most convincing arguments allow for the untidiness of life.

When McCaig quotes from published sources, her exegesis often bears only a passing resemblance to the original source. Thus, a statement by Munro that male writers are more often allowed to misbehave in public (the Norman Mailer principle) is transformed by McCaig into anxiety about appearing in *The New Yorker*. Elsewhere, small, ambiguous doodles that Munro penned in the margins of her papers are interpreted as evidence of an identity crisis.

Perhaps it is just as well that McCaig avoids old-fashioned close analysis of texts, since she is untrustworthy in reading even simple declarative sentences. The trouble is, outside the circle of family and friends who care for Alice Munro personally, the only reason Munro holds any interest is because she is a miraculous writer.

And, for a serious writer such as Munro, McCaig's avoidance of literary criticism is perhaps even more insulting than sniffing through old business letters.

It's not as if there is nothing to be said about Munro's writerly talents. As we've seen in 'The Office', Munro can render a character's transition from stammering hesitancy to subtly nuanced expressiveness within a few fluid sentences. Her entire body of work, 10 volumes so far, is filled with such verbal miracles. Aside from her mastery of prose, Munro has a landscape painter's sense of place: her small-town Ontario lingers in a reader's mind as a place we almost believe we grew up in. Equally admirable are Munro's narrative skills, which have become increasingly expert in recent years. Like a good magician, she knows how to hold the audience's attention by leaving the biggest trick to the moment of maximum anticipation.

But McCaig, oddly, seems to think literary value judgments (even the statement that Alice Munro's recent work is better than her early stories, for example, which McCaig makes a point of criticizing in her book) are always ideological impostures that need to be debunked. Aside from being silly, this line of thought is unnecessary for McCaig's thesis.

In the end, there is no reason why you can't argue that Alice Munro has adroitly manoeuvred in the literary marketplace and also that she is a very good writer who deserves her success. Certainly Pierre Bourdieu, the towering Marxist theorist whom McCaig relies on heavily for her analytical structure, was not averse to value judgements. In his book about television, Bourdieu heaps scorn on the junk that dominates the boob tube.

Too often, McCaig seems to resent Munro's high status and wants to replace the writer's fictional narratives with an academic interpretation. At one point, McCaig praises Munro's 'enviable artistry and authority'. Enviable seems to be the key word. 'I am, after all, not an eminent man of letters, but a mere slip of a girl barely out of college,' McCaig complains at another point. 'Like my subject, Alice Munro, I have had to wrestle with the lies, secrets, and silence that are my cultural inheritance, and have had to grant myself the authority to speak.... The real "beggar maid" in this story is not Alice Munro, but me.' ('Beggar maid' was, of course, Alice Munro's memorable description of her character Rose, from *Who Do You Think You Are?*, taken from a Tennyson poem.)

It's hard not to admire McCaig's audacity: using tatters of evidence from business letters, she wants to create a narrative so compelling it will supplant the work of Alice Munro. Not surprisingly, McCaig has failed, and merely created a literary curiosity.

National Post, May 11, 2002

CLARK BLAISE'S 'SOUTHERN STORIES'

The Florida that has been so much in the electoral news is not the Florida that Clark Blaise grew up in. Modern air-conditioned Florida is the land of retired snowbirds and Cuban exiles, the sanitized kitsch of Disney and the glittery kitsch of *Miami Vice*. The son of a French-Canadian father and an English-Canadian mother, Blaise's childhood in the late 1940s was spent in an Old South Florida much closer to William Faulkner than to Mickey Mouse.

Blaise remembers an 'impoverished Florida' that included 'the moss-pickers I went to school with, the worms in my feet that my mother treated with carbolic acid, and the worms she killed with dabs of acid on my rectum holding a flashlight as they churned out of my guts at night to spawn, the Ku Klux Klan (local politicians and businessmen who unmasked themselves every Confederate Memorial Day leading a cavalcade of convertibles with the high school band and beauty queens so we'd know who to vote for and where to shop).'

It's this gothic and grotesque Florida—a land where gawping hillbillies learn about sex at carnival peep-shows—that is the setting for Blaise's *Southern Stories*, the first of four geographically organized volumes reprinting his shorter fiction. Inheriting the wandering bug from his travelling salesman father, Blaise has been one of the most cosmopolitan of authors, so subsequent volumes will print his tales of the American North, Canada and India.

What makes Blaise a remarkable writer is that the breadth of his travels has not hampered the depth of his perceptions. He has the rare ability to be regional and cosmopolitan at the same time. He can conjure up Orlando as convincingly as if he has been a lifelong resident, but he can do the same for Montreal, Paris and Calcutta.

In describing a place, Blaise combines the visitor's attention to surface detail with the native's feeling of intense local attachment. As novelist Fenton Johnson notes in the introduction to this book, Blaise's portrayal of a dirt-poor South haunted by history belongs to an American literary tradition that includes Faulkner, Flannery O'Connor and Eudora Welty.

What needs to be added is that this Southern Gothic tradition has tendrils that reach all the way up to Canada. Aside from Blaise, there have been many reverse carpetbaggers, Southerners who have headed (or returned) north such as Leon Rooke, Douglas Fetherling and Elizabeth Spencer. Moreover, many prototypically Canadian writers such as Alice Munro learned their craft at the feet of Southern masters.

Like the American South, Canada has been a poor, rural land suspicious of outsiders and technological progress for most of its history. It's no accident that at the end of the American Civil War, Confederate leaders such as Jefferson Davis ended up in Canada.

Progressive and enlightened Canadians might not like to think so, but there is a deep emotional affinity between Canada and the American South. French Canadians in particular have felt the lure of the South. Long before the United States or Canada became nations, francophones were travelling down the rivers of North America, often ending up in Texas, Louisiana or Florida. That quintessential Texan Ross Perot is the descendant of these far-flung fur traders.

Outside of Quebec, French-Canadians are the hobbits of North America: a shy, diffident people who know how to hide from unfriendly outsiders. Part of Blaise's achievement is to tell the story of this hidden people, his father's people, who form an invisible thread that links Quebec with the Gulf of Mexico.

Blaise constantly plays off the parallels and differences between the American South and Canada. Here are the experiences of a young Canadian boy new to Florida: 'After a week in Hartley I developed worms. My feet bleed from itching and scratching. The worms were visible; I could prick them with pins. My mother took me to a clinic where the doctor sprayed my foot with a liquid freeze. Going on, the ice was pleasant, for Florida feet are always hot. Out on the bench I scraped my initials in the frost on my foot. It seemed right to me (before the pain of the thaw began): I was from Up North, the freezing was a friendly gesture for a Florida doctor. My mother held my foot between her hands and told me stories of her childhood, ice-skating for miles on the Battleford River in Saskatchewan, then riding home under fur rugs in a horse-drawn sleigh. My mother then consulted her old *Canadian Doctor's Home Companion*—my grandfather Blankenship had been a doctor, active for years in curling circles, Anglican missions, and crackpot Toryism—and learned that footworms, etc., "were unknown in Canada but sometimes afflicted Canadian travellers in Tropical Regions. Common to all hot climes," the book went on, "due to poor sanitation and the unspeakable habits of the non-white peoples, even in the Gulf Coast and Indians Territories of our southern neighbour".'

Two worlds are created in this passage: the Florida world of worms (a recurring and apt image, since Blaise himself is a writer who knows how to get under our skin) and the paternalistic world of the deftly described Saskatchewan grandfather. In another story, the same boy, after being acclimatized to Florida, returns to Saskatchewan. 'A cold spring gave way, in May, to a dry, burning heat, the kind that blazed across my forehead and shrunk the skin under my eyes and over my nose. But I didn't sweat. It wasn't like Florida heat that reached up groggily from the ground as well as from above, steaming the trouser cuffs while threatening sunstroke.'

Again, seen through the same eyes, Florida and Saskatchewan are both unexpectedly made fresh by Blaise's brilliant description.

Blaise has a mixed reputation in Canada. His best stories have been much anthologized and praised, but the very fact that so much of his fiction is set in other lands has prevented him from becoming a canonical Canadian writer. Yet this gathering of Southern stories, previously unpublished or scattered in other Blaise collections, should solidify his reputation as a major Canadian writer with a special achievement. More than any other writer, Blaise has shown how Canada is linked by geography, immigration and cultural affinity to the wider world, including the gothic world of William Faulkner.

National Post, December 30, 2000

LEON ROOKE'S 'LAST SHOT'

If you want to make any progress as a moral being, you have to own up to your biases and grapple with your unexamined assumptions. So in the spirit of self-correction, I'll freely admit that prior to reading Leon Rooke's *The Last Shot*, I was intensely prejudiced against pastiches.

I once thought that a pastiche is an inherently second-rate genre, a parasitical form redolent of self-satisfied bookish in-jokes. Pastiches, I believed, should be best left to the nerdy arrested-development types who try to map out the genealogies of Sherlock Holmes and Tarzan (sometimes proving that the great detective and the Jungle Lord are distant cousins). The attempt by various contemporary writers, working under the unhelpful rubric of post-modernism, to ennoble pastiche by making it subversive—I'm thinking here of the appropriation of genre tropes by Robert Coover, Jonathan Lethem and Michael Chabon—has generally left me cold since the novels they've produced lack either the unpretentious, light-hearted thrills of sincere pulp fiction or the emotional intensity of genuine literature. The core problem is that a pastiche is always literature about literature rather than literature about life, hence one step too far removed from the lived experiences that must, in however distorted or imaginative a form, make up the core truth that fiction is built around.

But, as Leon Rooke has shown time and again in a career nearly unprecedented in its inventiveness, there is no literary rule that can't be broken by a writer with enough daring and street smarts. 'Gator Wrestling', the novella that makes up the heart of *The Last Shot*, is a pastiche of the Southern fiction of Clark Blaise and echoes of Blaise's own loadstar William Faulkner. Yet there is nothing derivative or second-rate about the story. Readers of Blaise's superb novel *Lunar Attractions* or his essential collection *Southern Stories* will repeatedly experience déjà vu while reading 'Gator Wrestling', which features a torpid, musky small town Florida locale, complete with alligators and insects; wayward French-Canadian clans (with names like Thibidault and Coombs) who have made their way south; a furniture store that goes defunct leaving family disaster in its wake. One character uses the phrase 'a North American education' (title of a key Blaise story), another character is shamelessly named 'little Blaise' and there is even a 'Struthers' in the story (a tip of the hat to critic J.R. Struthers, who edited the volume of the journal *Short Story* which was dedicated to Clark Blaise, where Rooke's story first appeared).

All of this might make 'Gator Wrestling' sound hopelessly coy and self-referential, like a televised 'celebrity roast' where the stars rib each other for flubs they made decades ago on the set of a long forgotten B movie while the audience gawps in puzzlement. Yet 'Gator Wrestling' isn't just an expert joshing of a Blaise story but rather something much deeper than that, perhaps comparable to the musical genre of 'the cover'. Think of Joan Baez doing a cover of a Bob Dylan song, where she does more than just sing the same lyrics but also reveals new shades of meaning and comments on Dylan's influence on folk music. Or imagine Miles Davis doing a cover of a Duke Ellington number while also paying tribute to their common debt to Scott Joplin and you'll get an idea of what Rooke achieves by both covering a Clark Blaise story and also laying a wreath at the tomb of their common father, Faulkner.

Rooke can get away with doing a Blaise cover because the two men share a similar life-trajectory as reverse carpetbaggers, Southerners who have headed (or returned) north. Rooke was born in North Carolina, and Blaise spent his crucial formative years in Florida. Both men are haunted by the South in the same way a defrocked clergyman will remain haunted by Christ. 'Gator Wrestling' recreates the country of Blaise's youth to chronicle the shift from the Old South to the new. As so often in Rooke's fiction, generational conflict lies at the heart of the drama, in this particular tale the tension between the racism of the traditional South and the rise of a younger generation formed in the wake of the Civil Rights movement.

The characters in 'Gator Wrestling' aren't just crackers and hicks, they are self-conscious crackers and hicks, whose very dialect is knowingly exaggerated. As the narrator observes of two girls, 'No one could put [them] in the shade when it came to talking cracker talk.' So when a character refers to a car as 'a awe-tee-mo-beel' we're to think not just of Faulkner but also the long tradition of comic hillbillies such as Al Capp's Li'l Abner. The Old South is no longer a region but rather a giant open air theme park, and even the reactionary politics of the area has an aspect of play-acting. Ultimately 'Gator Wrestling' is an elegy, albeit a hilarious one:

the South of Blaise and Faulkner, for better or worse, is long gone, and the story offers up a high-spirited obituary.

Blaise and Faulkner are only two of the many writers alluded to, celebrated or even gently tweaked in *The Last Shot.* The first shot in 'The Last Shot' makes reference to almost all the major modern short story writers, from O. Henry to Raymond Carver. J.D. Salinger, no less, shows up in another tale, although he's only a teeny-bit more forthcoming in Rooke's tale than he was in real life. The process of writing gets foregrounded in the book, as witness titles like 'How to Write a Successful Short Story' (a phrase which gains an extra edge of irony when we realize that there is no one alive who can offer good advice on this topic better than Rooke) and 'All True Stories Have Loose Ends'.

I've mentioned my prejudice against 'literature about literature' and my distrust of post-modernism. Well, just as some of Rooke's Southerners overcome their racism and indeed transcend the condition of whiteness, Rooke has conquered my literary bigotry. With an author as wide-reading as Rooke, and as skilful as he is in doing riffs in the style of other writers, literature is part of life and a fit subject for stories.

With all its literary allusiveness, *The Last Shot* almost seems designed to provoke reflections on Rooke's own status in the pantheon of modern fiction. At this late date in his career, more than forty years after the publication of his first story collection, appraising Rooke's oeuvre seems both daunting and unnecessary. He belongs in the small, select company of Canadian masters, a peer of Alice Munro, Mavis Gallant and Clark Blaise. Like their work, everything he writes is, almost by definition, worth reading and re-reading.

Tellingly, reviewers faced with the task of surveying the Rooke phenomenon often resort to the same tactics used by hapless tour guides at Niagara Falls, statistics. Rooke has given us more than 300 stories, many but not all of which can be found in his eighteen collections, as well as seven novels, and sundry plays and poems.

Such quantitative measures tell us nothing about quality. More impressive is the fact that Rooke's prodigious prolificness is achieved without the vices of prolixity and repetitiveness. Although he's given over to swooping flights of rhetoric, Rooke's verbal virtuosity always serves a purpose. There is scarcely an unnecessary word in *The Last Shot.* The stylistic variety on display is remarkable: aside from his impressive resurrection of

Flannery O'Connor's flint-eyed portrayal of shiftless poor whites (in 'The Last Shot' and 'A Good Radio Voice') we also get a sentimental story about angels told by a narrator who is as bluff and breezy, as clubby and cool, as Anthony Trollope unfolding a tale about a small town vicarage.

What holds the collection together is a concern for family life. In 'Gator Wrestling' a family saga is summed up in a crisp sentence: 'Junior had been wanting to leave town since he was a boy, the father bound and determined to keep Junior under his thumb and properly beholden, as a child should be.' Here is Rooke's recurring concern, which is not just the way the old weigh down the young but also the way the young trap the old. Family life in Rooke's universe is like a spiderweb, both a home and a sticky constraint. And if they do escape from home, Rooke's people perversely desire to return there. This desire for home even affects Dark, the personification of death who is the hero of the last story in the collection.

The great cliché about Rooke is that he's primarily an oral writer, one who flourishes best when he's onstage. Anne Michaels has called Rooke 'a preacher' while Kent Thompson says he's a 'performance artist', a description echoed by John Metcalf. Like most clichés, Rooke-as-performer is true enough, but it allows readers to ignore the fact that he's as much an eye-writer as a tongue-writer. To simplify, tongue-writers are the great rhetoricians and monologuists of literature—Joyce, Faulkner, Philip Roth—who hold our attention with a torrential outpouring of words. Eye-writers are the cooler, more observant sorts who like to linger on the surface of things: Nabokov, John Updike, Nicholson Baker.

Rooke's skill as a tongue-writer has prevented readers and critics from noticing how visually attentive he is. In 'Gator Wrestling' a bicycle is limned with these words: 'a near-spokeless, wired-together bike, ... seatless but for a protruding metal spike, the bent pedals dragging the dust, the handlebar misaligned, as though an axe heel had been taken to it.' This remarkable bike is a thing of beauty not only in and of itself, it's a perfect emblem of an entire way of life and region. That region, the American South, gave birth to Leon Rooke, and is the ground of his being, the wellspring of his remarkable literary career. Just as Dark returns to his mother, Rooke has taken one last trip home, a journey that enriches us all.

Canadian Notes & Queries, No. 79, 2009

JOHN METCALF'S LITERARY WARS

In the chummy world of Canadian literature, where smarmy mutual praise is the reigning lingo, John Metcalf has a reputation as a troublemaker. Largely unknown to the general public, the British-born novelist and editor is legendary in bookish circles for his blunt honesty, cherished and reviled alike for his willingness to express strong and unpopular opinions.

As short story writer Patricia Robertson notes in *The New Quarterly*, if you haven't met Metcalf it is easy to be intimidated by his many caustic critical essays and biting book reviews. 'I had an image of a British pit bull, seizing Canadian literature by the seat of its pants and yanking it, kicking and screaming, in the direction of Mr Metcalf's School of Higher Literary Standards,' Robertson observed.

In his new autobiography, *An Aesthetic Underground*, Metcalf proves that the pit bull of CanLit still has some bite. Aside from many entertaining stories about boozing and skirt chasing by the literati, Metcalf's autobiography is filled with characteristically tart put-downs of revered literary figures. Morley Callaghan, Metcalf insists, was guilty of, 'stumblebum writing'. Margaret Atwood's influential nationalist tome *Survival* was, 'not only silly but dangerous'. *The Rebel Angels* by Robertson Davies was, 'a relentlessly bad novel' which won applause because the author's theatrical presence flummoxed dim-witted reviewers. 'Like the yokels at a medicine show, the audience was awed by the gravity of mien, the silver splendour of the beard, the Edwardian knickerbockers,' Metcalf writes, describing Davies's hammy public persona.

In responding to Metcalf's polemics, many otherwise genteel Canadian writers become querulous and ill-tempered. 'I think he is a bombastic Brit who came over here and tried to tell Canadians what they should think of their literature with absolutely no background in the subject whatsoever,' says W.P. Kinsella, author of *Shoeless Joe*. 'He's a jerk as far as I'm concerned.' Douglas Gibson, the diplomatic and civil publisher of McClelland & Stewart, once described a Metcalf essay as 'loony'.

According to poet Gordon Phinn, Metcalf has been 'bullshitting himself fearlessly for most of his adult life.'

Metcalf the curmudgeon has a position in Canadian literature comparable to Don Cherry among journalists: he's a mildly amusing crank whose opinions can be written off as the products of a warped personality. Yet for those who know him best, the dozens of writers he's helped nurture over a four-decade career, this reduction of Metcalf into a cartoon gadfly is an enormous cultural injustice. To his admirers, Metcalf is not eccentric but central, a brilliant prose-smith who has mentored an entire generation of fledgling authors.

'People think he's a grouchy bear,' complains Annabel Lyon, a young writer whose short story collection *Oxygen* (2000) was edited by Metcalf. 'But he's not like that at all. Everyone who has worked with him feels lucky. He's a brilliant editor who is very supportive of younger writers.' An impressive array of writers echo Lyon's words: Russell Smith, Andrew Pyper, Mary-Lou Zeitoun, Steven Heighton and Caroline Adderson all testify to Metcalf's nurturing influence. As Smith slyly notes, there is a 'maternal' and 'sensitive' side to Metcalf, which is well hidden by his public image as a hard-boiled scold.

Will the real John Metcalf please stand up? Is he a rude crank or a caring mentor? One of the benefits of reading his autobiography is that it lets us revisit the career of our most controversial living writer.

I first met John Metcalf three years ago after a public reading at Toronto's Harbourfront. Knowing Metcalf only from his prickly prose, I had to steel myself before I could talk to him. Yet after a few quick words, I realized my trepidation was misplaced. A compact, dapper man with a neatly trimmed beard and mellifluous British accent, Metcalf set me at ease with his courtly Old World manners.

To be sure, Metcalf in conversation can be as opinionated as he is in print. He'll express mock-outrage at the fact that 'fundamentally mediocre writers like Margaret Laurence and Matt Cohen have awards named after them.' About Kinsella, Metcalf simply notes that 'I just don't think he's a very bright man. I think of him as a commercial writer, and a clumsy one.' About Douglas Gibson's criticisms, Metcalf retorts that they are 'offensive and dishonest'. Yet the stridency of these put-downs is tempered by Metcalf's genial and puckish tone. Like a schoolboy pulling a prank, he knows he's being naughty and invites you, with a wink, to join in the fun.

In both his private conversations and his memoirs, Metcalf dwells on his English upbringing. Born the son of a Methodist minister in 1938, Metcalf rejected the religion of his parents but inherited their zealous do-gooding energy. As his memoirs make clear, Metcalf found in literature the salvation that his father received from the Bible and theology.

Metcalf came of age in the 1950s, when the afterglow of literary modernism still suffused the intellectual world. T.S. Eliot, Ezra Pound, Ernest Hemingway were among the idols of the day: from these writers Metcalf learned the importance of language and technique. The British literary culture of the 1950s was also a contentious place. In order to win a hearing for controversial writers like Eliot, critics like F.R. Leavis and William Empson had developed a combative public presence: in championing modernism, they weren't afraid of mocking the philistines who preferred to cling to old-fashioned Victorian literature. Metcalf's literary mentors believed that literature thrives on debate and argument, a position he continues to hold to this day.

Metcalf brought this legacy of battle-hardened modernism when he immigrated to Canada in the early 1960s. He came to Canada largely because he found the experience of teaching in England to be depressing because the schools were filled with an 'underlying viciousness and violence'. The year 1962 found the twenty-four-year-old Metcalf in Canada, where after a few dismal years of teaching high school he began a long, fruitful career as a literary critic, short story writer, novelist and editor.

Metcalf's aborted career as a teacher left a mark on his writing career. His two spirited satirical novels, *Going Down Slow* (1972) and *General Ludd* (1980), both focus on the deadening effect of education, as do many of his short stories. A beleaguered teacher facing down a sullen mob of students is perhaps the most characteristic scene in Metcalf's fiction.

When he first started out, Metcalf's novels and stories were almost universally praised. In the *Globe and Mail*, William French described *Going Down Slow* as 'trenchantly funny'. However, as Metcalf became a more outspoken critic in the late 1970s and '80s, other writers began to stop discussing his work and including his stories in their anthologies. This informal blacklisting has prevented Metcalf from gaining a wider audience.

Yet Metcalf's unpopularity in certain circles hasn't dampened his spirits. He has constantly sought, with great tenacity and energy, to find new writers. According to Leon Rooke, a Governor General's award-winning writer whose first Canadian book was published with Metcalf's help, Metcalf spends countless hours, 'poring over the lit mags, keeping his ears to the ground, discovering writers, getting their work into print.'

Given the loneliness of a literary life, even the small acts of kindness that Metcalf performs can have a lasting impact. In the late 1960s, Alice Munro was starting her career and feeling dejected. 'I had absolutely no status as a writer,' Munro recalled in an autobiographical essay. 'A creative writing teacher at the University of Victoria told me that I wrote the kind of things he used to write when he was 15.'

Then Munro received a letter of praise from Metcalf. 'I was stunned by it, really. He had taken the trouble to do this—to write so generously and thoughtfully, to a writer he didn't know, a writer of no importance.' Munro's description of her 'literary friendship' with Metcalf nicely distills the impact he has on many writers.

Since 1989, Metcalf has served as senior editor of the Porcupine's Quill, a literary press in Erin, Ontario—a position that allows him to do more than just praise writers. Now he can publish them as well. Over the last fourteen years, Metcalf has edited more than 100 volumes for Porcupine's Quill, many of them from young writers he first discovered in the pages of small literary magazines and writing schools. Metcalf's judgments as an editor have been vindicated time and again. Many of the writers he first published have gone on to win not just big awards but also lucrative contracts with large publishers.

Metcalf's achievements as an editor are based not only on his unequalled abilities as talent scout, but also on the sensitivity with which he handles his writers. Editors have real power, especially when dealing with young writers. Not surprisingly, some editors have fallen into the temptation to play God, using a writer's work as an outlet for their own frustrated creativity. In the 1930s, Max Perkins was accused of doing that with Thomas Wolfe; more recently, similar charges have been levelled against Gordon Lish, in his relationship with Raymond Carver.

Given Metcalf's strong views on literature, one might suspect that he's a domineering editor of that sort. Yet the writers who have worked with him are unanimous in praising the way he sensitively works to enhance their own voices.

'John does read his writers well,' Steven Heighton notes. 'And not just their vulnerability or toughness when it comes to criticism, but their special strengths or weaknesses as artists. The most cursory look at the writers he has edited will show that he never tries to make his writers sound like himself, as bad writer/editors do.'

For all his good works, Metcalf's reputation remains covered by a cloud of acrimony. This is undoubtedly for political reasons: Metcalf is a vocal critic of government cultural subsidies; he thinks nationalism corrupts literary judgment; he is skeptical of fiction that promotes 'progressive' causes like feminism and multiculturalism. Moreover, Metcalf believes that many of the alleged giants of Canadian literature (Morley Callaghan, Robertson Davies, Timothy Findley) were never very good and deserve to be knocked off their pedestals.

All of these positions are worth debating. In a healthier literary climate, Metcalf and his critics would be able to thrash out their difference in the court of public opinion. Unfortunately, Metcalf's ideas have usually been answered by catcalls, in part because he himself has a tendency toward invective.

Yet even if they don't like his ideas, readers should pay attention to Metcalf's words. As the title of his autobiography makes clear, Metcalf's primary concerns are aesthetic, not political. Metcalf hates the way Canadians talk about literature largely because he is a master of English prose and therefore offended by the sentimental blather that pervades our book chat.

Take the case of the poet Al Purdy. When Purdy died three years ago at the venerable age of 81, he was repeatedly praised as a decent, down-to-earth writer who voiced the everyday concerns of ordinary Canadians. 'He sounded, looked, acted and thought like your imagined average Canadian,' argued Purdy's publisher. 'That's why he's so beloved.'

Metcalf shared an office with Purdy at Loyola College in the 1970s and remembers a frisky poet, too lively to be called average. 'He'd boom and bellow about in the English department office for a while, groping unfortunate secretaries and filching letterhead and then he'd phone a nearby grocery store to get a case of beer delivered. A pizza would follow and soon he'd have the place comfortable with a fug of cigar smoke. His cigars were rank, plastic-tipped and dipped in port.'

In order to sleep off his daytime boozing, Purdy kept a collapsible cot in his office, a piece of furniture that apparently had numerous uses. 'On some afternoons I'd be further excluded from my office facing a locked door while on the collapsible cot he plumbed the depths of one of the female department members.

'With the advent of spring and the retreat of the snow under our office window, beer bottles began to surface, more and more every day as the sun gained strength, until they lay revealed on the playing field like corpses after a mighty battle.'

In a few quick paragraphs, Metcalf demolishes all the stifling clichés about Al Purdy as The Voice of the Common Person and replaces it with a much earthier image of the poet as a disreputable coot, both endearing and unmanageable. The beer bottles are nicely placed in the last sentence, right between the high rhetoric of 'the advent of spring' and an imaginary 'mighty battle'. Without saying so, Metcalf is suggesting that Purdy's beery muse deflated his poetic diction.

This little sketch of Purdy is a typical Metcalf performance: a strong and funny piece of writing designed to upend the conventional thinking of the Canadian literary world. *An Aesthetic Underground* vindicates Metcalf's long service as the troublesome conscience of Canadian culture, provoking debate in order to stir up thought. Instead of continuing to subject Metcalf to the silent treatment, perhaps his critics will now take up his long-standing offer to start talking about literature.

Toro, April/May 2003

ATWOOD'S 'MADDADDAM TRILOGY'

The imminent extinction of humanity is always good for a few laughs. While the death of any one individual inevitably inspires awe and dread at our common fate as mortal creatures, the extinguishing of billions of lives can, if presented deftly, produce an entertaining spectacle. Doomsday scenarios, whether in the form of marauding zombies or nuclear catastrophes, have long been a staple of popular entertainment, with the idea of universal destruction providing a frisson of anticipatory dread.

Margaret Atwood's *MaddAddam*, the concluding volume of an expansive trilogy of novels set in the not-too-distant future, deals with the aftermath of a genetically engineered plague that exterminates the vast majority of the human species, leaving a scattering of survivors fending for themselves in the face of an uncertain future.

Described in such bare terms, you might think this a very depressing book and it's true that the earlier volumes in the *MaddAddam* trilogy, although not without moments of mirth, are generally dour reading experiences. Yet *MaddAddam* is unexpectedly and frequently an exhilarating and hilarious novel.

How does Atwood wring comedy out of her nightmare scenario? Partially, it's a matter of tone. Her famously vinegary wit is always most pungent when scorning folly and venality, of which there is no shortage in the *MaddAddam* trilogy. The future imagined in these books is one where cupidity reigns supreme, with every appetite, no matter how debased and vile, ready to be fed for the right amount of money.

In the pre-plague world one of Atwood's characters spends time working for 'an anything-goes sex bazaar' where 'you could get everything … from chicken soup to nuts, on or off the bone, screams-for-sale extra. He spent a nervous four weeks on that deathstar working for a pod of seedy Russian pussy-smugglers who were tiring of the whininess and bleediness and need-to-feed of their human merchandise.' The frequent references to kiddie porn and child abuse reinforce a sense of a universe where decency has disappeared. After sharing Atwood's jaunty and unflinching gaze at such evils, a humanity-destroying plague comes as a welcome relief, like a cleansing Biblical flood.

One of the easiest ways to create comedy is to have a character who keeps doing the same thing over and over again even though the results are always disastrous. Think of Wile E. Coyote, forever coming up with elaborate schemes to catch the Roadrunner which always end with the mastermind falling off a cliff. In the *MaddAddam*s trilogy, humanity is Wile E. Coyote writ large, with nature being the elusive Roadrunner that seems within our grasps but in the end evades capture. The trigger for the disaster in the novel is the actions of one man, a rather implausible mad scientist named Crake, but the real villain is the species as a whole, which is not just omnivorous but also meanly gluttonous, willing to brush aside any respect for others in the pursuit of pleasure.

It's not just Wile E. Coyote's invariable failures that make him funny but also his resilience. Every near-death scrape is followed by a come-back. Part of the comedy of *MaddAddam* is that humanity, despite the best laid plans of the lunatic Crake, displays a cartoon character's ability to bounce back. The main movement of the novel concerns the re-formation of a working community that includes not just a hardy band of human survivors but also their genetically engineered neighbours, including a race of super-intelligent pigs (pigoons) and a disconcerting tribe of post-humans called Crakers (whose genes are sculpted to keep them from having vices like meat-eating and jealousy).

The reconciliation of these separate sentient species is abetted by the shared task they all face of staving off some of the less wholesome humans who have also survived the plague.

Atwood's great mentor Northrop Frye taught us that all of Western literature is based on the cultural DNA found in the Bible. Faithful to Frye, Atwood has, in the *MaddAddam* trilogy, essentially rewritten both the beginning and end of the Hebrew and Christian Bibles, giving us both a new Genesis and a new Apocalypse. The trilogy is rich not just in Biblical references and invented futuristic religions but also in the primordial themes of Genesis: nature as a garden, sibling rivalry as a microcosm of human strife, humanity as a perpetually disobedient child. Like the Biblical God, Atwood is often wrathful towards her (or Her) creation, punishing them for their transgressions. But as in the Bible, Atwood also offers a promise of transcendence, perhaps not a new Heaven but maybe a new earth where her creatures can live in peace.

Like its distinguished predecessors *Oryx and Crake* (2003) and *The Year of the Flood* (2009), *MaddAddam* gives ample evidence of Atwood's enviable literary talents. The fertility and ingenuity of her inventiveness keep us amused. The pigoons and Crakers will surely join the great bestiary of imaginary creatures that includes Jonathan Swift's Houyhnhnms, H.G. Wells's Elois and Morlocks, and Frank Herbert's Sandworms. The surefootedness of Atwood's narrative skills is also striking. In all three novels she weaves a complex plot that moves back and forth from the past to the future, yet the narrative momentum never abates.

Yet the *MaddAddam* books aren't without flaw. One major problem is that Atwood relies heavily on coincidences, with her small cast of characters constantly running into each other both before and after the catastrophe. In the world of the novel, there are only a dozen odd human survivors, yet one of them is reunited with no less than three women he knew at various stages of his pre-apocalyptic life. At one point a character argues that we live in 'a universe in which—rightly understood—there are no coincidences.' This bit of New Age hooey is unconvincing both as a philosophy and a narrative technique.

In her other fiction, Atwood is adept at creating plausible characters but in the *MaddAddam* trilogy her focus on inventing a credible future world seems to deflect her from imagining fleshed-out people. In an acute review of *Oryx and Crake*, John Clute, a commanding expert in the science fiction genre, noted that there was something 'pulpish' in the depiction of Crake as a mad scientist. A similar reliance on genre clichés can be seen in other leading characters like Oryx (an exotic and enigmatic foreign beauty) and Zeb (a major figure in *MaddAddam*, an adroit environmental adventure hero who seems like an improbable mix of Jason Bourne and David Suzuki).

Zeb's lover, Toby, a major figure in both *The Year of the Flood* and *MaddAddam*, is one of the few exceptions to the general thinness of characterization in the trilogy. A hardy and wary survivor who comes to love late in life, Toby has a complexity that is only fleetingly present in other characters in the series.

Atwood's ability to get us to care for Toby's fate is what redeems the trilogy in the end, giving it emotional gravity that was previously missing.

The sheer cleverness of the trilogy is entertaining but also makes the books at times feel cold and distant. Thanks to Toby, the trilogy gains a human dimension that the earlier books in the series lacked.

National Post, August 30, 2013

SHOAH BUSINESS: YANN MARTEL'S HOLOCAUST NOVEL

Few hypothetical scenarios are harder to imagine than a conversation between Theodor Adorno and Natalie Portman. Adorno was the highbrow's highbrow, the sage Thomas Mann turned to for advice while writing *Doctor Faustus*, the friend and long-time correspondent of Walter Benjamin, the champion of astringent creators like Arnold Schoenberg, the relentless foe of jazz and Hollywood, the mercilessly pessimistic Marxist critic of modernity whose 'negative dialectic' has enriched thousands of scholarly studies. Portman is perhaps best known for her turn as Queen Padmé Amidala in the more mediocre of the two *Star Wars* trilogies.

Yet on the subject of the Holocaust, Adorno and Portman, both of Jewish heritage, might have found some common ground. In a typically dense 1949 essay titled 'Cultural Criticism and Society', Adorno—a refugee from Nazi Germany who had lost the world of his youth to the Nazi genocide—bluntly declared that 'to write poetry after Auschwitz is barbaric'. Arguably, Portman is not as deep a thinker as Adorno (who died in 1969, twelve years before the actress was born), but the starlet has been impressively educated at Harvard and the Hebrew University of Jerusalem. Interviewed by the *Daily Mail* earlier this year, she complained, 'I get like twenty Holocaust scripts a month, but I hate the genre.'

Despite their shared discomfort with Holocaust art, an enormous historical and cultural gulf separates Adorno's statement from Portman's. When Adorno was writing, the murder of the European Jews was so fresh that there wasn't even a proper term to describe it. The catch-all name 'the Holocaust' hadn't yet gained the currency it would receive in the 1970s, 'Shoah' was largely confined to Hebrew speakers, and the word 'genocide' (coined in 1944) still carried with it the awkwardness of a neologism. In lieu of such terms, commentators most often relied on the infamous and very specific names of the camps: Auschwitz, Belsen, Buchenwald, Dachau, and many more. In the Portman era, not only is the Holocaust easier to talk about because it has been named; it has even become a genre, like the romantic comedy, the superhero film, or the road movie. As the saying goes, there's no business like Shoah business.

Adorno's brief, barbed, bitter comment—more a cry from the heart than a reasoned statement—is the single most quoted sentence in debates about Holocaust art. And Adorno himself is the inevitable jumping-off point for discussion, because he pinpointed the root dilemma every intelligent artist and critic has experienced: how can you make art about atrocities? Art, no matter how difficult and painful, always involves the aestheticization of reality; every artist is a mortician who prettifies the corpse so the public can look at it without the nausea and dread that death induces. Or, as Adorno said on another occasion, 'The so-called artistic rendering of the naked physical pain of those who were beaten down with rifle butts contains, however distantly, the possibility that pleasure can be squeezed from it.' In the face of the enormity of what actually happened at Auschwitz, isn't it better for art to maintain a dignified silence?

If Portman is right and the Holocaust is now a genre, we have to say that Adorno's worst fear has come true. Not only did poetry persist after Auschwitz, but poetry and the other narrative arts have conspired to make the Holocaust banal. It sometimes seems as if the Holocaust is for modern art what the Crucifixion was to medieval and Renaissance art: a common frame of reference and the quickest way to affect your audience. It would take the entirety of this article to list just the most famous novels, films, comics, and plays about the Holocaust: *The Diary of Anne Frank; If Not Now, When?; Sophie's Choice; See Under: Love; Maus: A Survivor's Tale; Schindler's List; Life Is Beautiful; The Pianist; The Shawl; The Reader.* Adorno's strictures are hard to follow. Even Natalie Portman once played Anne Frank on Broadway.

Some of these are brilliant works of art; others are unspeakably exploitive, especially that mawkish monstrosity *Life Is Beautiful.* But whatever quality they possess, they all must answer to Adorno's piercing question: After what actually happened, how can you presume to offer up a distillation of reality that is also, inevitably, a distortion of reality?

I must confess that when I heard that Yann Martel's new novel is about the Holocaust my heart, already Grinchily small, shrank just a little bit more. 'Does the world really need another Holocaust novel?' I wondered. 'Especially one written by a very goyish Canadian?' Upon reading the book, I realized that my misgivings were somewhat misplaced. Whatever other faults Martel has, he's not a sensation-monger or a cheap writer. His book is at worst a noble failure, a sincere attempt to write about a large and terrible subject in a fresh way, so the pain of the past doesn't recede into history. Interestingly, he takes up the Adorno question and puts it in the foreground. *Beatrice and Virgil* is not so much about the Holocaust directly as it is about the problem of representing the Holocaust in art. It's a meta-Holocaust novel, and as such more valuable for the reflections it provokes than for any literary merit it may posses.

As in Martel's previous book, the bestselling *Life of Pi, Beatrice and Virgil* opens with a writer at a literary crossroads. Henry's previous novel was an international bestseller that featured 'wild animals'. As a follow-up, he writes an avant-garde Holocaust story fused with an essay on the same subject to form a flip book. Henry's experimentalism is based on the argument that literature about the Shoah has been tyrannized by the dominance of one mode: 'historical realism'. Henry's editors aren't happy with what they see as his notion that 'we're supposed to throw our whole imagination at the Holocaust [and write] Holocaust westerns, Holocaust science fictions, Holocaust Jamaican bobsled team comedies.'

Rejected and dejected, Henry forswears the literary life and tries to sink back into anonymity by moving with his wife, Sarah, to an unnamed foreign city. There he encounters a fan and namesake, Henry the taxidermist, who wants novelist Henry's help with an experimental play about two talking animals, Virgil the monkey and Beatrice the donkey. The erstwhile writer forms an uneasy collaboration with the taxidermist, and both grapple with the issue that began the book, 'representations of the Holocaust'. Much of the novel consists of excerpts from the embryonic play the two Henrys work on. The two animals are paralleled by stuffed specimens in the taxidermist's workshop, and by a dog and a cat in the writer's home; doppelgängers abound.

This literary house of mirrors contains more rooms. Throughout the book, Martel carefully tries to preclude criticism by anticipating it. Many of the tart observations one could make about *Beatrice and Virgil* are voiced by characters within it, notably by Henry's editors, and by his wife, who dismisses the play-within-a-novel as 'Winnie the Pooh meets the Holocaust'.

Any bald-faced summary of *Beatrice and Virgil* will make it sound odd.

But some of the book's strangeness disappears if we see it not as an isolated mutation but rather as an outgrowth of the fecund field of Holocaust literature. Fiction about the Holocaust has proliferated to such an extent that literary critics have found it necessary, rather like zoologists in a particularly overpopulated rainforest, to start sorting out subspecies. In his helpful taxonomic study *The Holocaust Novel* (2005), Efraim Sicher offers the following groupings: survivors (notably Aharon Appelfeld, Primo Levi, Elie Wiesel); the Jewish American post-Holocaust novel (Saul Bellow, Cynthia Ozick); historical Holocaust novels (Thomas Keneally, William Styron, D.M. Thomas); second-generation Holocaust fiction (David Grossman, Art Spiegelman); and postmodernist Holocaust fiction (Martin Amis, Don DeLillo).

Martel clearly belongs in the postmodernist camp, although for all his storytelling gamesmanship he lacks the intellectual intensity and verbal firepower of the great postmodernists, like Thomas Pynchon, John Barth, Robert Coover, or Leon Rooke. Rather like Kurt Vonnegut, Martel is a populist postmodernist, a middlebrow magician whose sleight-of-hand tricks are entertaining diversions rather than deep-reaching challenges to conventional storytelling. Martel is a fabulist who's also an easy airport read, which perhaps explains his great popularity. As a writer, he is like one of those steroid-enhanced baseball players—say, Barry Bonds or Mark McGwire—who are impressively well developed in certain specialized body parts but not otherwise healthy, indeed even weak and impotent at times. He's very talented at description, as can be seen in a long passage where two characters talk about a pear for several pages and make you look on a familiar fruit with fresh eyes. Yet he has no skill for dialogue: all his characters, human and animal alike, talk with the same monotonous, expository suaveness as the narrator's. His forays into postmodern mythmaking add to the general unreality of his fiction.

The dangers postmodernism presents to historical reality need to be weighed against the possibility that it offers a promising solution to the problem of representing the Holocaust. The hallmark of postmodernism is a refusal to deal with subjects directly, and a preference for circumlocution, subterfuge and the sideways glance. Postmodernism has led to a flourishing of techniques like allegory, which allows the artist to deal with serious subjects without succumbing to the burdening weightiness of documentary realism.

Martel naturally turns to allegory as his preferred narrative technique. In one of his many acts of self-exegesis, he has a character refer to the idea of 'the Holocaust as allegory' to explain the taxidermist's anthropomorphic play. This is a shrewd connection: allegory has always been the lingua franca of oppression.

We know very little about Aesop, but legend holds that the fable writer was a slave. In more recent times, African American slave culture was rich in trickster tales about clever animals like the rabbit who outwits his foxy enemy. These animal tales are the forerunner not just of the stories of Br'er Rabbit, but also of George Herriman's *Krazy Kat* comic strip (1910–1944). A light-skinned African American, Herriman passed for white and used his cat and mouse characters to comment, subversively and slyly, on race relations. He inspired everyone from Walt Disney to Art Spiegelman, whose graphic Holocaust family history, *Maus*, also uses talking animals as symbols of a desperate human situation. As a work of art, *Beatrice and Virgil* pales in comparison to *Maus* or *Krazy Kat*, but it belongs to the same venerable and honourable tradition. Allegory's popularity in the wake of modern totalitarianism is no accident: Ernst Junger's *On the Marble Cliffs*, Camus's *The Plague*, and Orwell's *Animal Farm* are all early examples of artists turning to allegory as a way of writing about large public issues without resorting to journalistic clichés.

Perhaps this is precisely why postmodernism is a major mode of Holocaust literature. 'In ancient mythologies and religions there are things and beings that are not to be named,' Irving Howe noted in 'Writing and the Holocaust', a 1986 essay. 'They may be the supremely good or supremely bad, but for mortals they are the unutterable, since there is felt to be a limit to what man may see or dare, certainly to what he may meet. Perseus would turn to stone if he were to look directly at the serpent-headed Medusa, though he would be safe if he looked at her only through a reflection in a mirror or a shield.' Postmodern trickery and allegory are like the shield of Perseus: they allow the artist to approach the Medusa that is the Holocaust without looking directly at the monster.

Like the most annoying member of a graduate seminar or a book club, Martel likes to make great displays of his erudition. He's careful to spell out all his precursors, so we don't miss the fact that the original Beatrice and Virgil are from *Dante's Inferno*, or that an allusion to 'Birnam Wood moving to Dunsinane Castle' comes from *Macbeth*. He name-drops Spiegelman, along with many other Holocaust artists, just so the reader knows he understands the serious tradition within which he's working. Samuel Beckett is also checklisted, and this is particularly important: Beckett is, in a sense, the presiding spirit of *Beatrice and Virgil*. Like *Waiting for Godot*, the play within *Beatrice and Virgil* is mostly focused on two characters, set against a denuded, abstract background, who talk around an ominous subject without ever blurting out what is scaring them.

As it happens, Beckett was one of the few modern writers Theodor Adorno approved of. Beckett is not usually thought of as a Holocaust writer, but a few biographical facts are illuminating: normally apolitical, he was angered enough by the Nazis to join the French resistance, and he had friends who were tortured and killed by the Gestapo. As scholar Hugh Kenner has suggested, much of Beckett's work makes sense if we see it as a veiled allegory about Vichy France. '*Waiting for Godot* is very nearly a fable of the occupation,' Kenner wrote in a 1986 essay. 'In the play three people are led over the same story again and again, under spotlights. The Gestapo grillers reputedly made much use of such lights ... [Seeing] a Beckett play, reading a Beckett text, no one thinks, "The Occupation!" The "power of the text to claw"... arises from his way of unhooking it from historical particulars, leaving something as vivid as a bad dream, as oppressive, as inescapable.' So perhaps Beckett offers one solution for the problem of how the Holocaust can be represented without dishonouring the memory of the dead, by writing allegories so oblique that they capture horror without trying to glibly explain it or offering reassuring narrative comforts.

Beckett and Martel both universalize the Holocaust, but in diverging ways and to different effects. Martel's universalization is selective: Jewish voices are erased, as is the specificity of the Jewish experience—even the animals aren't quite kosher—but we still get the story of Nazi evil. Beckett's universalization was more extreme: everything historically specific is erased, and the Holocaust is unnamed. In its place, we get pure stories about torture, with characters reduced to the fundamental categories of victim and abuser. Because Martel's universalization is selective, it produces a lopsided effect, something Beckett's more radical art avoids.

While Adorno's famous admonishment about Auschwitz and poetry is often quoted, many commentators forget that late in life the philosopher had a slight change of mind. In his 1966 book *Negative Dialectics*,

Adorno wrote, 'Perennial suffering has as much right to expression as a tortured man has to scream; hence it may have been wrong to say that after Auschwitz you could no longer write poems.' The contradictory statements spring from the same unsolvable dilemma: it is impossible to write about the Holocaust, but it is also imperative that we continue to write about the Holocaust. Samuel Beckett is not normally someone to turn to for advice, but there is wisdom in his great injunction from *Worstward Ho* (1983): 'Ever tried. Ever failed. No matter. Try again. Fail again. Fail better.'

The Walrus, June 2010

LISA MOORE'S 'CAUGHT'

We all know what drug dealers are like: they're poor, they're scruffy, they're products of the urban ghetto, they're often foreign. In sum, they're not like us.

One of the few redeeming lessons to be gained from the ongoing scandals currently entangling Toronto Mayor Rob Ford is that drug culture doesn't necessarily take the shape that conforms to our most comfortably held ideas. When news broke of a video allegedly showing the mayor smoking crack, there was an attempt to fit these startling claims within our preconceived notions with chatter about 'Somali drug dealers'. But as we read reports about the history of the Ford family and illicit substances, it is evident pushers don't have to come from impoverished exotic climes. Your local hash merchant may well have been a wealthy white kid just down the street in suburban Etobicoke.

Why would a middle class Canadian kid get entangled with the narcotics trade? That's one of the big questions taken up by Lisa Moore in her surprising and superb thriller *Caught*. The novel opens briskly in 1978 with an escaped prisoner on the lam. David Slaney, a Newfoundlander serving time in a Nova Scotia prison for trying to smuggle a boatload of marijuana, is on the run and trying to hook up with his old partner in crime, Brian Hearn. Neither Slaney nor Hearn fit the profile of pushers as slum kids. Hearn, in fact, is a graduate student in English with designs on becoming a professor.

Caught is a literary adventure story, which is to say it is both action-packed and an investigation into character and motive. Moore gives us a gripping, detailed and wholly convincing account of the surreptitious but complex manoeuvres involved in bringing Colombian marijuana to Canada, but this compelling narrative is deployed in the service of figuring out what makes Slaney and Hearn tick. These are men who don't necessarily understand their own impulses; they deceive not just others but themselves, so the tense unfolding of the story always has at least a double purpose. In seeing how they behave in extreme situations, we're brought closer to figuring out who they are. While issues of trust and identity are human universals, they achieve a heightened intensity in the pressure-cooker world of serious criminality.

The tradition of literary adventure goes back to Homer and is more recently exemplified by Joseph Conrad and Graham Greene. Slaney is very much a wayfaring hero in the mode of Ulysses, in long exile from home and hearth, cagey in his ability to take on new identities in his travels, resourceful in adapting to adversity and occasionally lured from his main course by the temptations of the flesh. In keeping with the novel's broadly Homeric themes, Slaney even has to contend with a Cyclops (an RCMP surveillance satellite). Like many of Conrad's heroes, Slaney proves his manhood in the taxing toil of shipboard life, and in keeping with Greene's fiction, he comes into contact with his more instinctual self in the heat and dust of the southern hemisphere.

These echoes of older adventure stories not only provide a literary frame of reference for the novel but they're also a key to understanding the emotional drive that pushes Slaney and Hearn. As he criss-crosses the continent while being pursued by the authorities, Slaney the escaped prisoner meets many people trapped in their own lives, jailed in bad jobs, held captive in unhappy relationships or shackled by general dissatisfaction. The call of the outlaw's life is in part a siren song of freedom, a paradoxical fact since the liberty Slaney seeks is shadowed by the prison cell.

In a notorious 2009 column in the *National Post*, Barbara Kay excoriated Moore as a novelist of 'female grief' who wrote about 'nobly suffering women or feminized men: men immobilized in situations of physical, psychological or economic impotence … rather than demonstrating manly courage in risk-taking or heroic mode.' Even at the time, Kay's critique was not convincing: the columnist had only the most skimpy awareness of Moore's work and relied on a second-hand account. Moreover, there's nothing wrong with literature dealing with 'female grief'. Women, after all, make up roughly half the species and for many of us are the more interesting of the two major genders. And a literature shorn of grief would leave us with mindless pap: even comic and joyful works gain their authority by possessing a tinge of grief.

With *Caught*, we see an even more forceful rebuttal of Kay's argument. It's not just that Slaney is a rugged he-man who could set Barbara Kay's heart aflutter. More impressively, the novel transcends any simplistic or essentialist gender division. While the main characters and themes are masculine, Moore deploys the literary techniques stereotypically regarded as feminine: tact, sensitivity to emotional nuance, understatement and irony. This is neither a masculine novel nor a feminine one. Rather it's a supremely human book.

Although *Caught* is a strong novel that I wholeheartedly recommend, I did have a few reservations. While there are moments of wit, as in a scene where a Colombian and Newfoundlander compare the respective colonial suffering of their nations, most of the novel is told in a grave monotone that is sometimes oppressively uniform. Slaney and Hearn are both strongly grounded and plausible characters, but some of the secondary figures are less convincing. This is particularly true of Patterson, the police detective who doggedly tracks the drug dealers. Patterson is strangely overmotivated, given several different reasons for his pursuit of the smugglers (desire for a promotion, hatred of hippie culture rooted in alienation from his daughter, desire for more income to help a disabled brother). This stacking on of justifications suggests Moore hasn't fully thought through who Patterson is and where he's coming from. The novelist understands outlaws better than lawmen.

Despite these problems, *Caught* is an outstanding novel, combining the complexity of the best literary fiction with the page-turning compulsive readability of a thriller. Some of the most interesting writing of our time takes place at the intersection between genre and literature, with writers trying to merge the stylistic power of the modernist tradition with more vernacular storytelling modes. Notable examples include Margaret Atwood's various forays into science fiction, Michael Chabon's adoption of a noir voice, Cormac McCarthy's use of dystopian tropes. Moore's *Caught* can be shelved with the other fine books in this robust trend.

National Post, May 31, 2013

ANNABEL LYON'S 'SWEET GIRL'

Perhaps in a previous life Annabel Lyon was a commando, a tactical expert on surprise attacks and ambushes. I'm inclined to speculate along this line because in her current incarnation as a distinguished writer of short stories and novels Lyon's defining trait is her gift for unfolding stories in an unexpected way, for carefully camouflaging her narrative intent so that even the most alert reader is constantly caught off guard by unexpected plot turns and disclosures about her characters.

Lyon's early stories and novellas, collected in the volumes *Oxygen* and *The Best Thing for You*, stood out for their brainy audacity, their use of subterfuge and cunningly withheld information to force readers to be maximally attentive. You can no more relax while reading a Lyon story than you can while playing racquetball or climbing the side of a mountain. Fiction that requires every brain cell to be firing at full capacity can be as rewarding as a good workout. You become mentally healthier, sharper, quicker on the uptake.

With her first novel, *The Golden Mean*, Lyon bushwacked readers once again, this time with her choice of subject matter: a historical novel about the years the philosopher Aristotle spent as a tutor to the young Alexander the Great. While Aristotle was undeniably a towering intellect, he was also by reputation a bit of a plodder and hardly seemed like a fit subject for entertaining fiction. As against more flamboyantly poetic and debonair sages such as Plato or Nietzsche, Aristotle was a stolid and unsexy proto-scientist, a collector of facts, a dissector of data, a taxonomist happy to subdivide the world into neat categories.

Yet Lyon managed to animate a fictional Aristotle who was both humanly believable and a pleasure to be around. She did this in part by putting forward the radical but plausible hypothesis that to survive in the macho world of a warrior king's court, Aristotle had to adopt a tough guy pose himself. In *The Golden Mean* we meet an Aristotle who knows how to swear like a sailor.

In retrospect, Lyon's decision to reimagine Aristotle fit in perfectly with her persistent thematic concern with the limits of rationality. Philosophy is the attempt to cordon off a small clearing for reason in a world governed by prejudice, fear and superstition. From her earliest stories, Lyon has repeatedly told the story of what happens when sober, orderly people who try to hew the path of calm decency are confronted with irruptions of passion, often in the form of violence or lust. Reason, Jonathan Swift has taught us, 'is a very light rider, and easily shook off'. This quip can stand as an epigram for all of Lyon's work.

Lyon's new novel, *The Sweet Girl*, is a companion to *The Golden Mean*, although the two books can be read independently if the reader is so inclined. The title character of the novel is Aristotle's daughter, Pythias, who has inherited her father's wide-ranging mind but lives in a society that has no room for learned women. Expressed in such blunt terms, Pythias's story can be seen as a variation of the tale told by Virginia Woolf in her parable about Shakespeare's (imaginary) sister Judith, another bright-eyed girl doomed to a mute, inglorious fate.

While Woolf's Shakespearean hypothesis, found in her classic essay *A Room of One's Own*, remains a brilliant polemic, it is a mere sketch compared to the thickly and quirkily imagined world of ancient Greek women that Lyon gives us in her novel.

I'm loath to say too much about the plot of the novel, lest I prematurely and oafishly spring the many narrative traps that Lyon has so cagily prepared. Suffice to say that upon the death of her father, Pythias, known as Pytho, tries to maintain her independence in a world where the options available to unmarried women are few and tightly constrained. Through Pytho's eyes we get a tour of the distaff side of Greek culture, getting glimpses of slaves, midwives, priestesses and prostitutes.

Nietzsche famously argued that the ancient Greeks were dual-faced, both Apollonian and Dionysian, torn between sunny reason and ecstatic passion. *The Golden Mean* was an Apollonian novel, showing Aristotle using his supremely level intellect to navigate through the masculine public world of medicine, theatre, politics and military life. In *The Sweet Girl*, Aristotle's daughter tries to be loyal to Apollonian values but discovers the full and terrible force of the Dionysian passions, the earthy, furtive biological impulses that can overturn the order and discipline we impose on ourselves and our world.

One surprise is perhaps worth sharing. Unexpectedly, the novel turns out to be almost as much about slavery as about gender, or rather about the connection between the condition of slaves and that of free women. The American Confederate writer Mary Chesnut once asked, 'Who is more a slave than a wife?' Coming as it does from a slaveowner, it is easy to dismiss this as a self-serving bit of apologia. Yet our impatience with Chesnut's query perhaps hides our unease with seeing the linkage between different forms of oppression. It's a measure of Lyon's talent that she forces us to seriously confront the full implication of this question.

The Sweet Girl is a remarkable novel, not just a pleasure to read but also a book that I expect to reread several times.

National Post, September 21, 2012

ZSUZSI GARTNER, THE ANTI-MUNRO

Alice Munro was born into a world in which nature still existed. Her family were fox and poultry farmers. The felt reality of the barnyard and the forest, the persistence of elemental animal needs, is never far from her imagination. Typically her stories are rich in details about the green and hardy physical world that her characters inhabit and draw substance from. Even when humans interfere with nature, Munro's eyes are alert to older and more primordial biological patterns that still exist as archeological layers under human habitation. In Munro's masterful short story 'Meneseteung' we read about a 'raw countryside just wrenched from the forest.... The meandering creeks have been straightened, turned into ditches.... The trees have all been cleared back to woodlots. And the woodlots are all second growth.' In a deep sense, Munro writes organic fiction.

One quick way of defining Zsuzsi Gartner and explaining the novelty and force of her work is to say that she is the anti-Munro. This is not a question of literary quality as of basic worldview. Pure nature does not exist in Gartner's fiction. Her characters are immersed in a completely technological environment. Surrounded all their lives by a digital sensorium, when Gartner's people encounter nature, they see it through the prism of the man-made world.

In one story, a movie producer journeys into the backwoods of British Columbia where he sees 'a scaly creature lurch from the water, mythic, voracious, a Trump Tower of serrated teeth and shipwrecked breath.' The same producer also makes 'a number of promises he's already consigned to his cranial delete file'. In another story, a character thinks about her uterus as 'a dried gourd inside her, rattling like a maraca'. Animals with teeth like skyscrapers, brains that have delete files, and a uterus like a musical instrument: this is a very different way of perceiving the world than the biological and gardening metaphors that provide the grit and ground of Munro's fiction.

As against Munro's organic fiction, Gartner can be said to be writing plastic fiction. Hence the aptness of the title of Gartner's superb new story collection, *Better Living Through Plastic Explosives.*

As an organic writer, Munro's instinctive orientation is towards the past, and her fiction in recent years has become increasingly historical as she goes back to her family roots (to use an appropriate plant metaphor). As a plastic writer, Gartner turns her back to the past and looks to the future. Many of her stories have a science fiction and fantasy slant. One features a future America where motivational speakers have become enemies of the state. In another, angels take over the bodies of West Coast teenagers and discover the wonders of communing through texting. Even when Gartner's stories are set in the real world, it's a world where the digital paraphernalia of everyday life—email and iPods and texting—are so minutely described that we become aware, for the first time, just how alien our surroundings are.

Some critics have complained that historical fiction dominates CanLit. What's less often been noted is that there is an important countertradition, going back as far as Marshall McLuhan, of high order Canadian futurism. This futurist tradition includes novelists such as Margaret Atwood, Douglas Coupland and William Gibson. Gartner's previous book, *Darwin's Bastards*, made this futurist tradition more visible by gathering a strong collection of writers who work in this mode.

Literary people tend to have a biological bias. If you say a book is 'warm' and 'lively,' these terms are taken as praise. Conversely, saying a story is 'artificial' and 'plastic' sounds like abuse. But this preference for the biological needs to be questioned. Gartner's attentiveness to the artificial gives her prose a laser-like sharpness and precision that nothing organic is capable of.

Take as an example the opening sentence of a story about a young lady named Didi who is comparing an unhappy date she is on with a great party from the night before: 'What is she doing here watching this older man, practically an old man, briskly rubbing garlic against the insides of a wooden bowl in preparation for a Caesar salad when she could be at a real party like the party last night where that one guy said he was so angry (angry!) at her for having such a beautiful butt he couldn't help smacking it with the flat of his hand, and then he did so—so hard it stung Didi through her terry-cloth shorts, the same shorts that had everyone joking they should be using her as a hand towel, and didn't she finally let the freckle-faced little lesbian food stylist do just that to prove she had a sense of humour?' In the space of a sentence Gartner perfectly evokes how the frisky energy of a crowded party can linger in the mind.

A little while later, the aftermath of the butt-smacking is described thusly: 'his fingerprint still a low-voltage buzz on her backside'. The phrase 'low-voltage buzz' comes close to capturing the sensation of Gartner's own prose, although in fact she varies the voltage depending on the needs of the narrative.

Despite all that our species has done to nature and despite the dreams of the transhumanists, we remain poor biological creatures. We're born, grow over many years, hit puberty and menstruate, have the urge to mate and procreate, suffer sickness and death. The emotional weight of Gartner's stories comes from the contrast between the persistence of uncontrollable biological urges and an artificial universe. The emotional leitmotif that gets sounded throughout the book is disappointment. Almost all of Gartner's characters are dissatisfied with their lives, especially by the gap between their desires and their achievements. Marianne Moore once wrote that poets create 'imaginary gardens with real toads in them'. Gartner has given us an artificial world with real people living in it.

National Post, April 8, 2011

CANNIBALISTIC CANLIT

Is all the world obsessed with cannibals?' asks a character in Harry Whitehead's new novel, *The Cannibal Spirit*, which the author based on the true story of George Hunt, an ethnologist who reported on the alleged cannibalistic practices of the Kwakwaka'wakw people of British Columbia. In 1900 Hunt was himself accused of cannibalistic activity, and those charges serve as the inspiration for Whitehead's book, a thriller that imagines Hunt's son-in-law Harry Cadwallader (a real person, but heavily fictionalized in the book) searching for Hunt after he goes into hiding. Like Marlow's quest for Kurtz in *Heart of Darkness*, Cadwallader's journey reads like a feverish dream. The novel alternates between Hunt's wavering first-person account and the seemingly more objective third-person report of Cadwallader's mission. Both versions contain a supernatural undercurrent, with visits by characters who seem to be messengers from another world.

An instructor at the University of Leicester in England, with a master's degree in medical anthropology and a doctorate in creative writing, Whitehead has published several academic articles on the controversies surrounding Hunt's work. The latter's descriptions of First Nations cultures influenced Franz Boas, the eminent German American anthropologist and proponent of cultural relativism. The two men became collaborators, and Boas used Hunt's extensive testimony to theorize that the Kwakwaka'wakw tribe included four secret societies, one of which practised a cannibalistic ritual called *hamatsa*. The ritual, and what it entails, forms a central question in *The Cannibal Spirit*, as Hunt is both celebrated for his discovery and suspected, because of his half-Aboriginal heritage, of being a cannibal himself. And while the novel is rooted in the ongoing arguments among anthropologists about whether the ritual includes actual flesh eating, the story continues a long tradition of cannibalism-inflected Canadian literature.

Tellingly, the roots of the word 'cannibal' lie in colonial misunderstanding: when Christopher Columbus landed in Hispaniola in 1492, he assumed that he had arrived in Asia. Believing that a tribe he encountered were Mongols living in the kingdom of the Grand Khan, the befuddled seaman called them Caniba. A neighbouring group, the Arawaks, warned the explorer that the Caniba had a taste for human flesh, thus contributing to the tall tales about cannibalism in exotic climes. Since then, countless yarns about flesh-eating Indigenous peoples have been propagated by missionaries, soldiers and traders. Going by these accounts, you could hardly have set foot in Africa, Asia or the Americas without being pursued by a hungry headhunter or a shaman smacking his lips. Anticipating Boas, the Renaissance essayist Michel de Montaigne used the figure of the cannibal to argue for a cosmopolitan acceptance of cultural difference, but the more common attitude held that the custom of flesh eating justified the European mission to spread Christianity and civilization. Certainly, the grisly and widely circulated accounts of the Iroquois eating Jesuits helped drum up support for New France.

While doing fieldwork in Tanzania in 1968, University of Virginia graduate student William Arens noted that many of the Africans he met assumed that Europeans were cannibals, often casually smearing them with the Swahili word *mchinja-chinja*, which means 'bloodsucker'. This usage perhaps arose from the procedure of blood transfusion, which foreign doctors had introduced to African clinics and hospitals earlier in the twentieth century. Arens's African experience provided the germ for his influential 1979 book, *The Man-Eating Myth*, which argues that the vast ethnographic literature on cannibalism belongs to the human imagination rather than to real cultural practices. 'Rumors, suspicions, fears and accusations abound, but no acceptable first-hand accounts,' Arens wrote, adding that 'the idea of "others" as cannibals, rather than the act, is the universal phenomenon.'

The book ignited a fierce debate that caused scholars to cast a more skeptical eye on accounts of cannibalism. In the ensuing battles, Arens lost a few skirmishes, as medical and scientific evidence seemed to reveal cases of cannibalism in Papua New Guinea and the American Southwest, but he won the larger argument. Most traditions once deemed cannibalistic were increasingly revealed to be metaphorical, comparable to the Christian Eucharist. Far from being a nearly universal practice, cannibalism seems to have been strongly taboo in all but a handful of human societies.

Not everyone greeted Arens's arguments with ready assent. In 1981, the literary critic Marvin Mudrick snorted about 'a recent mealy-mouthed anthropological hypothesis concerning the practice of cannibalism: that there wasn't any, that there wasn't ever an extended or nuclear family anywhere that ate people day in and day out, it was nothing but loose talk by tribes on the other side of the mountain, who didn't eat people either. Well, once in a while they ate people, but only at Easter and Thanksgiving.' Post-Arens, the work of Hunt and Boas has been subjected to searching critiques. Boas has been accused of relying on hearsay, while Hunt's tales of his career as a shaman are rife with contradictions. Early on, Hunt wrote about his ecstatic visions and visits from his animal spirit; later, he appears to deny these experiences, writing as if he had always been a skeptical man of reason who studied shamanism in a purely clinical manner. Still, popular historians such as George Franklin Feldman and Jim McDowell continue to lean heavily on Hunt's accounts of flesh eating by Kwakwaka'wakw. Since the *hamatsa* ritual is a secret initiation rite, very little is known about it. By various accounts, young men are taken to the forest, where they invoke the spirit of a giant eater of human flesh and are visited by elders; eventually, they return to their village, where they perform the *hamatsa* dance and bite other members of the community.

In *The Cannibal Spirit*, Whitehead grapples with this tension by imagining Hunt's personal dilemmas. The son of a British trader and a Tlingit mother, Hunt married into Kwakwaka'wakw society. A natural shape-shifter and border crosser, he managed to exist in many cultures but was distrusted by all sides. In the novel, he must contend with white authorities who charge him with eating human flesh, as well as Aboriginal people who condemn him for another kind of cannibalism: the theft of Native stories for non-Native consumption. Although packaged as a thriller with a Joseph Conrad–inspired plot, *The Cannibal Spirit* is actually a psychological novel in disguise that works best as an empathetic portrayal of Hunt as a divided self. The book's strength lies in how it depicts Native magic as an experiential reality, respecting the mystery of rituals while avoiding the academic tendency to explain away the sacred.

Whitehead's novel is merely the latest in a long line of fiction set in Canada and devoted to eaters of human flesh. Whether dredging up tales from Native folklore or revisiting Arctic journeys that went badly awry, authors demonstrate an unexpected and persistent fascination with cannibalism. The reputation of Canadian literature for bourgeois blandness is belied by the way major writers have delved deeply into this most taboo activity. Ever droll, Margaret Atwood devoted an entire chapter of her 1987 anthology, *The Canlit Foodbook*, to 'Cannibalism Canadian Style'. Among the examples she serves up are Leonard Cohen's meditation in *Beautiful Losers* on Iroquois who dined on the hearts of Catholic priests; Dennis Lee's child-eating monster ('I eat kids yum yum!'); and her own anorexic *Edible Woman*, who bakes a woman-shaped cake. It's easy to conclude that CanLit actually stands for 'cannibal literature'.

Atwood returned to the subject in 1991 when she delivered a series of lectures on Canadian literature at the University of Oxford. 'The English, I knew, were very fond of cannibalism,' she explained when the talks were published as *Strange Things: The Malevolent North in Canadian Literature*, in which she traces two major thematic inspirations for our fixation with cannibalism. The first is a cycle of poems and narratives inspired by the doleful fate of the Franklin expedition, which set out in 1845 to open the Northwest Passage to Asia, and ended two years later with mass starvation and alleged cannibalism. Various Canadian writers found their inspiration in this story, from Gwendolyn MacEwen, whose blood-curdling verse drama *Terror and Erebus* amplified the heroism and horror played out on the expedition; to the sardonic mockery of Mordecai Richler in *Solomon Gursky Was Here*, in which a character postulates that Franklin's doomed crew included Jewish members.

Richler was particularly delighted that initial Inuit reports about cannibalism on the Franklin expedition were met with British incredulity: 'The fact that a Christian would accept the word of the Natives on such an insidious matter inflamed not only Lady Franklin, but also other Britons, among them Charles Dickens. The source of these stories, Dickens wrote, was a "covetous, treacherous and cruel" people, with a proven taste for "blood and blubber." Members of the Franklin expedition represented the "flower of the trained English Navy" and, therefore, "it is in the highest degree improbable that such men … would or could, in any extremity of hunger, alleviate the pains of starvation by this horrible means."' In pointing to this choice passage of Dickensian pleading, Richler provides excellent evidence to corroborate Arens's contention that cannibalism is often used to demarcate the difference between 'us' and 'them'.

Atwood's other major theme is the cluster of poems and stories about the Windigo, a cannibalistic monster from the mythology of Woodland

Crees and Ojibwas. Windigos appear in human form, and victims join their ranks by being bitten by one, by eating human flesh, or through a dream or an enchantment. Parallels can be drawn between the Windigo and the many ghouls who populate European culture, from vampires to zombies to Frankenstein's monster (after all, didn't Frankenstein steal human body parts to build his creature?). Indeed, the ubiquity of such legends around the world suggests that the cannibal is an ur-monster, the prototype for all our fears.

But what makes cannibalism such a pervasive theme in Canadian literature? Atwood's idea of the 'malevolent north' provides a clue. If, as Arens suggests, cannibalism provides a handy insult to throw at a rival tribe, then it follows that Canada, a nation where many cultures have come together in an often hostile environment, should serve as an especially hospitable home for tales of humans who devour each other. In *The Cannibal Spirit*, Hunt wonders, 'Ain't we all monsters in our darkest hours?' In the best books, eating human flesh constitutes a useful way to examine the monstrous side of human nature and the myths that spring up when we encounter people who are alien to us.

Cannibalism, then, isn't about whom you eat; it's about whom you meet.

The Walrus, October 2011

VEGETABLE SEX

Canadian filmmakers are notable for their interest in outré forms of passion, as displayed in the acrobatic sexual positions in the movies of Atom Egoyan, David Cronenberg, and Denys Arcand.

A similar fixation on erotic outrageousness is also a running theme in Canadian literature: after all, the Governor General's Award has twice been given to novels that raise the possibility of a woman having sex with a bear (an act that is consummated in Marian Engel's *Bear* and only raised as a hypothetical in Douglas Glover's *Elle*).

In many ways, bears make a natural sex symbol. With their hairiness, burliness, and wary aggression, bears embody a certain ideal of rugged Northern masculinity (notably among a subset of husky gay men). The image of ursine/human mating is redolent of both folklore (*Beauty and the Beast*) and mythology (the many occasions when Zeus took an animal guise in order to seduce a nubile maiden).

While the connection between bears and sex is easy to make, it is harder to suss out the erotic appeal of vegetables. My thoughts in this direction were prompted by the fact that I've recently encountered two separate short stories, both from first-rate Canadian writers, featuring sex and ... cucumbers.

In Cynthia Flood's 'Watching', from her 1992 collection, *My Father Took a Cake to France*, the narrator recalls, 'Hands. Allan's fingers. He did that for me maybe seven times in seven years. Once I took a real cucumber.' Lisa Moore offers an even steamier scene of cucumber arousal. In Moore's story 'Granular', from her 1995 debut collection, *Degrees of Nakedness*, we're told of this memorable event: 'You move the cucumber down the ridges of my neck, chest bone, circle one nipple, a shiny snail's trail down my belly. Icy on my clitoris, numbing. You hold it gently down against the opening of my vagina.'

Another example of vegetable love can be found in Caroline Adderson's story 'The Chmarnyk' in her classic collection *Bad Imaginings* (1993). A 'Chmarnyk' is a rain-man and in this story a family caught in the dust bowl believes in the folkloric power of cattail roots to make rain. Told from the point of view of an older woman remembering her youth, one passage reads: 'That night, to keep it moist, I brought [the cattail root] to bed and put it inside me.' Later we're told: 'I had given my innocence to a cattail root while you held its power.'

Of course, Canadians are not alone in getting an erotic charge out of plant life. As long ago as the 17th century, Andrew Marvell was wooing his coy mistress with the promise that 'My vegetable Love should grow/ Vaster than Empires, and more slow.' Scholars say that Marvell was making a metaphorical mind-bender, as was the wont of metaphysical poets. Still, the phrase 'vegetable love' is suggestive, especially when linked to the provocative verb 'grow'.

More recently, Philip Roth has also explored the pornographic potential of the garden. In Roth's 1974 novel, *My Life as a Man*, we're told of Nathan Zuckerman's youthful adventures with Sharon, a young lady, daughter of a businessman known as the Zipper King, gifted at 'introducing various objects into herself'. Here is Roth's account of Sharon's talents:

> Transfixed ... Zuckerman would stare down the hallway at the nude girl writhing, just as he had directed her to, upon the plastic handle of her hairbrush, or her vaginal jelly applicator, or once, upon a zucchini purchased for that purpose earlier in the day. The sight of that long green gourd (uncooked, of course) entering into and emerging from her body, the sight of the Zipper King's daughter sitting on the edge of the bathtub with her legs flung apart, wantonly surrendering all five feet nine inches of herself to a vegetable, was as mysterious and compelling as any Zuckerman had ever seen in his (admittedly) secular life.

A full academic analysis of cucumber love would discuss why these delicious edibles, so essential for salads and sandwiches, are also so sexy. Partially it has to do with their organic nature and vaguely phallic form. If you think about it, the grocery store offers more sexual aids, natural and cheap ones too, than the adult toy shop. Also, eating and sex are overlapping activities. Many sex acts are described by metaphors taken from the kitchen and dining table.

Some attention, too, would have to be given to national differences. Why are (at least two) Canadian writers so taken with cucumbers? Why is the American Roth more passionate about zucchinis? This is a fruitful topic which I hope others will examine in greater detail.

There might also be neurological and cognitive factors at work. Judy Dutton, author of *Secrets from the Sex Lab*, has cited research which shows that the smell of cucumber, when combined with other appealing odours such as Good & Plenty candy, has a measurable effect in arousing women. Could it be that in depicting sex with cucumbers, Flood and Moore were anticipating the latest findings of sex researchers? It wouldn't be the first time that imaginative fiction prefigured scientific discoveries.

Ogden Nash once offered this advice to men on the make: 'Candy is dandy/But liquor is quicker.' A modern-day versifier would have to find a rhyme for garden.

The Walrus blog, September 16, 2010

SMUT AND LITERATURE

Despite its name, the Gutter Press only recently achieved a reputation as a purveyor of porn. Founded in 1992 by Toronto cultural entrepreneur and scene-maker Sam Hiyate, the Gutter Press for most of its first decade had been known as a scrappy upstart publishing house willing to take chances on young writers with edgy and unusual books. While some of these books were raw and nervy, the publisher really started raising eyebrows in CanLit circles with its 2001 release of Tamara Faith Berger's *Lie With Me*, a novel that looks like a dainty kids' book but is definitely adult-only reading. '[The] man raised my dress as I climbed him,' Berger writes in the first of many sex scenes. 'My naked ass was exposed and I felt it clench in his hands.' Fulminating in *The Globe and Mail*, Michael Posner dismissed Berger as a 'professional pornography writer' whose book is 'unabashedly XXX-rated—virtually every page describes sexual activity in language that would make even a Scandinavian blush.'

Despite some scowling book reviews and snickering press coverage, *Lie With Me* was a hot seller. In the wake of its success, Russell Smith, the novelist who had discovered Berger and shepherded her book into print, announced that he was editing a second erotic novel for the Gutter Press. Released in the spring of 2003, *Diana: A Diary in the Second Person* was, ostensibly, another torrid erotic novel told from a female point of view.

'You know he is looking down on you, holding onto your hips, controlling your movement, the globes of your ass quivering with every thrust, your asshole open and exposed, and you can feel this exciting him,' wrote the novel's author Diane Savage in one of the book's tamer moments.

Soon, however, it turned out that Diane Savage was a pen name for Russell Smith. 'Russell wanted to write this book basically based on what happened with *Lie With Me*,' explains Ed Sluga, who recently took over control of the Gutter Press from Sam Hiyate. 'Russell was so jazzed up by the whole notion of it. He and Sam had been talking about erotic books for a long time, so Russell thought, I want to take a shot at it but I want to write it from a female perspective, under a pen name.'

'I don't think the book stands up as a novel and it's not intended to be a novel,' Smith admits. 'Its goal is plain and simple: to titillate. I'm happy to be writing pornography.'

Smith's authorship of *Diana* raises all sorts of interesting questions about men pretending to be women and well-known authors taking pseudonyms. But perhaps the most intriguing fact about the novel is how it reveals the hidden affinity between porn and highbrow literature. Why would an ambitious author like Smith want to write a porn book? Why would the Gutter Press publish it?

With its rage to classify every book in an appropriate category, the publishing industry sometimes resembles South Africa in the days of apartheid. In order to remain fine and pure, good writers are supposed to keep their distance from those grungy pulp writers who inhabit the slums and shantytowns of literature. And, at the very bottom of the publishing hierarchy is porn, which carries the dank and unwholesome reek peculiar to a teenage boy's bedroom.

In the normal course of the publishing world, serious literature—published in upscale hardcovers or trade paperback—has little traffic with porn (usually marketed as tawdry paperbacks under pseudonyms). However, just as the ideology of apartheid was always undermined by the existence of millions of mixed-race individuals, in the real world where writers have to earn a living, porn and literature have a history of playing footsy. Long before the Gutter Press made a sideline publishing 'erotic fiction', serious writers often found themselves trafficking in the red-light district of prose.

In 1911, H.L. Mencken took over the editorship of *The Smart Set*, a failing literary magazine. A brilliant editor and essayist, Mencken soon revitalized *The Smart Set*, aesthetically if not financially, by bringing on board writers like Joseph Conrad, Theodore Dreiser and James Joyce. Unfortunately, too few readers appreciated the fine jewel Mencken had crafted and the magazine was always on the verge of losing money. In 1915, Mencken decided that if 'the morons' couldn't appreciate fine literature, he would give them the swill they deserved.

According to biographer Terry Teachout, Mencken's solution was to start up pulp magazines: *Parisienne Monthly Magazine*, which featured 'trashy short stories and novelettes set in France'. *Parisienne Monthly* was successful enough to spawn two other Mencken-edited pulps, *Saucy Stories* (where the smutty action takes place in the United States) and *The Black Mask* (featuring hard-boiled detective stories).

Mencken funnelled the profits he made from these magazines into *The Smart Set*, rather in the spirit of a drug dealer who drops large bundles of cash into the church collection plate. Mencken always gave the back of his hand to *Parisienne Monthly* and its siblings, calling them 'the louse magazines'. Yet these cash cows (or cash lice) had more merit than their haughty editor was willing to allow. *Parisienne Monthly* was often targeted by the puritans in the United States Post Office, which was the agent of government censorship at the time. In order to keep publishing stories about sexy flappers in Paris, Mencken often had to battle against government censorship and soon became a feisty and committed civil libertarian, willing to use his resources to defeat the prudes who tried to thwart publication of writers like Dreiser and Herbert Ashbury (the author of *Gangs of New York*).

Moreover, after Mencken happily sold off *The Black Mask* in the mid-1920s, the pulp magazine would go on to publish the early work of Dashiell Hammett and Raymond Chandler, the authors of such classic thrillers as *The Maltese Falcon* and *The Big Sleep*. The very stone rejected by Mencken became a cornerstone of American popular culture.

The Mencken formula—using profits from sex to finance more serious work—remained a standard technique in the publishing industry for the rest of the 20th century. In the 1920s, the Random House impresario Horace Liveright published such modernist classics as T.S. Eliot's *The Waste Land* and Ezra Pound's *Personae*.

It would take years for Eliot and Pound to find their audience. In the meantime, Liveright specialized in 'naughty' books like *Replenishing Jessica* and *Flaming Youths* to pay the rent. One of his biggest successes was a collection of the smutty excerpts from the Roman historian Petronius, priced at $30 U.S. (about $300 in today's money) so that it could only be bought by scholars, collectors and 'other mature and incorruptible persons'.

Liveright's scam of republishing historical and classic porn to give a patina of respectability was later used by Barney Rosset, who founded the legendary Grove Press in 1951. Rosset, a war veteran who was disappointed with the reactionary drift of American life in the early Cold War, was willing to publish anything that shook people up. He specialized in books by black radicals (notably *The Autobiography of Malcolm X*) as well as giants of late modernism like Samuel Beckett and Jorge Luis Borges. The real staple of the Grove Press line, however, was old-fashioned erotica.

Rosset was a collector of Victorian pornography. With the help of scholar Stephen Marcus, Rosset amassed a huge collection of dirty books that had been covertly and shamefacedly published in the 19th century. To his delight, Rosset found he could make money reprinting dusty titles like *My Secret Life* (allegedly the private diaries of a Victorian gentleman who enjoyed having his way with chambermaids) and *Harriet Marwood, Governess* ('a whip-me-shame-me-make-me-write-bad-cheques Victorian flagellation novel', according to former Grove Press editor Gilbert Sorrentino).

Grove Press's great rival in the 1950s and 1960s was the Olympia Press, under the stewardship of Maurice Girodias. Like Rosset, Girodias was a man of high culture and refinement who enjoyed low things, including a taste for the retro porn of the 18th and 19th centuries. Both men were genuine heroes in the cause of cultural freedom, fighting lengthy court battles to publish books that more prissy publishers refused to touch. Aside from Vladimir Nabokov's great novel *Lolita*, which had been rejected by every mainstream publisher in New York, Girodias published books like *Under the Birch: The Story of an English Governess* by Miles Underwood (actually a pseudonym for the Canadian writer John Glassco) and *There's a Whip in My Valise* by Greta X (an anonymous writer who has never been identified).

However, in order to keep their presses running, Rosset, Girodias and other porn publishers had to rely on an army of pseudonymous writers to keep churning out an ever-fresh supply of lewd material. Who were these unknown writers who wrote quickie paperbacks like *Love Addict* and *The Sins of Seena*?

Not a few of them, as it turns out, were science fiction writers whose careers eerily resemble that of Kilgore Trout, the fictional sci-fi hack who keeps popping up in the novels of Kurt Vonnegut, Jr. As readers of *God Bless You, Mr. Rosewater* and *Slaughterhouse-Five* will remember, Trout dreamed of being taken seriously as a writer but his pulpy sci-fi stories (with titles like 'Pan-Galactic Three-Day Pass') always ended up in the back pages of tawdry men's magazines like *Black Garterbelt*.

Many real-life science fiction writers earned money the Kilgore Trout way, by supplying fodder for the porn industry. *The Sins of Seena*, for example, was written by Robert Silverberg, now a highly regarded science fiction writer who hopes people will forget the nearly two hundred porn novels he published under pen names like Don Elliott from the late 1950s to the early 1970s. In his peak year of 1962, Silverberg was writing a porn novel every two weeks (in addition to a large number of mysteries, westerns and sci-fi potboilers).

In *Campus Sex Club* (1960), Silverberg told the torrid tale of co-eds who run an exclusive salon devoted to invitation-only orgies.

'Marge kneeled in the middle of the floor—nude, as were the circle of eager watchers,' runs the description of the initiation rite for the sex club. 'Les Haberman, a tall muscular senior, stood over her cupping her breasts in his hands and gently massaging the already-swollen tips.'

Harlan Ellison, a close friend of Silverberg, is now famous for his short stories and television scripts (including popular episodes of *Star Trek* and *The Twilight Zone*). However, in the early 1960s he was a struggling writer who, under the pen name Cordwainer Bird, wrote 'numerous extremely soft-core stories in such magazines as *Adam, Knight, Adam Bedside Reader* and other Los Angeles–based girlie journals.' Typical Ellison/Bird titles include *The Girl with the Horizontal Mind, Tramp* and *The Fine Art of the 15-cent Pick-Up*. Ellison remains slightly embarrassed by these stories. 'While they could bring me a desperately needed two or three hundred per appearance, they were—how shall I put it—less memorable works,' he once recalled.

Ellison's friend and fellow science fiction writer Barry Malzberg is equally queasy about his days of youthful porn writing. Malzberg's first two books—*Oracle of a Thousand Hands* (1968) and *Screen* (1970)—were both written for Olympia's porn line. Like Silverberg, Malzberg wrote his porn novels with astonishing speed. He tossed off one novel, *Diary of a Parisian Chambermaid* (1969), in sixteen hours.

When I tried to contact Malzberg to find out about his days writing for Olympia, he rebuffed my requests for an interview. 'I don't know if I want to do this,' he emailed me. 'I do know that I don't want to be characterized as Would-Be Literary Writer ... [who] Wrote Porn!'

Despite their shame, writing porn probably helped Silverberg, Ellison and Malzberg develop as writers. Up until the 1960s, science fiction had been a singularly sex-less genre. Bug-eyed-monsters might put their throbbing tentacles around blond heroines, but the heroes of sci-fi rarely seemed to have any sexual passion themselves. All this started to change when Silverberg and company started hitting their stride in the late 1960s, writing an array of taboo-breaking books that remain shocking in their audacity. Silverberg's *The Book of Skulls*, Ellison's *Deathbird Stories* and Malzberg's *Beyond Apollo* are passionately written books filled with lurid sex. Arguably, writing porn gave these men the courage to achieve their best work.

Younger writers and artists are much less embarrassed about doing both porn and serious work. To get a sense of the contemporary scene, I met up with Ho Che Anderson, a Toronto-based cartoonist who just finished his decade-long work on *King*, a much-praised graphic novel retelling the life of Martin Luther King, Jr. At the very start of his career as an alternative cartoonist, Anderson had done a very different work, *I Want to Be Your Dog*, a graphic graphic novel about sadomasochism, set in a Toronto black community.

Although named by his parents after Ho Chi Minh and Che Guevara, Anderson, with his horn-rimmed glasses and steely manliness, reminded me of another great radical: Malcolm X. Quaffing back beers at a grungy downtown bar, Anderson told me about how desperate he was as an aspiring young cartoonist to land a job, leading him to answer an anonymous call for submissions from a firm called Eros Comix in 1991. (Eros, as it turned out, was the porn wing of Fantagraphics Books, a leading alternative publisher that would bring out *King*.)

Anderson had no qualms about working for Eros. 'Finally someone was offering me a job,' Anderson recalls. 'I was trying to break into the business for years before that and been getting nowhere. Finally someone said if you want to do something for us here is your opportunity. Plus, I like sex. I like drawing naked people doing the deed.'

When talking about porn, Anderson exudes an unflustered confidence very different from earlier writers, who seem like blushing teenagers taking a peek at *Penthouse* in the corner newsstand. As with other porn writers, Anderson was liberated by his experience. Writing and drawing porn taught him to be honest, a quality that shines through his more mainstream work. Unlike most biographies of Martin Luther King, Anderson avoids the trap of hagiography. He deals, for example, with King's raw sex life. 'The way I see it, nobody wants to read about a saint,' Anderson says. 'I sure as hell don't. I can relate to a person who messes up as much as everyone else. I want to read about a real person, not someone who is saintly all the time. I don't think because your character is flawed in certain ways it makes you a bad person. In fact, I think it enriches your character. It makes you one of us.'

Anderson's self-assurance is shared by the many young feminists who are now taking a crack at the porn lit biz.

I got a taste of the new female take on porn when I went to a Queen Street bistro to meet Jenn Bowers and Kate Gilliam, two twenty-something activists who plastered downtown Toronto with posters asking for submissions to their new magazine, SMUT. 'We were talking about doing a magazine and then we thought, who are we kidding?' Gilliam explains. 'What people want to read is smut, what we want to write is smut, so let's just call it SMUT.'

In their unabashed enthusiasm, Bowers and Gilliam are emblematic of the new wave of pro-porn activists. The fact that they are young women is equally characteristic: it's a known fact in the publishing industry that the majority of porn writers and readers these days are women. This feminization of porn-writing has many causes (the fact that men can now easily down-load hard-core images from the web which makes reading seem too slow, the fact that women are more likely to read books of any genre than men, the convincing arguments made by pro-sex feminists which have made many young women friendlier to erotica). A genre which was once the domain of dirty old men now has an energetic female readership.

'Smut should be fun,' Gilliam notes. 'It should be used to provoke humour, laughter and experiments. It should loosen people up a little bit. People get really get excited when we say we're making a magazine called SMUT.'

Earlier writers and editors used porn to finance their careers and fought censorship wars to make erotica available. But these pioneers were ashamed of the very freedoms they had won: they always kept the porn separate from their serious work. Now a new generation of creators, heirs to a hard-won liberty, are willing to fuse porn and serious art as never before.

'I do think that there is something happening in that porn and literature are converging,' Smith notes. 'What I would hope to do is eventually erase the barrier between them.'

Toro, August/September 2003

THE MESSIAH IS THE MESSAGE: MCLUHAN'S RELIGION

Appropriately enough, a century after his birth in 1911, Marshall McLuhan has found a second life on the Internet. YouTube and other sites are a rich repository of McLuhan interviews, revealing that the late media sage still has the power to provoke and infuriate. Connoisseurs of Canadian television should track down a 1968 episode of a CBC program called *The Summer Way*, a highbrow cultural and political show that once featured a half-hour debate about technology between McLuhan and the novelist Norman Mailer.

Both freewheeling public intellectuals with a penchant for making wild statements, Mailer and McLuhan were well matched mentally, yet they displayed an appropriate stylistic contrast. Earthy, squat and pugnacious, Mailer possessed all the hot qualities McLuhan attributed to print culture. Meanwhile, McLuhan adopted the cerebral and cavalier cool approach he credited to successful television politicians like John F. Kennedy and Pierre Trudeau, who responded to attacks with insouciant indifference.

Early on in the program, McLuhan and Mailer tackle the largest possible issue, the fate of nature:

McLuhan: We live in a time when we have put a man-made satellite environment around the planet. The planet is no longer nature. It's no longer the external world. It's now the content of an artwork. Nature has ceased to exist.

Mailer: Well, I think you're anticipating a century, perhaps.

McLuhan: But when you put a man-made environment around the planet, you have in a sense abolished nature. Nature from now on has to be programmed.

Mailer: Marshall, I think you're begging a few tremendously serious questions. One of them is that we have not yet put a man-made environment around this planet, totally. We have not abolished nature yet. We may be in the process of abolishing nature forever.

McLuhan: The environment is not visible. It's information. It's electronic.

Mailer: Well, nonetheless, nature still exhibits manifestations which defy all methods of collecting information and data. For example, an earthquake may occur, or a tidal wave may come in, or a hurricane may strike. And the information will lag critically behind our ability to control it.

McLuhan: The experience of that event, that disaster, is felt everywhere at once, under a single dateline.

Mailer: But that's not the same thing as controlling nature, dominating nature, or superseding nature. It's far from that. Nature still does exist as a protagonist on this planet.

McLuhan: Oh, yes, but it's like our Victorian mechanical environment. It's a rear-view mirror image. Every age creates as a utopian image a nostalgic rear-view mirror image of itself, which puts it thoroughly out of touch with the present. The present is the enemy.

It's a measure of McLuhan's ability to recalibrate the intellectual universe that in this debate, Mailer—a Charlie Sheen–style roughneck with a history of substance abuse, domestic violence and public mental breakdowns—comes across as the voice of sobriety and sweet reason. Mailer once observed that McLuhan 'had the fastest brain of anyone I have ever met, and I never knew whether what he was saying was profound or garbage.' Many others were similarly divided. It was easy to be overawed by McLuhan's quick-wittedness, his startling erudition, and his ability to describe the familiar world in shockingly fresh language while remaining uncertain about the ultimate value of his ideas.

McLuhan has strong claims to being the most important thinker Canada has ever produced. In his first book, *The Mechanical Bride*, published in 1951, he established himself in the emerging field of cultural studies by offering a caustic survey of the dehumanizing impact of popular magazines, advertising and comic strips. By the 1960s, he had widened his lens to examine the power of media as a whole. In *The Gutenberg Galaxy*, he offered a map of modern history by highlighting the hitherto-unexplored effect of print in shaping how we think. This was followed by *Understanding Media*, which prophesied that new electronic media would rewire human consciousness just as effectively as print once did, giving birth to a 'global village' where people all over the world would be linked via communication technology.

McLuhan has also long been a fiercely polarizing figure, especially during the height of his fame in the 1960s and '70s. For instance, the American novelist and social critic Tom Wolfe praised him in the most extravagant terms: 'At the turn of the nineteenth century and in the early decades of the twentieth there was Darwin in biology, Marx in political science, Einstein in physics, and Freud in psychology. Since then there has been only McLuhan in communications studies.' Meanwhile, the German essayist and poet Hans Enzensberger denounced McLuhan as a 'reactionary' and a 'charlatan', a shallow theorist who attempted to 'dissolve all political problems in smoke' and promised 'the salvation of man through the technology of television'.

One of the most contentious aspects of McLuhan's life and work was his devout Catholicism, which some critics saw as antithetical to his academic pursuits. In 1971, the British intellectual Jonathan Miller published a short monograph on McLuhan as part of Fontana Books' Modern Masters, a series of pocket guides on important thinkers. Unrelentingly hostile, Miller argued that McLuhan's ideas were rooted in a reactionary Catholicism and had little basis in science. According to Miller, the 'hidden bias' of McLuhan's work was that it was 'strongly animated by Catholic piety'. He claimed that 'McLuhan found it necessary to elaborate a psychological theory which owes considerably more to the unacknowledged authority of St Thomas Aquinas than it does to any of the scientific sources he openly refers to.' A running theme of Miller's book is that McLuhan's ideas were cloaked in the impartial language of science, but carried with them implicit moral values based on his Catholicism.

Since McLuhan's death in 1980, there has been an outpouring of biographical and exegetical texts, ranging from a hefty collection of his letters, to a superb biography by Philip Marchand, to insightful explications of his work by writers like Douglas Coupland. Arguably, this thriving book industry is paradoxical for an author associated with the death of print culture. But the benefit of this ever-growing body of literature is that it allows us to revisit the debates about McLuhan's work with a fresh batch of evidence. As it turns out, his relationship with Catholicism was more complicated and layered than his critics allowed, serving not as a hidden bias but rather as a spur toward creativity. His faith provided him with special insights that enabled him to become the Marx of the media age and the Darwin of the digital revolution.

Critics like Miller are dead accurate on one point: the absolute centrality of Catholicism to McLuhan's intellectual life. McLuhan was born in Edmonton to a generically Protestant family. His father, a good-natured but unsuccessful businessman, was a Methodist, while his mother, a strong-willed public speaker and actress, was a Baptist. He grew up in Winnipeg and would later claim that much of his personal life was shaped by his horrified reaction to that industrial city, which led him to search for a more humane culture in Europe.

In a 1935 letter to his mother explaining his increasing interest in Catholicism, McLuhan noted that 'I simply couldn't believe that men had to live in the mean mechanical joyless rootless fashion that I saw in Winnipeg.' The young McLuhan was a romantic anti-industrialist who came to conclude that Protestantism was to blame for the ills of the modern world. His thinking was much influenced by the Catholic apologist G.K. Chesterton, who advocated 'distributist' politics that sought to restore the guild ideals of the Middle Ages as a counterforce to both capitalism and socialism. In the same letter to his mother, McLuhan noted that 'I need scarcely indicate that everything that is especially hateful and devilish and inhuman about the conditions and strain of modern industrial society is not only Protestant in origin, but it is their boast(!) to have originated it.'

In converting to Catholicism in 1937, McLuhan was joining a Church he saw as a refuge from the ills of modernity, a litany of evils that included everything from sexual promiscuity to wives bossing around their husbands. At the time, the Church was under the sway of Pius IX's 'Syllabus of Errors', an 1864 proclamation condemning the idea that 'the Roman Pontiff can, and ought to reconcile himself ... with progress, liberalism, and modern civilization.' McLuhan admired the fascist Spanish dictator Francisco Franco as a necessary bulwark against godless communism and anarchism. He thought that feminism and the 'homosexual cult' were working in tandem to undermine the natural authority of men over the family.

If he had remained so reactionary, his ideas would have been no more intellectually challenging than those of Michael Coren or Pat Buchanan, cartoon Catholics for whom Church doctrine is largely useful as a blunt instrument with which to attack political foes. McLuhan's great saving grace, however, was his ceaseless curiosity, which led him to expand his intellectual framework. Even in the years before his conversion, he wrestled with theologians whose thinking challenged his own prejudices.

He made an extensive study of his contemporary Jacques Maritain, who was attempting to update the philosophy of St Thomas Aquinas as a way of making a rapprochement between Catholicism and modernity. As a neo-Thomist, Maritain argued that Catholic social thought was compatible with pluralism and democracy (in the abstract) and contemporary North American society (in particular). These ideas were radical in the 1930s and '40s, but they would eventually influence the direction of the Church in the great doctrinal revolution of the 1960s, Vatican II.

Maritain frequently lectured at St Michael's College, at the University of Toronto, whose faculty McLuhan joined in 1946. McLuhan was attracted to the 'lucidity and order' with which Maritain expounded the ideas of Aquinas. If McLuhan had any critique, it was that Maritain did not go far enough to integrate Catholicism with developments in the social sciences. McLuhan also took inspiration from the avant-garde theology of Pierre Teilhard de Chardin, a Jesuit scientist who argued for a congruence between evolutionary theory and the doctrine of redemption. In a 1952 review of *The Mechanical Bride*, Father Walter Ong, a Jesuit intellectual who studied under McLuhan, drew connections between McLuhan's theories and de Chardin's concept of a 'noosphere' where 'the whole world [is] alerted simultaneously everyday to goings-on in Washington, Paris, London, Rio de Janeiro, Rome, and ... Moscow.'

McLuhan's pioneering studies of popular culture were part of a sea change in Catholic intellectualism, as the Church gave up the siege mentality of earlier decades and tried to offer a more nuanced and positive account of modern life. As well, the Church began to move away from its defence of authoritarianism to support pro-democracy political movements around the world. McLuhan underwent his own political evolution: the young man who admired Franco became the academic who engaged in a long correspondence with Pierre Trudeau. And while *The Mechanical Bride* condemns the comic strip *Blondie* for undermining the patriarchal ideal of the man as the natural head of the household, in later writings, such as *Understanding Media*, McLuhan deliberately eschewed traditionalist strictures, because he thought it was more important to understand the world than to condemn it. As he told an interviewer in 1967, 'The mere moralistic expression of approval or disapproval, preference or detestation, is currently being used in our world as a substitute for observation and a substitute for study.'

On moral matters, he remained very conservative. He was adamantly anti-abortion, for example. But part of his achievement as a mature thinker was his ability to bracket off whatever moral objections to the modern world he might have had and to concentrate on exploring new developments—to be a probe. Indeed, although he joined the Church as a refuge, his faith gave him a framework for becoming more hopeful and engaged with modernity. This paradox might be explained by the simple fact that as he deepened in his faith he acquired an irenic confidence in God's unfolding plan for humanity. In a 1971 letter to an admirer, McLuhan observed, 'One of the advantages of being a Catholic is that it confers a complete intellectual freedom to examine any and all phenomena with the absolute assurance of their intelligibility.'

Indeed, his faith made him a more ambitious and far-reaching thinker. Belonging to a Church that gloried in cathedrals and stained glass windows made him responsive to the visual environment, and liberated him from the textual prison inhabited by most intellectuals of his era. The global reach and ancient lineage of the Church encouraged him to frame his theories as broadly as possible, to encompass the whole of human history and the fate of the planet. The Church had suffered a grievous blow in the Gutenberg era, with the rise of printed Bibles leading to the Protestant Reformation. This perhaps explains McLuhan's interest in technology as a shaper of history. More deeply, the security he felt in the promise of redemption allowed him to look unflinchingly at trends others were too timid to notice.

A century after his birth, what is McLuhan's status as a thinker? Much more robust than his critics would have expected. Consider again the statement that so shocked Mailer: 'Nature from now on has to be programmed.' Living as we do in an age grappling with climate change and proposals to control the planet's temperature through geoengineering, McLuhan's observations seem like a sober recital of facts. His core insight was a simple one: technology isn't just an external tool; it also changes how we think. 'The medium is the message' means that each new technology humanity has invented, from the wheel to the alphabet to the Internet, creates new mental habits and new patterns of thought. Anyone addicted to Facebook understands what he meant: our tools aren't separate from us but rather interact with us and alter, be it ever so slightly, who we are.

As a scholar, McLuhan had a multitude of flaws. He was often sloppy and made many factual errors. But to judge him simply in terms of whether all his quotations and citations are accurate is to misunderstand the role of a master thinker. Like Marx and Freud, he was an intellectual agitator, a conceptual mind expander, the yeast in the dough. After Marx, we can no longer ignore the reality of class difference; after Freud, we can't pretend that our mental life isn't saturated with sexual impulses; after McLuhan, we can't imagine that technology is just a neutral tool. Moreover, like Darwin and Marx, McLuhan is no longer just one man but rather a living and evolving body of thought. The literary critic Guy Davenport once argued that McLuhan was a 'half-mad genius' and 'one of those strange figures whose brilliance can be articulated by others though not by themselves.'

Davenport may have gone too far: works like *The Gutenberg Galaxy* remain fertile reading. But it is true that to fully appreciate the profoundness of McLuhan's thinking, you need to read books like Hugh Kenner's *The Mechanic Muse*, Walter Ong's *Orality and Literacy: The Technologizing of the Word*, and Nicholas Carr's *The Shallows: What the Internet Is Doing to Our Brains*. These sober, scholarly works about the interaction between technology and culture build on McLuhan's work while avoiding his tendency toward blunt hyperbole. Kenner shows how modernist literature emerged out of industrial culture, and Ong demarcates how the shift from orality to literacy changed the way we think, a process Carr sees as being replicated as we move on to electronic communication. Taken together, they demonstrate the solidity of the intellectual framework McLuhan created. In this new century, countless other thinkers will find inspiration from his work; he has become an inescapable part of the world's intellectual heritage.

The Walrus, July/August 2011

HUGH KENNER, RIP

Hugh Kenner, who died in late November 2003 at age 80, began his career as a great literary critic in a characteristically eccentric way, by reading a book smuggled in by a priest and visiting a genius locked away in a madhouse. To understand why the book and the genius changed Kenner's life we have to return to Kenner's formative years, in the provincial backwater that was Canada in the 1940s.

From a young age, Hugh Kenner was equally interested in the arts and the sciences. As an undergraduate entering the University of Toronto in 1941, he had to decide whether he wanted to major in mathematics and physics or literary studies. Literature won out over science but Kenner would remain blissfully free of the sniffy disdain for technology that so many cultured people confuse with humanism.

Canada was an inhospitable place for a budding scholar of modernism: the University of Toronto curriculum stopped dead-cold at 1850. More contemporary books were not only disdained, they were often forbidden by the government. At Canada's skittish border, certain novels by Balzac, Zola, D.H. Lawrence and James Joyce were kept out of a country that feared much that was foreign and new. One modern masterpiece that Kenner did have access to was Joyce's *Finnegans Wake*, tolerated because it was deemed incomprehensible.

Excited by *Wake*, Kenner discovered that Joyce's *Ulysses*, otherwise verboten in Canada, could be found in the restricted access section of the University of Toronto library. However, in order to take a look at the illicit text, Kenner needed to secure two letters of reference: one from a religious authority and one from a medical doctor. Kenner knew a priest who could vouch for his morals, but, unfortunately, was not able to find an MD who could attest that reading Joyce would not corrupt him. Ultimately, Kenner had a family friend, a Jesuit priest, smuggle into Canada a copy of the greatest novel of the 20th century.

Compared with the traditional literature of pre-1850 vintage, Joyce seemed wild and chaotic. A friend of the young Kenner argued he shouldn't expect to find coherence in modern culture—'just let it hit you'. This despairing notion haunted Kenner, raising what he called 'the generic 20th-century problem, discontinuity'. As Kenner notes in his book *Bucky*, reading Joyce and the other modernists forced him to wonder whether we 'still have lines of communication open with Jefferson, Socrates, Christ? Or have we spot-welded about ourselves a world we can't think about? Must you just let it hit you?'

Kenner was never willing to write off contemporary culture as something beyond understanding and he soon found a mentor who shared his hope of finding an underlying order beneath the surface chaos of modern life and literature.

Frye and McLuhan were Kenner's Canadian mentors. From them, Kenner learned invaluable lessons, both positive and negative. Not only were they more alive to 20th-century literature than their academic peers, they were also up on the novel techniques of literary criticism developed to deal with modernism: the 'close reading' of texts promoted by F.R. Leavis and the New Critics.

Yet while he was respectful of Frye's encyclopaedic intelligence, Kenner distrusted the arrogance that went with it. Frye had the hubris of an intellectual conquistador for whom explicating literature became subsumed to the larger task of system-building. As his first book *Fearful Symmetry* (1947) was about to be published, Frye casually remarked to Kenner, 'What a pity that Joyce and Yeats did not live to read my book, it would have saved them so much time.' For Kenner this arrogation of the critic's role (taken to an even further extreme by Frye's disciple Harold Bloom) is supremely wrongheaded: the critic should help readers gain a better understanding of the writer but not eclipse literature with flashy and irrelevant displays of intellectual pyrotechnics. Like a good tour guide, the critic exists to illuminate our experience of art, not to supplant it with overbearing commentary.

Frye, Kenner once mildly noted, did 'have a taste for systems and "key", something it's easy to think of as Canadian (his contemporary Marshall McLuhan comes to mind).' Frye's systems were built on Linnean categories, Jungian archetypes and biblical myths; McLuhan's systems were elaborate historical narratives that combined conspiracy theories with technological determinism.

McLuhan, later famous as a gnomic media guru, was a young English professor interested in the parallels between literature and mass culture in the late 1940s. Sharing a fascination with technology and modern culture, McLuhan and Kenner became fast friends. In the warmth of their initial enthusiasm, they had planned to co-write several books, including studies of T.S. Eliot and the cartoonist Al Capp. (Kenner would write the Eliot book alone and the Capp project never came off, although Kenner eventually wrote a book on an animation director, Chuck Jones.)

Both Kenner and McLuhan felt the great modernists did not represent a permanent break from the past. Rather, they argued, writers such as Joyce and Eliot helped readers reconnect with tradition, and re-energized the stories found in Homer and Shakespeare for our times.

More than intellectual interests drew Kenner and McLuhan together. Both men were born Protestants but became Roman Catholics. McLuhan converted in 1937 and Kenner would do the same in 1964 (although he had clearly felt the gravitational pull of Catholicism for many years prior). As Catholics enthusiastic about modernist culture and even some forms of lowbrow popular entertainment, Kenner and McLuhan cut against the grain of their adopted faith.

After all, Roman Catholicism at that time still lived under the shadow of Pius IX's 1864 'Syllabus of Errors', which condemned the idea that 'the Roman Pontiff can, and ought to, reconcile himself... with progress, liberalism, and modern civilization.' Kenner would lament the fact that 'middlebrow Catholic intellectuals' of the early 20th century 'found a facile role in condemning modernity en bloc.... Alienation from the whole century could be made to seem a Catholic English layman's moral duty.' In their own work, Kenner and McLuhan heralded the newer and more confident Catholic mood of Vatican II, where the Church sought to reconcile itself with modernity.

In June 1948, Kenner and McLuhan made a fateful trip to visit Ezra Pound, then incarcerated as a mental patient at St Elizabeth's Hospital in Washington, D.C. After his wartime support for Mussolini and his alleged descent into madness, Pound's personal and literary reputation was at a low. Yet Kenner found in Pound's company a sane genius. 'Enthralled by the master, I resolved that if no one else would make the case for Ezra Pound as a poet, then I would,' Kenner once recalled.

With McLuhan as an intellectual ally and Pound as a poet needing a champion, the trajectory of Kenner's career was set Kenner would always remain a loyal Poundian. His book *The Pound Era* (1971) is by far the best tribute that poet has received and a classic in 20th-century literary criticism. By contrast, Kenner's friendship with McLuhan would fray. Because Kenner was always a much more fluent and readable writer than McLuhan, his early essays and books got a great deal of attention. Quite unfairly, McLuhan accused Kenner of stealing his ideas.

The reality was that McLuhan was at his best as an oral thinker, rather like Socrates, who developed his sharpest thoughts in conversation with bright students. When McLuhan tried to transcribe his thoughts, the results were usually a mess, half-developed notions splattered all over the page. McLuhan needed Kenner to complete his thoughts and give them form. Plato had performed a similar function for Socrates.

Kenner and McLuhan were both interested in how technology interacted with culture, but Kenner, unlike his erstwhile mentor, actually had a sense of how science works. If you want to build a geodesic dome, you could do worse than to turn to Kenner's *Geodesic Math and How to Use It* (1976). This book has recently been reissued by the University of California Press, after many years of being the most requested out-of-print book in their catalogue. English professors don't normally moonlight as the authors of practical engineering guides, but Kenner was always a bundle of contradictions: a technophile, a Catholic convert, a political and social conservative, a cultural radical, an explicator of recondite poetry and a celebrator of animated cartoons.

'As a teacher at the University of California at Santa Barbara, and later at Johns Hopkins and the University of Georgia, Kenner sought to impart his way of seeing to students,' recalls John Wilson, a former student, now the editor of *Books & Culture*. 'Chain-smoking, spreading his long fingers to illustrate a point, with his hair seemingly electrified by sheer brainpower and his odd, synthesized-sounding voice (the result of childhood influenza that left him almost completely deaf), he could appear as a slightly alien if benign presence, a member of a species closely related to humans yet clearly superior in intelligence. In the classroom, he quoted from memory whatever he needed to cite.'

Kenner's polymathic writing earned him a wide array of admirers in unlikely places. (For many years he was one of the most popular columnists in *Byte* magazine.) Yet among academic literary critics, Kenner was always an odd man out. Because of his offbeat approach, he belonged to no lit-crit school and had no followers. You can't be a Kennerite the way you can be a Leavisite or a Derridean. Moreover, Kenner's politics made many people nervous. Many of the modernists Kenner celebrated, notably Ezra Pound and Wyndham Lewis, had been fascists. And so there was occasional suspicion that he was in sympathy with their ideology as well as their aesthetic. In 1958, Leslie Fiedler wrote that the typical young conservative critic was 'a limp, Hugh Kennerish admirer of Ezra Pound or Wyndham Lewis, dreaming that all their manly spite and vigour are his own; and writing careful exegeses of the *Cantos*, in which he conceals certain bitter political comments for the initiated.'

This notion of Kenner as a covert fascist is simply absurd. Among other things, Kenner was as much inclined to praise a left-wing poet, such as George Oppen or Robert Duncan, as the Tory modernists. In short, Kenner was a slippery writer who evades any easy political labelling. Rather than placing him on the left-right spectrum, it would be better to describe him as a collector of marginalized thinkers and artists: he loved to demonstrate that figures who were dismissed as cranks or freaks did work that has coherence and value. During his lifetime, Kenner's crank collection included Marshall McLuhan, Louis Zukofsky, Buckminster Fuller and Chuck Jones, as well as Pound and Lewis. Some of these people were right-wingers, but what they have in common is that they tend to be undervalued or misunderstood.

Kenner can, indeed, be described as a conservative, but he was an eccentric one. In the late 1950s, Kenner befriended William F. Buckley. The two men shared a passion for boating and for good prose. Buckley recruited Kenner as poetry editor for the *National Review*, but the assignment proved awkward. Kenner was as much an anomaly at the *National Review* as he would have been at any other magazine. The only difference was the *National Review*, then a fledgling publication without a fully coalesced editorial point of view, had room for distinctive writers. In bringing Kenner on board, Buckley demonstrated the high literary aspiration he had for his magazine. During the 1950s and 1960s, under the guidance of the editor Frank Meyer, the *National Review* had an excellent arts section, featuring such writers as Guy Davenport, Joan Didion, Arlene Croce and Garry Wills—all of whom had voices as distinct as Kenner's own.

In his few political articles and stray comments, Kenner showed himself to be broadly conservative but never partisan or predictable. Early on, he mocked Ronald Reagan's fake 'aw shucks' populism and warned Buckley against becoming mired in the moral quagmire that was the Nixon presidency. In his book on Buckminster Fuller, Kenner decried environmental degradation. As a social conservative, he praised a collection of essays by Joseph Sobran that attacked legalized abortions, gay rights and feminism.

McLuhan could sometimes coin snappy phrases ('the global village' and 'the medium is the message') but his densely written paragraphs could be hard to suss out. Kenner, by contrast, was a sparkling writer. His best expository prose hummed with energy and shone with wit. Consider Kenner's celebration of Buster Keaton's films as an example of physics in action, which starts by deftly contextualizing their 1920s sensibility:

> You could understand how a thing worked by looking at it. A locomotive, a steam shovel, Calvin Coolidge hid nothing from the mind; they did not require to be explained as all subsequent technology has required endlessly to be explained.... Trajectories Everyman intuited with ease, and the Parallelogram of Forces irradiated his mind as Love does an angel's. The collaboration between audience and kinetic mime was nearly ideal. No one had trouble understanding how a snagged log with Buster clinging to its end could pivot up like a mast and then out over a waterfall's lip like bowsprit; nor why, swinging down from its end on a rope to rescue the girl, he launched himself not toward her but away from her; nor by what conversion of potential to kinetic energy he is carried up, having snatched her from her ledge, exactly to that handy shelf of rock.

The characteristic Kenner touches are all present: the vigorous syntax and rich diction, the confident leaping through time and space, the unexpected juxtapositions (the steam shovel with Coolidge), the linkage between technology and culture, and even a slight hint of his religious convictions.

Kenner's genius was always in doing the unexpected: showing that Pound's poetry illustrated the principles of fractal math, arguing that Alexander Pope anticipated the techniques of Pop Art, demonstrating that Bugs Bunny cartoons gained their speed and energy from tight-fisted economic policies at the Warner Brothers Studio.

All of these are unlikely connections, yet Kenner made them real and convincing. He never simply accepted the world as it appeared, but always looked for deeper patterns that demonstrated coherence and order. Perhaps Kenner's Catholic faith gave him confidence to carry out his inquiries, sure in the ultimate goodness of creation. Yet even those of us who don't share his faith can still cherish the beautiful patterns he uncovered.

National Post, January 24, 2004

RIGHT-WING POLITICS

THE PHILOSOPHER: LEO STRAUSS

Odd as this may sound, we live in a world increasingly shaped by Leo Strauss, a controversial philosopher who died in 1973. Although generally unknown to the wider population, Strauss has been one of the two or three most important intellectual influences on the conservative worldview now ascendant in George W. Bush's Washington. Eager to get the lowdown on White House thinking, editors at *The New York Times* and *Le Monde* have had journalists pore over Strauss's work and trace his disciples' affiliations. *The New Yorker* has even found a contingent of Straussians doing intelligence work for the Pentagon.

Yet while the extent of Strauss's influence is wide, his writings are frequently obscure, and his legacy is hotly disputed by admirers and critics alike. Certainly, Strauss was no ordinary Republican idea-maker: steeped in ancient philosophy, he had dark forebodings about democracy, religion, technology and nearly everything else that can claim the allegiance of the contemporary conservative (or liberal, for that matter).

At first glance, a University of Chicago professor who spent most of his life pondering old books would seem an unlikely master-thinker for the policy wonks, career bureaucrats, and pundits who make up Washington's unelected elite. Strauss held that politics was a central human activity, but he also believed that 'all practical or political life is inferior to contemplative life.' He participated in the battle of ideas not by issuing political manifestos or angling for bureaucratic power, but by writing recondite and difficult books.

A typical Strauss volume is a densely packed commentary on a classic text like Plato's *The Laws* or Machiavelli's *The Prince*, festooned with footnotes drawing on an array of hard-won languages from ancient Greek and Latin to medieval Arabic. It's often difficult to discern where Strauss's paraphrases of dead writers leave off and his own views begin—and this has only deepened the mystery that attaches to his work.

Despite his life of quiet scholarly obscurity, Strauss has exerted a strong posthumous sway among those who bustle through the corridors of power. Washington Straussians have included Robert A. Goldwin, who had the bizarre and unenviable task of organizing weekly seminars in political theory and practice attended by President Gerald Ford in the mid-1970s; Carnes Lord, National Security Council adviser in the Reagan administration; and William Galston, deputy domestic policy adviser in the first two years of the Clinton administration. Irving Kristol, an intellectual whose name is virtually synonymous with neoconservatism, has named Strauss as a major influence, and Straussian writers and ideas regularly grace the pages of magazines like *National Review, Commentary* and *The Weekly Standard*, which is edited by Irving's son William Kristol. The Bush administration's Straussians include the Pentagon officials Paul Wolfowitz and Abram Shulsky, who studied with Strauss at the University of Chicago, and the bioethics adviser Leon Kass, a colleague at Chicago.

Strauss also claims a large, if rather clubbish, following in the academy, especially among scholars of political theory and American constitutional history. And yet even those academics who know Strauss's work best often sharply disagree about its fundamental meaning. There are East Coast Straussians, West Coast Straussians, and even some Straussian Democrats. Clifford Orwin, a professor at the University of Toronto strongly influenced by Strauss, describes him as a wise teacher who counselled prudence and moderation. But Shadia Drury, a professor of political science at the University of Calgary and the author of *Leo Strauss and the American Right*, completely disagrees. For her, Strauss was nothing less than 'a Jewish Nazi' whose pretense of American patriotism and piety hid a cynical and extremist antidemocratic ideology.

Was Leo Strauss a friend of liberal democracy, or an elitist who wanted society to be ruled by a secretive cabal? An ardent opponent of tyranny, or an apologist for the abuse of power? An atheist or a pious Jew?

To understand Strauss, we need to look beyond the famous students and self-styled acolytes and examine the man himself.

Born in 1899 to an Orthodox Jewish family in Germany, Leo Strauss learned at an early age that religion and philosophy are always vulnerable to the threat of political persecution. As a young man, Strauss was a liberal rationalist who nursed the hope, widespread in German Jewish circles, that assimilation into a liberal democracy would end anti-Semitism. As an undergraduate at the University of Marburg, his mentor was Hermann Cohen, a philosopher whose reconciliation of Kant's philosophical ethics and biblical morality seemed to suggest that there was no contradiction in being a German Jewish liberal.

In the 1920s Strauss became increasingly disillusioned with modern liberalism. Philosophically, he was shaken by his encounters, at the University of Freiburg, with Martin Heidegger, the philosopher whose powerful critique of rationality's delusions seemed to undercut the guileless liberalism of Kant and Cohen. Politically, the instability of the Weimar Republic and the rise of Nazism proved to Strauss that liberals were also weaklings in practical matters, unable to protect society from explosions of popular fanaticism. Furthermore, the rise of a new and more virulent strain of anti-Semitism demonstrated that assimilation had failed to solve the problems of German Jewry.

These political and philosophical problems were fused in the 1930s, when the Nazis came to power—and won the applause of Heidegger. By this point Strauss had left Germany for France, where he was studying medieval Jewish and Islamic philosophy on a Rockefeller scholarship, but he continued to view events in his native country with dismay.

Strauss believed that Martin Heidegger possessed the greatest mind of the 20th century. But unlike those Heidegger admirers who excused the philosopher's flirtation with Nazism as a mere personal failing, Strauss believed it showed that modern philosophy had gone deeply astray. Orwin explains: 'Strauss's question always was, "What was it about modern thought that could have led Heidegger to make these disastrous practical misjudgments?"'

In Strauss's mature work, he would argue that Plato and Aristotle were wiser than modern thinkers like Machiavelli and Heidegger. This exultation of ancient thought wasn't merely a nostalgic celebration of the good old Greek days. As the political theorist Stephen Holmes observes, Strauss believed that classical thinkers had grasped a still-vital truth: inequality is an ineradicable aspect of the human condition.

For Strauss, the modern liberal project of using the fruits of science and the institutions of the state to spread happiness to all is intrinsically futile, self-defeating, and likely to end in terror and tyranny. The best regime is one in which the leaders govern moderately and prudently, curbing the passions of the mob while allowing a small philosophical elite to pursue the contemplative life of the mind.

Such a philosophical elite may discover truths that are not fit for public consumption. For example, it may find that its city's prosperity derives ultimately from 'force and fraud', or that the gods do not exist. Aware that Socrates was executed for blasphemy, ancient thinkers realized that philosophy was dangerous: it had to be kept for the intelligent few rather than the ignorant many. Therefore ancient philosophers (and their medieval followers) wrote in code. Using metaphors and cryptic language, they communicated one message, an 'esoteric' one, for an elite of wise readers and another, 'exoteric' one, for the unsophisticated general population. For Strauss, the art of concealment and secrecy was among the greatest legacies of antiquity.

Although Strauss's ideas had been developing for years, they really coalesced when he moved to London in 1934, and then to the United States later in the decade. Like many European émigrés, he found refuge at New York's New School of Social Research, where he taught from 1938 to 1948, and then at the University of Chicago, where he remained until his retirement in the late '60s. While his teachings and books bewildered mainstream American social scientists and drew many hostile comments, students flocked to this odd and beguiling refugee scholar.

Many would go on to become important academics in their own right, including the philosopher Stanley Rosen (a leading light at Boston University), the historian Harry Jaffa (who later wrote speeches for Barry Goldwater), and Allan Bloom, whose 1987 bestseller, *The Closing of the American Mind*, would—paradoxically—bring Strauss's thought to a mass audience.

Mindful of the collapse of Weimar Germany's fragile democracy, Strauss was distrustful of American liberals; he believed they were too weak-minded and trusting to fight communism. In fact, Strauss believed that the United States shared certain ills with Soviet communism: both societies put the material well-being of the masses ahead of the cultivation of virtues among an elite. But Strauss also saw America's constitutional government as the last, best hope for excellence in a modern world besotted with egalitarianism. Many of his students would go on to champion the U.S. Constitution—with its separation of powers and its provision for a strong executive branch—as a political masterpiece that put limits on popular rule.

Stanley Rosen observes that Strauss's earliest students were often indifferent to politics and interested mainly in philosophy. Robert

Goldwin became one of the first Straussians to work in practical politics when he joined the campaign of Charles Percy, a Republican candidate for the governorship of Illinois, in 1964. As it turned out, this migration of Straussians into the world of politics helped fill a vacuum in the Republican party, which, aside from free-market economists like Milton Friedman, had few well-educated intellectuals to fill policy-making positions. Once in Washington, Straussian conservatives could carry on their war against modern liberalism's moral relativism at home and naive pursuit of détente with the Soviet Union abroad.

The Straussian milieu was a closely knit one, where professors and pundits cultivated their favourite disciples with devotion. As Holmes points out, Strauss once wrote of 'the love of the mature philosopher for the puppies of his race, by whom he wants to be loved in return.'

With his teachings about philosophers who write in code and secret doctrines for the elect, Leo Strauss can seem like a conspiracy buff. In fact, some of Strauss's followers like Allan Bloom and Willmoore Kendall do use the word 'conspiracy' to describe the history of Western thought. Not surprisingly, conspiracies have flourished around Strauss himself. The followers of Lyndon H. LaRouche, the fringe presidential candidate who believes that the world is governed by Jewish bankers inspired by a Babylonian cult and that the Queen of England is a drug dealer, argue that Strauss is the evil genius behind the Republican Party. More sensible folk, like the *New York Times* writer Brent Staples, who earned a doctorate in psychology at Chicago in the 1980s, have also decried the 'sinister vogue' of Strauss.

Certainly, Strauss's embrace of obscurity is part of his appeal. When it comes to religion, the obscurity can get especially thick. Strauss, who wrote on Jewish issues all his life, held that atheism was not a viable public philosophy. And yet he often interpreted religious figures in an impious way. He suggested once that the great medieval Jewish scholar Maimonides secretly believed that reason and revelation were incompatible while pretending to reconcile the Bible with philosophy. In his book *The Anatomy of Antiliberalism*, Stephen Holmes maintains that, in Strauss's view, only philosophers can handle the truth: that nature is indifferent to human values and needs.

So where did Strauss really stand? 'He was an atheist,' says Stanley Rosen flatly. 'They [Straussians] all are. They are epicureans and atheists.'

While some Straussians dispute the idea that the master was a godless cynic, it does seem that Strauss wanted a regime where the elite lived by a code of stoic fortitude while governing a population that subscribes to superstitious beliefs. 'He agreed with Marx that religion was the opium of the masses,' says Shadia Drury. 'But he believed that the masses need their opium.' Sociologically, Strauss's approach would seem to work well for the Republican Party, which has a grass-roots base of born-again Christians and a more secular elite leadership—at least in its foreign-policy wing.

Some traditional and religious conservatives have become deeply wary of Straussians. 'They certainly believe that religion may be a useful thing to take in the suckers with,' notes Thomas Fleming, editor of the right-wing journal *Chronicles*. 'Exoteric Straussians are taught to repeat mantras about democracy, liberty, and republican government which the inner-circle Straussians don't appear to hold to. One of Allan Bloom's students told me that Professor Bloom had taught them that Plato was just an American-style democrat. This is just absurd. Plato taught the rule of a tiny elite, which is what the Straussians actually believe.'

Clifford Orwin sees nothing objectionable in the alliance between Strauss-inspired neoconservatives and fundamentalist Christians. 'The Republican Party, like the Democratic Party, is a big tent in which a great many people have to coexist who disagree on a great many things,' notes Orwin. 'There is nothing sinister about that.'

But just how 'sinister' was Leo Strauss himself? The answer depends on how a reader approaches his books. If you read Strauss with a well-disposed spirit, he can be interpreted as a genuine friend of American liberal democracy. He worked to create an elite that was sufficiently free of illusions about the goodness of man to fight the totalitarian enemies of liberal democracy—be they fascists, communists or Islamicist fundamentalists.

But if you read Strauss with a skeptical mind, the way he himself read the great philosophers, a more disturbing picture takes shape. Strauss, by this view, emerges as a disguised Machiavelli, a cynical teacher who encouraged his followers to believe that their intellectual superiority entitles them to rule over the bulk of humanity by means of duplicity. The worst thing you can do to Leo Strauss, perhaps, is to read his books with Straussian eyes.

Boston Globe, Ideas, May 11, 2003

ADDENDUM TO STRAUSS: THE CLASSICS AND THE CLOSET

For centuries, classical scholarship was fuelled by homoerotic desire. The Greeks, as every schoolboy who paid attention knows, didn't have the Jewish, Christian and Islamic prohibition against same-sex desire. Because the church respected the ancients despite their vices, Latin continued to be taught into the monotheistic centuries and ancient Greek enjoyed a rebirth. Hard-won languages that could only be understood by an elite (which until very late in the game was also an exclusively male club), these dead tongues existed as a kind of code. You could say things in them that were otherwise unspeakable, things that could get you killed if voiced in the vernacular. The sanction of the church created, in effect, a closet space in the Western tradition, a place to hide but also a place of comfort.

Allan Bloom, himself a closeted gay, loved to emphasize the covert nature of the Western tradition, the concealed ideas wrapped up in esoteric texts that were passed down from generation to generation in whispers. Bloom, of course, learned esoteric reading from Leo Strauss and if you look at the Straussian movement closely you'll see that if it's not homoerotic it certainly is homo-social. Did Strauss ever have a female graduate student? Occasionally you hear Straussians suggest that women, with their icky biological urge to procreate, are incapable of philosophy. Certainly this boys' club is conducive towards the forging of tight male friendships.

Everywhere you look in the history of classical scholarship, especially as it overlapped with literature, you see evidence of what we would now call gayness. There were the Uranian poets who flourished at Oxford and Cambridge in the late 19th and early 20th century who celebrated boyish bodies with Virgilian ardour (Oscar Wilde was the great popularizer of this coterie and its sensibility). For these poets, Hellenism and homosexuality went hand in hand. The Uranians were also the precursors to A.E. Housman, the star Latin scholar of his age and a great poet of unspoken and thwarted desire. In his book *One Hundred Years of Homosexuality*, the scholar David Halperin recounts a fascinating story about how even Housman's scholarly work on classical homosexuality had to stay in the closet. When, in 1930 Housman 'proposed to clarify the meaning of various sexual acts mentioned in Roman literature and, in particular, to explicate Roman attitudes to sex between males'—a topic to which he brought a personal as well as a scholarly interest—he chose to express himself in Latin rather than in English; Housman's intricate Latin style, however, was still too explicit for the Board of Management of the *Classical Quarterly*, which forbade the editor to publish Housman's essay (the essay had already been set up in type, but that was as far as it got). Housman ultimately published his essay abroad, in the German classical periodical *Hermes*: it appeared in 1931, still in Latin.

Lesbians are part of this story as well. Is it any accident that Edith Hamilton, bestselling author of *The Greek Way* (1930), lived for many years with the investment banker Doris Fielding Reid? Or that Marguerite Yourcenar and Mary Renault, both of whom had female lovers, wrote historical novels about the ancient world?

Michel Foucault represents the culmination of this tradition in more ways than one. He was not closeted at all (at least not in his last years). This allowed him to tackle the subject of Greek sexuality with a frankness previously impossible. What Housman had to hide in Latin, Foucault could freely discuss in French. But it also meant that he wasn't interested in the Greeks as imaginary ancestors. The upshot of his work is to emphasize how different ancient Greek sexuality was from that of the modern world, including same sex desire. For the Greeks, the relevant categories were active and passive, not male or female. This meant they experienced sex in a way we moderns don't.

The question is, after Foucault and the end of the closet, what will happen to the classics? One of the main emotional wellsprings for classical scholarship has been lost. Repressed sexual energy was a great motivator for the hard work of mastering very difficult texts. It's difficult to imagine young men and women looking to the Greeks with the same yearning that animated Housman and Hamilton.

This might explain why Allan Bloom was so adamantly opposed to the gay rights movement, to the open proclamation of a gay identity. Somewhere deep in his bones he must have felt that the end of the closet could also mean the end of the classics.

Sans Everything, October 26, 2007

HILTON KRAMER: A DISSENTING OBITUARY

Hilton Kramer, the art critic and founding editor of *The New Criterion*, who died at age 84 on March 27, 2012, rather enjoyed his own reputation for being fearsome and formidable. Take a look at the back cover of his essay collection *The Revenge of the Philistines* (1985) where Kramer presents himself to the world as a very severe killjoy, almost like a caricature of the critic as hanging judge. 'Would it kill him to crack a smile?' a friend asked when he saw that photo.

Yet as off-putting as he could seem from afar, Kramer enjoyed many close collaborators and admirers, who are already bearing witness to his virtues. Since others writers are making the case on behalf of Kramer, I want to enter a few dissenting notes about his writing and public presence.

Back in his salad days in the early 1950s, Kramer's big break came from publishing in *Partisan Review* and he saw himself as heir to that magazine's stance of being both politically and aesthetically engaged. Unfortunately, his politics were absurd. He started off as a cold war liberal (with perhaps a few social democratic sympathies). In the early 1960s he even served as art critic for *The Nation*, an alliance that both he and the magazine would later regard with bemused puzzlement. In reaction to the turmoil of the late 1960s Kramer became a very fierce and unbending neo-conservative, of the sort that prefers ideological purity to any acknowledgement of reality.

In a 1987 essay on Sidney Hook, Kramer, with his characteristic obtuse overconfidence, argued that Mikhail Gorbachev was a far bigger threat to the free world than Joseph Stalin had ever been. 'Under Stalin, both the military power of the Soviet Union and its vast espionage apparatus were seen to constitute a danger to every non-Communist society in the world—yet Gorbachev commands a far greater war machine than any Stalin ever had at his disposal, and if recent revelations are any guide, a no less effective espionage network,' Kramer asserted. 'By every significant measure, the Soviet Union is a far more formidable adversary today than it was forty years ago, and one of the things that makes it more formidable is its unbroken record of conquest in the intervening years. It already enjoys an unchallenged hegemony in more parts of the world than it did forty years ago, and the momentum of its drive to seek further conquests shows no sign of abatement.' Equally in keeping with his impervious intellectual manner was the fact that when Kramer reprinted this essay in his 1999 collection *The Twilight of the Intellectuals* he carefully excised this passage, displaying an appropriately Soviet willingness to rewrite history.

The same perverse ideological prism that allowed Kramer to see Gorbachev as worse than Stalin also made him regard the various social movements of the 1960s (feminism, gay rights, the Black Power movement, the anti-war movement, environmentalism) as agents of subversion and destruction rather than attempts, however partial and flawed they might be, to build a more decent and equitable society.

Perhaps the worst part of Kramer's worldview was his rigid gender politics, which infected his criticism with an intellectually debilitating homophobia and sexism. Kramer, of course, would have rejected any designation of himself as a homophobe and sexist. As he once told *New York Magazine*, 'Some of the people I've been closest to in my life have been homosexuals.' But whatever his personal conduct might have been, as a public figure Kramer stood in steadfast opposition to the idea that gays should be open and equal citizens in a democratic polity. He did this moreover not by making any rational arguments against gay equality but by constantly and snidely assuming that the very practice of gay sex was naturally repugnant to all right-thinking people.

Derisive hooting and cheap shots were his favourite rhetorical modes, as when he referred to the gay rights movement as 'orifice politics'. A finicky fear of anal sex is a recurrent theme in Kramer's criticism. In 1965 he lamented that 'nothing seems to interest the reading public quite so much these days as anal sex.' In 1977, Kramer upbraided Gore Vidal for 'proselytizing for the joys of buggery'. In 1990, Kramer attacked progressives for wanting to teach grade school kids about 'the niceties of anal intercourse'. On another occasion Kramer offered this account of the artistic style known as camp: 'the origins of camp is to be found in the subculture of homosexuality. Camp humor derives, in its essence, from the homosexual's recognition that his condition represents a kind of joke on nature.' I hate to be pedantic about such matters but Kramer seemed to be unaware of certain biological and social facts that many clever high-school students are able to figure out these days: that not all gays engage in anal sex while many heterosexuals do and that gay relationships, like straight ones, can be cemented by love as well as by sex. Notoriously, Kramer's distaste for public displays of gay identity fuelled his tireless crusade against Robert Mapplethorpe's late-period photography but I would argue that there is a gay-fearing subtext to virtually every essay he wrote on a gay artist or writer.

All this gay-baiting occasionally exacted a personal toll. The very conservative gay critic Bruce Bawer loved Kramer as a father figure and published in virtually every issue of *The New Criterion* for nearly a decade. Yet even Bawer broke with *The New Criterion* and Kramer when the journal published a cruelly mocking account of a gay pride march in 1993.

As for Kramer's gender politics, it is hard to forget the absurd claim he made in a 1991 *Partisan Review* symposium that 'orthodox feminism' dominated television, offering as evidence 'the ads in which the women are all so much smarter than the men, and the general depiction of women in their social roles, in their vocational roles now determined by the feminist agenda.' About one of America's most prominent female intellectuals Kramer wrote, 'In the end, Mary McCarthy's politics were like her sex life—promiscuous and unprincipled, more a question of opportunity than of commitment or belief.' When writing about sexually active heterosexual male intellectuals (notably McCarthy's ex-husband, Edmund Wilson) Kramer somehow avoided the word 'promiscuous'. Like a schoolyard bully, Kramer knew that slut-shaming is reserved for girls.

If Kramer's politics were distasteful, his better self occasionally shone through in his art criticism and editorship. He was a very gifted journalistic art critic, with the rare skill of being able to write intelligently about aesthetic matters under the constraints of newspaper deadlines and word counts. During his long tenure at *The New York Times* from 1965 to 1982, he elevated the paper's cultural coverage, bringing to the daily press some of the brainy excitement of *The Nation* and *Partisan Review*.

His great strength as a critic was his forthrightness. He knew his mind and never hedged or equivocated. When describing the art he loved best—the masterpieces of high modernism created by European and American artists from 1890 to 1960—his blustery prose achieved a hard-edged eloquence.

As unlikely as this may sound, Kramer's distinctive prose style represented a popularization of three of his cultural heroes, the critic F.R. Leavis, Henry James and John Milton. Leavis was the immediate precursor. Anyone who reads Kramer's mixture of tart sarcasm and high solemnity, his barely controlled rage that is held in check and given form by Latinate abstraction, his complex, serpentine sentences that curl around the subject before starting strangulation—anyone, that is, who reads Kramer with care will hear the echo of Leavis's prose.

It was the discovery of Leavis that a modified version of Henry James's studied involution could allow a critic to pursue an argument sedulously and forcefully while maintaining an urbane air. Kramer followed Leavis in imitating James's syntax. To put it another way, Kramer's stuffed shirt was a hand-me-down.

Even beyond Leavis, Kramer's literary roots go deeper into the history of style and sensibility. Consider these typical items from the Kramer lexicon: 'horrid', 'baleful', 'pernicious', 'despicable', 'malign' and 'ghastly'. For an art critic, these are odd words, deliberately archaic and pointedly moralistic. Kramer's diction is quite literally and literarily Puritan. Milton repeatedly used such words in that Puritan masterpiece *Paradise Lost*.

The diction of judgment and damnation moves with surprising ease from its religious home into the domain of art criticism, where souls are condemned to the eternal perdition of kitsch. *Paradise Lost* was not only the title but also the theme of Milton's famous poem. A similar vision of the fall from Eden informs Kramer's account of art history. The 1950s, for Kramer, was the paradise of high modernism when God-like artists like Picasso and Jackson Pollock walked the earth creating beauty *ex nihilo*. Alas, our feckless common parents (Andy Warhol and Susan Sontag) ate the apple of camp and pop art. By giving in to temptation, they doomed us all to the fallen world of postmodernism.

Kramer's over-reliance on the didactic language of moral reproach hampered his critical acumen. He once defined postmodernism as 'modernism with a sneer, a giggle, modernism without any animating faith in the nobility and pertinence of its cultural mandate.' By this account, postmodernism is simply a result of artists being naughty. Even if one agrees that postmodernism represents a falling off from the lofty ambitions of high modernism, Kramer's explanation of where postmodernism comes from is almost pathetically inadequate. To really understand why modernism metamorphosed into postmodernism we need to turn to a much more theoretically savvy analyst like Fredric Jameson, who persuasively sees postmodernism as the cultural working out of late capitalism.

Passionate and hard-working though he was, Kramer simply couldn't measure up to the genuinely front-ranking art critics of his era. He lacked Clement Greenberg's theoretical reach, Harold Rosenberg's phrase-making brio, Wendy Lesser's playful ability to upturn our received ideas, or Arthur Danto's grounding in philosophy (to name only a few distinguished contemporaries). Unlike Kramer, these critics wrote journalism that makes the same lasting claims on our attention as the best literature.

As an editor Kramer left a similarly divided legacy. *The New Criterion* opened shop in 1982 and for roughly a decade it offered meaty, argumentative cultural analysis month after month. While at times infuriating in its cultural politics, *The New Criterion* did take art seriously and gave a venue to many fine writers, notably Jed Perl, Karen Wilkin, Donald Lyons and Bruce Bawer. It is a sign of how relatively catholic the magazine was in its early days that many of these writers didn't share Kramer's politics. The situation changed in the 1990s when the Cold War gave way to the Culture Wars and *The New Criterion* became much more of a party-line right wing rag, sharing an editorial outlook that made it indistinguishable from *Commentary* or *National Review*.

In *Humboldt's Gift*, Saul Bellow gave a typically malicious portrait of the young Hilton Kramer, shown in the novel to be a shallow careerist. The real Kramer was a more interesting and admonitory figure. He started off loving art and had a talent for explaining his passion but never became the first-rate critic he could have been as he started to see paintings and novels as weapons in a cultural war against enemies that existed largely in his own mind. He once described Jacques Barzun as 'a grim example of liberalism turning reactionary'—an accurate epithet for Karmer himself. The gap between what Kramer could have achieved and his paltry legacy is immense and worth mourning.

Sans Everything, March 30, 2012

JOSEPH EPSTEIN: NOSTALGIA FOR EMPIRE AND THE CLOSET

Joseph Epstein is the most congenial of neo-conservatives, perhaps the only major one. He is a top-notch personal essayist, who has revived the ruminative, free-ranging tradition of Montaigne and Hazlitt. Among more modern essayists, he's the peer of Virginia Woolf, James Baldwin and Gore Vidal (not company he'd be completely comfortable with, sadly). He's also a very entertaining short story writer. Mind you, if literature were organized the way baseball was, Epstein wouldn't be playing with the New York Yankees against heavy-hitters like Alice Munro or Mavis Gallant but would have to content himself with life on a farm team in Albany or Akron. Still, the Akron Aeros have some good players and Epstein's fiction has given me a great deal of pleasure.

Epstein has his limits, which can be seen most clearly in his literary criticism. One mark of a first rate literary critic is the ability to transcend partisan politics. Hugh Kenner was a conservative Catholic in the *National Review* mould, but he was wonderfully appreciative of Louis Zukofsky and George Oppen, left-liberal Jews with a strong Marxist past. The socialist Irving Howe was equally insightful, and even good-naturedly affectionate, when writing about Kipling. And Fredric Jameson's Marxism hasn't prevented him from being a persuasive advocate on behalf of Wyndham Lewis, who can fairly be described as a fascist fellow traveller.

Kenner, Howe and Jameson all had strong political commitments but they also possessed the gift of empathy, the literary critic's essential skill of entering into a writer's mental universe and appraising it from within before passing judgment. For all his erudition, for all the wit and fluidity of his prose, Epstein lacks the ability to read empathetically, which leaves his critical essays severely limited.

If you know a writer's politics you can pretty much figure out how Epstein will react to him or her. If a writer is right wing or politically quiescent, Epstein will give him or her at least a respectful hearing and often high praise: the Esptein nod of approval has gone to Evelyn Waugh, Philip Larkin, Henry James, Barbara Pym, Max Beerbohm, James Gould

Cozzens, Somerset Maugham, George Santayana, V.S. Naipaul and others of their ilk. But if a writer is a liberal or leftist, Epstein has nothing to offer but the back of his hand: he's been scornful of Mary McCarthy, Joan Didion, Pauline Kael, Norman Mailer, Philip Roth, John Updike, Gabriel García Márquez, Edmund Wilson and like-minded souls. A kind of anti-leftism even infects Epstein's appraisal of classic writers like Hazlitt.

The few exceptions to this rule are telling: Epstein did write essays scoring points against William F. Buckley and celebrating A.J. Liebling but that was when Epstein's own politics were much more liberal than they are now. For many years Epstein was a member of the H.L. Mencken fan club, only letting his membership lapse when evidence of the extent and scabrousness of Mencken's anti-Semitism proved too overwhelming to ignore. And Epstein has many times praised Theodore Dreiser, whose politics were too muddled to be easily categorized. But really, these are pretty minor exceptions.

Every literary judgment Epstein makes is heavily filtered through his political concerns. A good example of this is his essay on E.M. Forster, which ran earlier this year in *The Weekly Standard* (and recently got highlighted by *Arts and Letters Daily*). The essay essentially restates arguments Epstein made in his article 'One Cheer for E.M. Forster' which was published in *Commentary* in 1985, later reprinted in Epstein's collection *Partial Payments*. (Epstein's conservative politics don't prevent him from being an adept recycler.) In both pieces, Epstein concludes that Forster is a minor writer because of his liberal politics. Near the end of the *Weekly Standard* essay Epstein writes: 'But in the end Forster's chief contribution has been to that continuing project of reinforcing liberals' feelings of self-virtue owing to their lovely imaginative sensitivity and courageous distaste for social injustice.'

Epstein is particularly upset by two aspects of Forster's 'emancipatory liberalism': the novelist was an anti-imperialist who bolstered the cause of Indian independence and he was an important precursor to the gay liberation movement. Both of Epstein's objections are worth examining in detail.

ONE OF HISTORY'S GRANDEST ADVENTURES

In his essay 'Anglophilia, American Style' Epstein admits to feeling 'nostalgia' for the British Empire, which he describes as 'one of history's grandest adventures'.

Given these Kipling-esque sentiments, perhaps rooted in too credulous a reading of *Kim* or a desire to emulate the life of T.E. Lawrence, Epstein has little use for a novelist who detailed the systematic cruelty of the British rule in India, as Forster did in *A Passage to India*. In the *Weekly Standard*, Epstein wrote, 'Whatever one's views of British imperialism, one has also to admit that Forster, the milquetoasty blocked novelist, the long-repressed homosexual, probably contributed, through *A Passage to India*, as much as anyone short of Gandhi, to justifying before the world Indian independence.'

In his *Commentary* piece, Epstein lays out the argument more explicitly:

> And [the portrayal of the Anglo-Indians in *A Passage to India*] came through accompanied by serious political consequences.... Paul Johnson, in *Modern Times* ... writes: 'In 1924 E.M. Forster published *A Passage to India*, a wonderfully insidious assault on the principle of the Raj, nearly turning upside-down the belief in British superiority and maturity which was the prime justification of the Indian Empire.'
>
> Books are created in history, and through the events of history is our reading of them influenced. Here it must be noted that history has dissipated much of the glory of *A Passage to India*, by revealing that the treatment of the Indians by the British had been nowhere nearly so cruel, indeed murderous, as the treatment of the Indians by one another, beginning with the massacres following upon independence and continuing even today with the bloody dispute between the Indian government and the Sikhs.

There is much that can be said about Epstein's arguments. I'll start by noting that I have a personal interest in these issues because I was born in the Punjab in India, where some of the worst fighting during partition took place. Despite India's troubled history, I have yet to meet a South Asian—be they Hindu, Sikh, Muslim, Buddhist, atheist, Christian or of any other form of belief or non-belief—who shares Epstein's nostalgia for the grand adventure of the British Empire. Nor indeed have I ever met any 'native' from Asia or Africa who is nostalgic the way Epstein is. Among Indians there is a general awareness of a fact that Epstein is probably not cognizant of: that the violence of the partition grew out of the long-standing British policy of divide-and-conquer. But there is an easy response to such anti-imperialist arguments: the natives don't know what's good for them. That's what Kipling believed and perhaps Epstein of Chicago (heir to Lawrence of Arabia) would agree.

But if anecdotes are unconvincing perhaps scholarship will do the trick. If Epstein would take the trouble to read credible scholars of India (i.e., people not named Paul Johnson) he would discover the true extent of British cruelty. In particular I would recommend Amartya Sen, the Nobel prize–winning economist and political theorist. As Sen has demonstrated in many publications, notably the 1999 book *Development as Freedom*, throughout the period of British rule India was racked by terrible famines which cost millions of lives. These famines were not just natural disasters but had a strong political dimension: because the British Empire was un-democratic and committed to laissez-faire ideology, relief efforts were constantly half-hearted or thwarted. Sen draws extensive parallels with the well-known history of Ireland. Since gaining independence and democracy, both Ireland and India have conquered the problem of famines.

Sen's compelling arguments can be usefully supplemented by the late Christopher Thorne, who in his masterful 1978 book, *Allies of a Kind*, demonstrates that the ethnic hubris of British leaders like Winston Churchill had real consequences on policy, notably in the low priority that was given to famine relief in the 1940s (at least a million Indians starved to death during those years). Tales of hunger and misery in India were often occasions for Churchill and his cronies to make quips. On one occasion, urged to release food stocks to alleviate a famine, 'Churchill responded with a telegram asking why Gandhi hadn't died yet.'

Thorne's summary of how Churchill's government handled Indian policy is worth quoting: 'It was not simply that these affairs showed up a side of Churchill that was ignorant, ugly and at times vicious … or that they revealed something of the way in which Cherwell approached the sufferings of the coloured peoples he found so distasteful. The Cabinet as a whole, with obvious exceptions such as Bevin, were wont to discuss India's problems, be they starvation, communal strife, or the country's economic structure, in a manner which, as we have seen, Wavell for one found appalling in its insouciance.'

But perhaps Epstein would have a hard time trusting that Sen and Thorne can both be described as academic liberals and hence slippery chaps, as Wodehouse or Kipling would say. In that case, perhaps he could listen to his fellow neo-conservative Nathan Glazer. In a letter published in the January 1986 issue of *Commentary*, Glazer took issue with the idea that India was better off under the Raj:

> What can Joseph Epstein possibly mean by writing that E.M. Forster's dislike of the 'Anglo-Indians' (*A Passage to India*) 'came through accompanied by serious political consequences'? Mr Epstein goes on to quote Paul Johnson to the effect that the novel undermined 'belief in British superiority and maturity'. Is the 'serious political consequences' that Britain did not put forth the effort (which was in any case beyond it, materially and morally) to maintain rule over India after 1947? Isn't that nonsense? At a time when the Western episode of colonialism is over, when no Western country has colonies, and all consider themselves better off without them, what would lead anyone to take up the defence of colonialism and regret its demise? Only, I am afraid, a narrow and distorted view of India....

But Glazer can be dismissed just as easily as Sen and Thorne. He's rather squishy as neo-conservatives go and he has an Indian-born wife, so maybe he's gone native.

There's one more voice to turn to for someone who won't trust Sen, Thorne or Glazer. Andrew Roberts is a very conservative historian, who has been known to keep company with George W. Bush and Dick Cheney. Roberts is as much a fan of the British Empire as Epstein is. Yet in his 1994 book *Eminent Churchillians*, Roberts recorded this revealing story:

> During the 1943 Bengal famine, in which over a million Indians died, [Churchill] reassured the Secretary of State for India, Leo Amery, that they would nevertheless continue to breed 'like rabbits'. After such an outburst in 1944, Amery was prompted to tell the Prime Minister that he 'didn't see much difference between his outlook and Hitler's'.

The Bengalis who starved to death because of Churchill's haughtiness probably did not think they were living through 'one of history's grandest adventures'. Interestingly, Amartya Sen is himself a survivor of the Bengal famine.

Given all these facts, I think Forster's anti-imperialism looks much better than Epstein's nostalgia for the grand adventure of Empire.

As a side note, Epstein and Paul Johnson almost certainly over-estimate the political impact of Forster's novel. Indeed Epstein contradicts himself by stating that Forster was second only to Gandhi in making the cause for independence while also saying that as late as 1943 Forster was 'a small-public writer, known chiefly to the cognoscenti'. There were many other writers, both Indian and British, who had more of an impact in discrediting the Raj than Forster.)

HOMO-UNEASE

In his *Commentary* essay, Epstein insists that Foster should be read through the prism of sexual politics in a way that damages the writer's reputation:

> It is no longer possible to think of Forster as a writer who happened to have been a homosexual; now he must be considered a writer for whom homosexuality was the central, the dominant, fact in his life. Given this centrality, this dominance, it hardly seems wild to suggest that the chief impulse behind Forster's novels, with their paeans and pleas for the life of the instincts, was itself homosexual....
>
> As for his teaching about the instinctual life—the sanity of passion, the holiness of desire, and the rest of it—here, too, his side, that of emancipatory liberalism, has known no shortage of victories. If, then, his writing today seems so thin, so hollow, and finally so empty, can it be in part because we have now all had an opportunity to view the progress of emancipationism in our lifetimes, the liberation that was the name of Forster's most ardent desire, and know it to be itself thin, hollow, and finally rather empty?

I'm not sure that most readers would agree with Epstein in thinking that emancipatory liberalism, the great project that has given women control over their reproductive lives and overturned the laws that once made it a crime to practise gay sex, has been such a failure. But perhaps this is a good occasion to review Epstein's larger relationship with gay rights and indeed gayness itself, both issues that have long troubled him.

'If I had the power to do so, I would wish homosexuality off the face of this earth,' Epstein wrote in a notorious 1970 *Harper's* article. 'I would do so because I think it brings infinitely more pain than pleasure to those who are forced to live with it; because I think there is no resolution for this pain in our lifetime, only, for the majority of homosexuals, more pain and various degrees of exacerbating adjustment; and because, wholly selfishly, I find myself completely incapable of coming to terms with it.' This article was very controversial when it was first published and remains so today; it was to gay rights what Norman Podhoretz's 'My Negro Problem—and Ours' was to civil rights.

'That is an essay that has followed me around,' Epstein once told an interviewer. 'I hope I don't have a reputation as a homophobe, which is really a stupid word.'

Epstein's twitchy discomfort with gays has occasionally led him to make near-libellous statements. 'Two friends have told me about Richard Poirier's performance at the MLA,' Epstein wrote in a letter to Robert B. Heilman on January 9, 1980. 'I used to think him a silly twerpish fellow, but I suspect that things go further—I suspect that he really does want to bring down the house and make the world safe for pederasty.' (For the record, there is no evidence that the late Richard Poirier, an astute literary critic who edited the valuable journal *Raritan*, was a pederast. Epstein's letter, and many other revealing and damaging correspondences, can be found in *Robert B. Heilman: His Life and Letters*, University of Washington Press, 2009.)

Despite these comments it wouldn't be quite fair to say that Epstein is a homophobe. I'm sure he has many gay friends. And indeed he's willing to praise gay or sexually ambiguous writers so long as they are either politically conservative or apolitical, hence his high regard for Henry James, Willa Cather, Somerset Maugham, Marguerite Yourcenar, Marcel Proust, C.P. Cavafy, among others. What Epstein can't abide are gay writers who are open and proud of their sexuality such as Paul Goodman or Gore Vidal. Rather than homophobia, I think it's more accurate to say that Epstein suffers from homo-unease, a feeling of discomfort at any overt references to gay sex, a desire for the good old days of the closet.

There is an interesting parallel between Epstein's nostalgia for the Empire and his nostalgia for the closet. In both cases there is a curious tendency to idealize an institution that has been rendered forever obsolete by history. Epstein is a romancer of lost causes, a not uncommon form of conservative fantasy.

E.M. Forster is an interesting test case because he was closeted (homosexuality was a crime throughout the vast majority of his lifetime in England). He rarely made public references to his sexuality, aside from in posthumously published works like *Maurice*. Still, Forster's themes anticipate the gay liberation movement, which is why Epstein is now so dismissive of a novelist he once greatly admired.

Politics, not literary merit, is the core of Epstein's objections to Forster.

CONCLUSION

Having spent so much time on Epstein, it might be worth essaying his larger importance. His way of thinking is not unique. He is a cherished contributor to the two leading neo-conservative journals, the *Weekly Standard* and *Commentary*. Both these magazines had a large—indeed incalculable—influence on the George W. Bush administration. And isn't it the case that a nostalgia for empire and a nostalgia for the closet can be seen in many recent Republican policies, ranging from the war in Iraq to the desire to hold on to the 'don't ask, don't tell' rule in the military? Which is another way of saying that Epstein is a much more deeply political writer than his graceful essays might let on.

Sans Everything, March 25, 2010

TORY STORIES: NEO-CON NOVELS

George W. Bush has been called many things, but he's rarely described as a literary maven. Quite the reverse: the U.S. president has carefully cultivated the image of a non-intellectual everyman, someone whose untutored common sense makes him more reliable than eggheads who spend too much time in the library. Given his populist persona, Bush often seems ill at ease with simple literacy, let alone literature. Not surprisingly, when *Slate* magazine surveyed the political views of thirty-one leading novelists in the run-up to the last election, Bush garnered only four bookish endorsements.

Yet, despite the disdain of the literati and his own linguistic difficulties, Bush presides over an administration chock full of novelists, particularly among the neo-conservative faction surrounding vice-president Dick Cheney. Lynne Cheney, the vice-president's wife, has written three novels, as well as several children's books. Before becoming the vice-president's chief of staff, Lewis Libby made his literary debut with a historical romance set in early 20th-century Japan. And, Richard Perle, who has been a formidable advocate for an aggressive foreign policy as the erstwhile chairman of the Pentagon's Defense Policy Board (DPB), is the author of a Cold War thriller. At the DPB, Perle shares the table with Newt Gingrich, who also has a thriller to his credit, an alternative history novel set during World War II. When the Bush administration sought the Pope's blessing for the Iraq war, they sent over a special diplomatic delegation to the Vatican headed by Michael Novak, a prolific Catholic political philosopher and author of two autobiographical novels about his religious experiences.

The presence of so many novelists in the corridors of power raises all sorts of questions. For starters, is there some hidden link between a powerful imagination and real-world power politics? And, what do these novels tell us about how political decision-makers really see the world?

Like many accomplished authors, Lynne Cheney blushes at her early efforts. She has steadfastly stilted attempts to republish her second novel,

Sisters (1981), a historical work of fiction about the American West. This self-suppression, combined with rumours that the novel is filled with lurid sex, has made *Sisters* a hot-ticket item in the used-book trade; it typically sells for around $500 U.S. a copy.

The only copy I was able to get my hands on was a pirated *samizdat* edition circulating on the Web. Reading *Sisters*, it becomes obvious that the author is less embarrassed by the prose of the novel (wooden but serviceable) than its sexual politics. Surprisingly, *Sisters* is not a nostalgic celebration of the wholesome days of yore in the tradition of *Little House on the Prairie;* rather, the novel offers a dark and unsettling vision of frontier America.

Its heroine, Sophie, uncovers that her sister Helen had a female lover, and later finds steamy letters between Helen and her female lover, a Sapphic schoolmarm. 'How I long to see you again, to hold you, to kiss you a thousand times,' the schoolteacher wrote to her beloved. 'My darling, my own precious darling. What I would whisper in your ear were you here this moment with me.'

Although she maintains that she prefers the company of men, Sophie lets her imagination run free, picturing what her sister's sex life might have been like: 'There could be no tearing off one's clothing and lustily hopping into bed, not if one would preserve the love-religion. But the loving words and the warm embrace were permitted, and the kiss before sleep, the arousal gentle enough so that its nature would not have to be acknowledged.'

Many have been taken aback that Cheney, the second most prominent Republican woman in America and an outspoken champion of family values, once wrote a book filled with intimations of sweaty girl-on-girl action. Yet two points have to be made about Cheney's pulp novel. First, good fiction has a complexity that polemical writing lacks (although, as we'll see, some novels are simply disguised polemics). As the chair of the National Endowment for the Humanities, and a writer for magazines such as *Commentary*, Lynne Cheney has been a forceful advocate of a neo-conservative point of view; but like many writers, Cheney investigates, through fiction, possibilities and sensations that real life doesn't offer.

Second, the radical and subversive subtext of *Sisters* exists in tension with a more conservative theme. Sophie is intrigued by the homestead homoeroticism between pioneering women, but her own preference is clearly men. She falls in love with her late sister's husband—even though the lout had abused Helen and defends lynching—simply because she's drawn to the 'vitality' of 'rich and powerful men'.

In retrospect, *Sisters* was a trail-blazing book, clearing the path for a Republican lesbian literary genre. There have been press reports that Mary Cheney, Lynne and Dick's out-of-the-closet daughter, is working on a memoir. Patti Davis, Ronald Reagan's daughter, also has literary plans, having announced that her second novel will be about a straight woman who has a lesbian affair. These books will have to compete with Australian writer Cate Swannell's debut novel, *Heart's Passage* (2003), which focuses on a love triangle that includes the lesbian partner of a Republican senator.

Lynne Cheney's other novels—*Executive Privilege* (1979) and *The Body Politic* (1988, co-written with Victor Gold)—lack the internal division of *Sisters* and are therefore less interesting. They offer a satirical take on Washington mores, mocking the press and politicians alike, but they are driven more by ideas than passion. Though there is an intriguing subplot in *The Body Politic* that has raised eyebrows. In that novel, a Republican vice-president dies of a heart attack while making love to a sexy reporter, not his wife. The VP's widow, conspiring with his staff, turns his death to her advantage, and by the end of the novel is herself the vice-president.

It is true that, like the widow in the novel, Cheney has always been politically ambitious and unwilling to stand in her husband's shadow. It is also the case that Dick Cheney has had a long history of cardiac problems, including four heart attacks. However, Lynne Cheney's loyal co-author Victor Gold has posted a message on Amazon.com reassuring readers that he was the one who came up with the idea of having the VP's wife gaining power over her dead husband's body. But we might be skeptical of Gold's protestations since his own novel shows that political underlings are quick to stretch the truth to serve their employers.

A strange and even twisted little book, *Sisters* packs a genuine emotional punch. But what happens when a novel doesn't have internal tension, and presents a single-minded world view? Richard Perle's *Hard Line* (1992) is one such novel.

A Washington fixture for more than three decades, Perle can be described as the hawk with the sharpest talons. As an aide to Senator

Henry Jackson in the 1970s, Perle was one of the strongest opponents of Henry Kissinger's policy of negotiating treaties with the Soviet Union to ease international tensions. Serving as assistant secretary of defence from 1981 to 1987, Perle repeatedly skewered arms-control negotiations with the Soviets, earning the nicknames 'Darth Vader' and 'the Prince of Darkness' at the State Department. More recently, Perle has been one of the most outspoken advocates of pre-emptive war, in the halls of the Pentagon and in his book *An End to Evil* (co-written with David Frum).

In *Hard Line*, Perle re-fights the Cold War one last time. The hero of the novel is Michael Waterman, an assistant secretary of Defense who is suspicious of arms control. In 1986, Waterman has two enemies: The first is the new Soviet premier Victor Novikov (a thinly veiled caricature of Mikhail Gorbachev), who is lulling the naive West into a false sense of security with promises of glasnost and perestroika. Even more dangerous than the communist leader is Daniel Bennet, the pusillanimous assistant secretary of state, a pencil-pushing wimp who is willing to make any compromise to cut a deal with the Russians.

In Perle's retelling, the real heart of the Cold War was a bureaucratic battle between two mid-level government officials. Unlike traditional thrillers that focus on spies and soldiers, *Hard Line* is an ode celebrating desk jockeys of power, who are described in terms befitting epic heroes. 'Urbane guerrillas in dark suits, they fought not with AK-47s but with memos, position papers, talking points, and news leaks. It was unrestricted warfare; there was no rule book. And no two antagonists in this administration had gone at it more regularly than Michael Waterman and Daniel Bennet.'

The battle of these titans is retold in minute detail, making the book about as much fun as filling out your taxes. 'The logical order of things would be to get the HLG paper approved by NATO members—or at least by the HLG—and to get ACDA's verification paper agreed to first,' Waterman says at one point. 'Then we can develop negotiating options that reflect those papers. We're certainly in no position to comment, since we haven't formulated any position.'

Amid this relentless welter of acronyms and memos, Perle tries to flesh out some human interest by recording Waterman's faltering marriage, but here again bureaucratic jargon takes over. 'It sounds like you're writing me a memo,' Waterman's wife, Laura, complains at one point. Fortunately, the hero proves to be very loving. 'Now, he looked at his marriage in much the same way he had examined the intermediate-range missile question.'

Books like *Hard Line* are sometimes described as 'insider novels'. They offer the reader the frisson of getting the straight dope, learning what really happened at important events. Richard Perle is a genuine Washington insider, but perhaps that is what makes *Hard Line* such a terrible novel. To understand the book at all, you already have to have a detailed knowledge of the internal wrangling of third-tier U.S. officials, circa the mid-1980s. Which means that this is a book that can be appreciated by about twenty readers, most of whom have recorded their own versions of the events.

Lewis Libby is as much a creature of the Washingtonian political scene as Richard Perle, but in his novelistic debut, Libby made an interesting decision to write about a distant time and place. As an undergraduate at Yale in the early 1970s, Libby enjoyed classes with a young teacher named Paul Wolfowitz. A decade later, Wolfowitz recruited Libby to join the Reagan administration. A fan of non-fiction spy books like *A Man Called Intrepid*, Libby was eager to join the government. Aside from the intermission of the Clinton years, Libby is often at the forefront of those arguing for a hyper-aggressive foreign policy. In 1992, Libby helped draw up a position paper stating it should be the goal of the United States to remain the permanent sole superpower in the world, always working to suppress any potential rival.

Given his key role in forging the neo-conservative vision of an American-dominated planet, you would expect from Libby a Perle-style insider novel. Instead, in his first and only work of fiction, *The Apprentice* (1996), Libby followed the path of Lynne Cheney and penned a historical romance. Indeed, he went even further than Cheney by writing about a period that seems even more remote from the bustle of today's headlines: rural Japan in 1903.

The Apprentice tells the story of Setsuo, a young hick from the mountains in the north of Japan who is training to become an innkeeper. While his master is away, Setsuo takes care of the inn, although he is awkward and unsure of himself. Then, during a snowstorm, he finds himself thrown into a world of intrigue when a guest is murdered near the inn. At the same time, he falls in love with another guest, a travelling performer named Yukiko who arrives for the spring festival.

Evoking a world where all relationships are circumscribed by rituals and tiny gestures of deference, the novel carefully registers how attentive the apprentice is to the smallest gestures of Yukiko. Here is his first sight of her: 'Then the girl reached into her mountain trousers and tugged at her clothing. The young apprentice could see the movements of her hands inside her pants.' The prose here is deliberately understated, giving us a sense of how even a brief glimpse can be charged with desire. Their second encounter with Yukiko and her friend takes the same tone but makes it just a little bit more intense: 'The girls were flushed and clean from the baths. Their collars stood open from their necks and the skin showing there looked pale in the dim lamplight.'

As a work of prose, *The Apprentice* is easily the best of all neo-conservative novels ever written. A dismal compliment, you could say, given the competition. Still, Libby has written a strong first novel that convincingly re-creates an exotic world, something the majority of historical fiction fails to do.

Libby wrote his novel during the Clinton years, his brief reprise from government service. Perhaps that explains the quiet, almost Zen-like mood of the novel, which seems to be an argument for the primacy of personal life over politics. But of course, when George W. Bush became president in 2001, Libby resumed his policy-making career and the world lost a promising novelist.

It's always tempting to look for the link between fiction and biography—all the more so with authors who are public figures like Cheney, Perle and Libby. Novelists are often badgered by readers wanting to know what the real deal is behind their stories. Biographers typically spend many pages tracing the parallels between the facts of a writer's life and the fiction that resulted. This dirty laundry approach to literature gives us the feeling, often illusory, that we're getting closer to a truth that the writer attempted to cover up with fake names and polished prose. The interest in biography is a measure of our distrust of fiction.

Yet, as we read neo-conservative novels, as poor as some of them are, we realize that fiction is not simply a form of disguised autobiography (although it can be on occasion). It's the element of fantasy and desire obliquely related to the lives of the authors that gives a spark of life to novels such as *Sisters* and *The Apprentice*. The sexual daydreaming of *Sisters* is an obvious case, but *The Apprentice* offers an even more intriguing example of the discrepancy between life and fiction. The power fantasy is a common type of novel: the work of a wimpy writer imagining that he's a world-conquering hero. In *The Apprentice*, we have the reverse: a fantasy about powerlessness.

Written by someone who has exercised high public office, *The Apprentice* is about finding bliss in being anonymous, free from the responsibilities of authority. Although some neo-conservative novels are clearly written to push an agenda, books such as *The Apprentice* unexpectedly turn out to be arguments against partisan politics of any sort. Rather, they affirm the autonomy of the imagination as a realm with its own rules.

Toro, May 2005

ROB FORD AND REXDALE

In Punjabi, 'pind' literally means 'village'. The word has intense associations: a pind is your hometown, the seedbed from which you sprang, the environment that shaped you as much as your family did. When meeting a fellow Punjabi speaker, rarely are you asked 'What do you do?' Rather, the invariable question is 'What's your pind?'

For me, the factual answer to the question is Dadyal, an obscure speck in Punjab. Yet I have few memories of Dadyal—I left at the age of five. And the more accurate answer is Rexdale. I grew up in Rexdale, where virtually the entire able-bodied population of Dadyal moved in the 1970s and 1980s.

I now live part of the year in Regina, where my wife teaches, and part of the year in Rexdale. My mother, brother and innumerable cousins, uncles and aunts are Rexdalers. Most of the people I know in Rexdale are, like my family, working-class immigrants who moved here in recent decades: Somalis, Italians, Jamaicans. There is a strange irony in the fact that one of the main streets in Rexdale is Kipling: an imperialist bard commemorated in a post-colonial district.

Rexdale is of course now internationally famous as the district where Rob Ford smoked crack in one of his drunken stupors. The wolf pack of accused criminals who hang around Ford as if he's their den master are either Rexdale natives or from other Etobicoke neighbourhoods. And, like Etobicoke in general, Rexdale is Ford's political base, the original home of Ford Nation. After news of the crack video first broke, I heard more than a few Rexdalers defend Ford as a native son being attacked by 'them'—the people from downtown. If Rexdale is my 'hood, then perforce Rob Ford is my homie.

Because of Ford's antics, Rexdale has become a major journalistic stomping ground. Although newspapers like the *Toronto Star* and *The Globe and Mail* have done a top-notch job of exposing Ford's many nefarious deeds and habitual mendacity, I'm appalled by the way they've depicted Ford's milieu. Journalistic accounts of Rexdale are written in the same tone of anxious amazement as Victorian explorers' reports from Africa.

The *National Post* once described Rexdale as 'blighted and violence-plagued', and on another occasion alluded to 'the wilds of Islamic Rexdale'. The *Globe*'s publisher has said his newspaper is only interested in readers who make more than $100,000 a year, which by implication means his paper isn't for the cab drivers and factory workers who live in Rexdale.

Despite his buffoonery, Rob Ford's political prowess should never be underestimated. He doesn't reflexively look down on Rexdale. He knows his way around it all too well. Ford once promised to make 'Rexdale the new Rosedale'. This typical Fordian flourish earned him many a snide laugh in downtown Toronto yet endeared him to his core constituency. He might be promising the stars, but at least he takes Rexdale seriously. Ford's right-wing populism derives its power from understanding the aspirations of Rexdalers for projects like the expansion of Woodbine Racetrack into a shopping and casino complex. Although the billion-dollar project fell apart, Ford's efforts on its behalf earned him street cred. What do Ford's opponents have to offer Rexdale, aside from austerity and condescension?

Multiculturalism is often a vacant word; if it has any substantial meaning, it involves people not just preserving their cultural traditions but also sharing them with their neighbours. In my experience, genuine multiculturalism occurs more in Rexdale than in downtown Toronto. Rexdale is where I hear impassioned conversations about the prospects of the Toronto Maple Leafs conducted in Punjabi. Rexdale is the home of a magnificent Hindu temple, brought over piece by piece from India. Rexdale is the place to find Punjabi pizza, a sumptuous curry-inflected dish that my Bulgarian-born partner prefers to the Italian version. Rexdale is where my mother, who worked for decades laundering hospital bedsheets, acquired conversational skills in Italian and Tagalog from her co-workers. Although she would be uncomfortable around the publisher of the *Globe*, my mother is at ease with the microcosm of the world she's found in Rexdale.

Cultural mixing always runs the risk of generating strife as well as affectionate familiarity. Growing up in Rexdale, I sometimes heard the words 'Paki' and 'nigger' from the mouths of working-class white kids. I've also heard racist anti-black comments from Punjabi elders. As terrible as this racism is, it comes from people who are more comfortable with other ethnic groups than are those who live in the sheltered enclaves of expensive downtown condos. Ford exemplifies the paradox. He often says dunderheaded, racist things, but few white politicians are more visibly at home at a multi-racial social event.

Sooner or later, Rob Ford will disappear from public life. But Fordism will endure beyond its dishevelled and oversized avatar. To defeat it, politicians will have to let go of their urbanite snobbery and learn to listen to Rexdale.

Toronto Life, January 2014

SCIENCE FICTION

ROBERT HEINLEIN: ABANDONING THE FUTURE

The science-fiction writer Robert Heinlein once described himself as 'a preacher with no church'. More accurately, he was a preacher with too many churches. Rare among the many intellectual gurus whose fame mushroomed in the 1960s, Heinlein was a beacon for hippies and hawks, libertarians and authoritarians, and many other contending faiths—but rarely at the same time. While America became increasingly liberal, he became increasingly right wing, and it hobbled his once-formidable imagination. His career, as a new biography inadvertently proves, is a case study in the literary perils of political extremism.

Heinlein's most famous novel, *Stranger in a Strange Land* (1961), was a counterculture bible, its message of free love inspiring not just secular polygamous communes but also the Church of All Worlds, a still-flourishing New Age sect incorporated in 1968. Heinlein was equally beloved in military circles, especially for his book *Starship Troopers* (1959), a gung-ho shout-out for organized belligerence as the key to human survival. A thoroughly authoritarian book, it included an ode to flogging (a practice the American Navy banned in 1861) and the execution of mentally disturbed criminals, yet Heinlein became a hero to libertarians: Milton Friedman praised Heinlein's 1966 novel, *The Moon Is a Harsh Mistress*, which chronicled an anti-statist rebellion on a lunar colony, as a 'wonderful' book and commended Heinlein for popularizing the slogan TANSTAAFL ('There ain't no such thing as a free lunch'). Friedman's son David, a self-described anarcho-capitalist, would go further: in 1971 the younger Friedman gave a speech at Harvard all pimped up with a large medallion engraved with a dollar sign and TANSTAAFL.

Heinlein, who died in 1988 at age 80, lived a large, complex, and contradictory life. His friend and fellow science-fiction writer Arthur C. Clark once noted that Heinlein was 'very protean. Heinlein was everything—like Walt Whitman.' The publication of the second volume of a mammoth Heinlein biography by the late William Patterson is, alas, only partially helpful in getting a grip on this complicated writer. Authorized by the Heinlein estate and fannishly worshipful, Patterson lacked sufficient distance from his subject to tackle the central puzzles of Heinlein's life.

Take, for example, the crucial issue of Heinlein's political evolution. Heinlein went from being a left-wing New Dealer in the 1930s and 1940s to flirting with the John Birch Society in the late 1950s and supporting Barry Goldwater in the 1960s—and yet he insisted that his politics were unwaveringly consistent. 'From my point of view what has happened is not that I have moved to the right; it seems to me that both parties have moved steadily to the left,' Heinlein wrote his brother in 1964. Patterson, as was his wont on all major issues, sides with his subject and maintains that Heinlein's politics remained fundamentally unchanged through his life. Heinlein was no 'rightist', Patterson assures us, but a lifelong 'radical liberal' with a 'democratic soul'. Patterson never explains how that 'democratic soul' came to believe that the right to vote should be severely restricted, a position Heinlein advocated not just in *Starship Troopers* but also in non-fiction works.

Contra Patterson, Heinlein was not a lifelong liberal, and this biography offers little insight into the science fiction writer's mad dash across the political spectrum. Weak tea as analysis, it nonetheless is a useful warehouse of facts about Heinlein, giving us a sturdy chronicle that allows us to ask—and sometimes answer—the questions the biographer avoids.

Robert Heinlein was a solipsist and an extrapolationist. These two components of his personality—his tendency to see reality as an extension of himself, and his compulsion to push ideas to their logical conclusion—were evident in his personality at a very young age. In later life, sometimes these tendencies would war with each other and sometimes they were fused, but they seem to have been present from early on.

To be a science fiction writer is to be born too soon, to yearn for a birth-date later than the one fate has decreed. Until the nostalgic spell he fell into late in life, the space/time co-ordinate that Robert Heinlein wanted to escape from was Butler, Missouri, in 1907. He was the third of seven children. The family often shuttled back and forth to Kansas, Missouri, where they ended up settling before the First World War. L. Frank Baum's Oz books were favourite childhood reading in part because they promised a wondrous world beyond the grayness of the prairies. The bookkeeper's salary that Heinlein's father earned kept the family barely afloat on the sea of poverty.

The solipsism set in at an early age, perhaps a form of escape from a bleak environment. As Heinlein wrote in 1955 to a friend, 'I have had a dirty suspicion since I was about six that all consciousness is one and that all the actors I see around me … are myself, at different points in the record's grooves.' Heinlein's high school yearbook offered this prescient tagline: 'He thinks in terms of the fifth dimension, never stopping at the fourth.'

At age twelve, Heinlein fell in love with the scientific romances of H.G. Wells, which offered not only a compelling vision of the world to come but also an irresistible political program. For Wells, socialism and science fiction were natural partners, both attempts to constructively imagine the future. As a teen, Heinlein signed on for the full Wellsian program of economic planning, sexual liberation, internationalism and secularism. Political radicalism, with its call to build a collective future, offered Heinlein a necessary corrective to his instinctive self-obsession, his ingrained inability to accept the reality of other people.

Poor as they were, the Heinleins had strong connections with the Pendergast machine that ran Missouri. These connections, combined with his strong grades, earned Heinlein a slot as a midshipman at Annapolis in 1925. Heinlein loved the Navy as a new family despite its often cruel practices. In 1928, Heinlein's fiancée, Alice McBee, only 21 years old, died of appendicitis. Heinlein's request for leave to attend her funeral was denied. It was a mortifying experience. 'I was crying [in the Commandant's presence] and midshipmen aren't supposed to do that,' Heinlein recalled.

Weeping before an officer was a rare lapse. Usually Heinlein was very good at compartmentalizing the divergent strands of his personality. He was capable of being both a disciplined officer at sea and a free-spirited bohemian on land.

Throughout his life Heinlein was attracted to wildly unconventional women, who shared his detachment from the expectations of monogamy. In 1929, shortly after receiving his Navy commission, he married his high school sweetheart Elinor Curry, who turned out to be even more independent than he expected. She refused to take his name or give up her job, and rejected his plans for her to move in with him. As an added flourish, she slept with another man during her honeymoon. The marriage soon broke up but Heinlein's explorations of non-mainstream sexuality were just beginning. In 1930 on shore leave, Heinlein rented a studio in Greenwich Village and tried to seduce a lesbian. He failed but they became friends and would cruise for women together.

His Sapphic misadventure aside, the young Heinlein was catnip for women (and possibly some men as well). He was tall, slim and possessed debonair good looks that called to mind Clark Gable. He had the courtly bearings of a naval officer and the lusty heart of a Henry Miller character.

For Heinlein, sex always seemed to involve more than two people. Heinlein and his close Navy buddy Caleb 'Cal' Laning (later a Rear Admiral) would often go 'double dating in bed' (in Laning's terms). In January of 1932, while Heinlein was stationed in Los Angeles Laning told Heinlein about a wonderful woman he'd met named Leslyn MacDonald, who worked as an assistant director in the music department of Columbia Pictures. Laning was so smitten by the artistic and intelligent MacDonald that he was thinking of marrying her and he wanted his pal Heinlein to meet her. The three had dinner and Laning left early, perhaps in keeping with his longstanding practice of sharing lovers with his friend. Heinlein and MacDonald continued talking and ended up in bed. The next morning the threesome reunited for breakfast and Heinlein shocked both Laning and MacDonald by proposing marriage. Laning would occasionally grumble that 'Robert stole my girl' but he was forgiving. Heinlein and MacDonald married a few months later.

For at least the first decade of their marriage, Robert and Leslyn Heinlein were superbly well mated. They shared an equal commitment to sexual liberation (including recreational nudism) and political reform, both were non-communist radicals on the left-wing of the emerging New Deal coalition. They would often finish each other's sentences and joked that they possessed a group mind. After Heinlein took up writing in the late 1930s, he described Leslyn as his indispensable 'collaborator' and 'story-doctor'.

If his health hadn't intervened, Heinlein would likely have had a distinguished naval career. At Annapolis in 1929, he graduated 20th in a class of 243. Many of his friends went on to become admirals. In the early 1930s as a junior officer on the *Lexington*, Heinlein served under Captain Ernest J. King, who became the Commander in Chief of the United States Fleet during the Second World War. According to Heinlein, King knew how to get his men to 'worship the deck he trod' and was 'the most nearly perfect military officer I have ever known' in part because he possessed 'the voice of command'—the ability to make listeners follow without question. King was a profound inspiration for Heinlein's fiction. Not only was naval officer the prototype of the seminal Heinlein figure (the crusty old salt who initiates the young into wisdom) but Heinlein's distinctive prose style consisted of bringing 'the voice of command' to the written page.

Heinlein's once promising naval career was cut short when he was diagnosed with tuberculosis in 1934. Retired from the Navy, he was given a pension worth two-thirds of the pay he would have received if he had stayed in service. Heinlein's naval pension was the indispensable life jacket that made his entire career as a writer possible. Thanks to the pension, Heinlein and his wife not only weathered the Great Depression but also pursued a wide variety of interests before settling into science fiction. From 1934 to 1939, Heinlein (often with his wife's help) speculated on a silver mine, took graduate science courses, sold real estate, tried his hand at architecture and became a leading left-wing activist in California Democratic policy. Aside from his naval pension, Heinlein also took money from the Works Progress Administration (WPA) to study art.

Even when he was fully launched as writer, Heinlein still depended upon his Navy pension as an indispensable source of income when publishers were slow to pay, when markets dried up, when he pursued new and uncertain venues for his fiction, when he went through a writer's block or when he suffered a family crisis. Later in life as a libertarian he would preach the doctrine of 'there is no such thing as a free lunch' but in his leftist days he knew how much he depended on the government. As he acknowledged in a 1941 letter, 'This country has been very good to me, and the taxpayers have supported me for many years.' The popularizer of TANSTAAFL ate more than his share of subsidized meals.

In the 1930s, Heinlein considered himself a 'pragmatic socialist'. He and Leslyn became leaders in the End Poverty in California (EPIC) movement led by the novelist Upton Sinclair. While Sinclair lost his bid to become governor of California in 1934, EPIC greatly augmented the strength of the Democratic party and the populist left in California. In his EPIC days, Heinlein protested police brutality, wrote reports on the persecution of the Okies that prefigured Steinbeck's *The Grapes of Wrath* and tried to unseat a reactionary state senator. We don't know the full extent of

Heinlein's radical political activism because he destroyed most of the documents connecting him to the left during the Cold War.

He also promoted the ideas of social credit, an unorthodox economic system that is too often linked to crackpot right-wingers like Ezra Pound. In fact, Heinlein's version of social credit can be seen as a form of vernacular Keynesianism: it was rooted in the accurate belief that capitalism suffered from a mismatch between production and consumer power, which could be eased by fiscal means.

As with his hero H. G. Wells, Heinlein's science fiction was inextricably linked with his politics. In later life, Heinlein came up with a deceptive origin story, portraying himself as someone who went into pulp writing to earn some cash. In fact, while Heinlein didn't mind earning money for his writing, right from the start he had a didactic intent. His first sustained work of fiction was a utopian novel *For Us, The Living* (1938) that combined standard Wellsian themes (internationalism, secularism) with some emerging Heinlein obsessions (anti-racism, social credit, nudism, space travel). *For Us, The Living* didn't find a publisher at the time and late in life Heinlein and his third wife, Virginia, tried to destroy all manuscript copies, mostly likely because it bore the mark of a radical past. It was only published posthumously in 2003. Yet the book is the seedbed for Heinlein's career, the first budding of many of his characteristic themes.

Starting in 1939, Heinlein found more success writing for pulp magazines, especially *Astounding Science Fiction*, where his first published story appeared. As edited by the genre-transforming autocratic John W. Campbell, Jr., *Astounding* looked for stories that remained true to actual scientific principles and had logical plots. The magazine was then in the process of revolutionizing the field, thanks in part to such gifted writers as Isaac Asimov, Theodore Sturgeon and L. Ron Hubbard. Within his first few stories, Heinlein was already the leading writer in the field, a huge influence on the entire genre because he had figured out a new way to tell stories about the future.

Before Heinlein's groundbreaking stories, most science fiction (including Heinlein's own abortive *For Us, The Living*) was exposition heavy: the future or alien worlds were described at laborious length. What Heinlein figured out, thanks to the lessons of Captain King's 'voice of command' was a way to sound authoritative without spelling out all the details. Heinlein wrote about the future as if he lived in it already, so all he had to do was drop a few hints and the reader could figure out the rest. The excellent engineering education he received in the Navy gave these stories an imposing scientific accuracy.

A simple and much-cited three sentence-phrase from Heinlein's early novel *Beyond This Horizon* (1942) distills his characteristic effect: 'the door dilated'. Heinlein didn't bother to spell out that this is a world where doors work like a camera's aperture, nor is the history and function of dilating doors explained. We're simply dropped into a different reality and must figure out the details as best we can, just as if we were tourists in a foreign country. Heinlein's commanding voice is so persuasive that we gradually acclimatize ourselves to his visions.

Heinlein's numerous connections with the nascent military-industrial complex infused his understanding of the future. In 1934, Heinlein befriended Robert Cornog, a young student who would go on to become a physicist and work on the Manhattan Project. Thanks to Cornog's tips, Heinlein wrote such prescient stories like 'Blowups Happen' (1940) predicting 'the most dangerous machine in the world—an atomic power plant' and 'Solution Unsatisfactory' (1941) about how possession of atomic weapons would transform America into a global empire.

As with all science fiction, these stories got most of the details of the future wrong (neither the United States nor the world has yet ended up with the military dictatorship foreseen in 'Solution Unsatisfactory'). They weren't prophesy but invigorating attempts to think through emerging problems by plausible extrapolation, thought experiments for sharpening the mind in order to live through cataclysmic changes. Occasionally he would write an oddball solipsistic fantasy like the story 'They' (1941), where the narrator correctly figures out reality is a sham. But in his early career, this type of solipsism was mostly a vacation from the main business of creating an imaginatively inhabitable future.

After Pearl Harbor, Heinlein desperately wanted to return to military service, ideally in combat. Normally in a wartime situation the Navy would have found some use for someone as talented as Heinlein but he was blacklisted because of his radical politics. Barred from official military activity he worked as a civilian engineer at the Philadelphia Naval Shipyard in Pennsylvania, where Leslyn also found war work. (Heinlein didn't want his wives to have paid employment but he made a wartime exception.) As Leslyn noted, Heinlein chaffed at being a 'p.f.c.—"a poor f——civilian".'

(The dashes are in the original quote from Leslyn Heinlein.) The rabid militarism of such future Heinlein works as *Starship Troopers* was partially a backwash of misplaced guilt over not having had a chance to serve in a time of war.

Even while the Navy disowned Heinlein, his friends in the service found his science fiction pertinent to their duties. As commander of the USS *Hutchins*, Caleb Laning reconfigured the ship's Combat Information Center so that it could organize battle plans in real time. Laning credited Heinlein's science fiction for inspiring such fresh approaches to using technology in war. In a similar manner, Robert Cornog and other scientists described radio and radar jamming techniques as 'the Heinlein effect' in honour of the author who inspired them. At Philadelphia, Heinlein supervised the creation of the high-altitude pressure suit, a precursor to the space suit. Both during the war and after, Heinlein was the Pentagon's unofficial intellectual ignition system.

Patterson goes too far in arguing that the 'policy think tank' is the 'step child' of science fiction. What is more accurate is that after the shock of Pearl Harbor the Pentagon never wanted to be surprised again and so adopted the habits of futuristic thinking taught by science fiction. The Rand Corporation and many similar think tanks always had a science fiction element. It's no accident that Heinlein would later befriend Herman Kahn, the nuclear theorist and futurist. Science fiction was the dreamlife of the military industrial complex.

Heinlein met L. Ron Hubbard in 1940 and was immediately enamoured. In fact, Heinlein was so fond of Hubbard that he encouraged Leslyn to bed with the future author of *Dianetics*. 'He almost forced me to sleep with his wife,' Hubbard marvelled. Heinlein shared his wife's sexual favours with his male friends with the same generosity another man might display by giving the keys to his cottage to his buddies. Sharing the sexual favours of the same woman was a kind of bonding experience. Quite possibly, Heinlein and Hubbard had a closer link. Leslyn suspected the two men were lovers (a theory that Patterson judges as possible but not likely).

Was Leslyn happy with the open marriage arrangement she had with Heinlein? That's a crucial question which Patterson skirts. In an endnote, Patterson notes that Leon Stover, in his unpublished Heinlein biography, argued that Leslyn's alcoholism, signs of which were evident during World War II, was a product of her unhappiness at enforced wife swapping.

Patterson idolizes Heinlein too much and is too psychologically incurious to pursue this line of thought. Patterson's unempathetic treatment of Leslyn (described at one point as behaving in a 'psychotic' manner) is a major flaw in the biography.

Leslyn's drinking problem had multiple roots. Her dad had been an alcoholic. World War II was stressful for her, with close family members trapped in the Philippines under Japanese occupation. It's possible that discontent at the open marriage was a factor, but more subtly the fertility problems she and Heinlein suffered from might have made open marriage a dicier proposition. Perhaps what upset her was not the open marriage but the threat of being replaced by a younger rival who could bear children.

In 1944 while working at the Naval Shipyard in Philadelphia Heinlein met Lieutenant Virginia Gerstenfeld, who was twenty-eight years old, attractive and athletic (a competitive figure skater) and science smart (an organic chemist and biochemist). In many ways Virginia was similar to Leslyn, but younger and with a different political inclination. Heinlein and Virginia hit it off and she became a frequent visitor to the Heinlein household.

After the war the Heinleins moved back to Los Angeles, and Virginia soon followed. In 1946, she moved into the Heinlein household as a 'family member'. This wasn't the first Heinlein ménage à trois but it was far less stable than earlier ones. According to one friend, 'Leslyn slept in the studio while [Heinlein] and the femme fatale cavorted in the master bedroom.' (This writer of the letter was echoing what she heard from Leslyn.) Feeling threatened in her position as wife, Leslyn demanded that Virginia leave.

Forced to choose between the two (current) women in his life, Heinlein divorced Leslyn in 1947, lived with Virginia on the sly for a year and married her when the divorce was finalized in 1948. Before marrying Virginia he wrote a letter advising her that she was to expect that he might sleep with other women after they tied the knot. The speed and ferocity with which Heinlein cut off Leslyn, a woman he had loved and who was experiencing serious psychological problems, was creepy, almost reptilian in its cold-bloodedness. He destroyed almost all the personal documents from his marriage with Leslyn, so it is difficult to even recover her perspective and voice.

Heinlein desperately wanted to have children, a blessing that continued to elude him even in his long marriage to Virginia. The couple tried to adopt but he was deemed too old. Issues of fertility and genetic inherence loom large in Heinlein's fiction. The author who couldn't have children created Lazarus Long, who lives for many centuries during which he creates countless families that go on to populate the galaxy. One comfort was the successful career he found in writing 'juveniles' (books for readers twelve and over) in the late 1940s and 1950s. Heinlein's juveniles, which treat teenage readers as smart enough to handle complex ideas and real science, are among his best works.

The marriage to Virginia lasted till his death and was a happy one. Heinlein believed that he and Virginia had a genuine telepathic link (his scientific rationality went out the window on subjects like telepathy and reincarnation).

Whereas Leslyn was a liberal Democrat, Virginia was a conservative Republican. Some of Heinlein's friends speculated that his shift in politics was connected to his divorce and remarriage. That's too simplistic an explanation, but Heinlein acknowledged that Virginia helped 're-educate' him on economics.

In truth, Heinlein's shift to the right took place over a decade, from 1948 to 1957. In the early 1950s, the Heinleins travelled around the world. The writer was already a Malthusian and a eugenicist, but the trip greatly exacerbated his demographic despair and xenophobia. 'The real problem of the Far East is not that so many of them are communists, but simply that there are so many of them,' he wrote in a 1954 travel book (posthumously published in 1992). Even space travel, Heinlein concluded, wouldn't be able to open enough room to get rid of 'them'. Heinlein treated overpopulation as a personal affront. The sheer abundance of other people, so many of whom it was difficult to relate to, seems to have been a shock to Heinlein's ego.

Heinlein had caught a bad case of the Cold War jitters in the late 1940s. Heinlein's anti-communism increasingly manifested itself as paranoia and exterminationist blood lust. The victim of blacklisting became an informal Red-hunter, accusing liberal friends, including the film director Fritz Lang, of being Stalinists. He accurately described his 1951 novel *The Puppet Masters* as a 'thinly-disguised allegory, a diatribe against totalitarianism in all its forms'.

In the novel the allegorical counterpart to communism is an alien species of mind-controlling parasites who can only be defeated by genocide. 'Puppet masters—the free men are coming to kill you!' the novel ends. 'Death and Destruction!'

With Heinlein's great talent for extrapolation, every East–West standoff seemed like the end of the world. 'I do not think we have better than an even chance of living, as a nation, through the next five years,' he wrote an editor in 1957. The USSR's *Sputnik* launch in 1957 and Eisenhower's moves toward a nuclear test ban the following year both unhinged Heinlein, who called Ike a 'slimy faker'.

At the same time, the recipient of a generous Navy pension started to rail against Aid to Dependent Children and professional 'loafers'.

The turning point came in 1957. After that year, Heinlein's books were no longer progressive explorations of the future but hectoring diatribes lamenting the decadence of modernity. A recurring character in these books—variously named Hugh Farnham, Jubal Harshaw or Lazarus Long—is a crusty older man who's a wellspring of wisdom. 'Daddy, you have an annoying habit of being right,' runs an actual bit of dialogue from *Farnham's Freedom* (1964). In the worst of Heinlein's later books, Daddy not only knows best, he often knows everything. The early Heinlein was an authoritative writer, but as he aged he became simply authoritarian.

Heinlein developed an uneasy relationship with the far right. He described Joseph McCarthy as 'a revolting son of a bitch' and the John Birch Society as a 'fascist organization' but he also thought they were far preferable to liberals or moderate conservatives. 'But if I am ever forced to a choice between the John Birch Society and its enemies, I know which side of the barricades I belong on,' Heinlein wrote a friend in 1961. 'I'll be on the same side the John Birch Society is on—because my enemies are on the other side.'

With the rise of Barry Goldwater, Heinlein found a mainstream political figure he could support almost wholeheartedly (although he preferred Lyndon Johnson on Civil Rights). In the 1980s, Heinlein was a vocal cheerleader of Ronald Reagan's 'Star Wars' missile defence system. Heinlein's last political fling was his failed attempt to get Jeanne Kirkpatrick to run for president in 1988.

Yet despite his alliance with the GOP, Heinlein was never a

conventional conservative. As censorship laws eased in the 1950s and 1960s, his novels increasingly explored and advocated sexual diversity, and he remained scornful of religious fundamentalism in all its forms.

On the issue of sex Heinlein did remain faithful to the radicalism of his youth, with some of his late books portraying a future where bisexuality is the norm. Yet even on sex, late-period Heinlein is an untrustworthy guide. Many readers have been disturbed by the pro-incest arguments found in such books as *Farnham's Freehold*, *Time Enough for Love* (1973), and *To Sail Beyond the Sunset* (1987). Perhaps the best that can be said on Heinlein's behalf is that incest served as an objective correlative to his libertarianism and solipsism. What better way of being an independent free agent than by sleeping with your closest kin?

Going further: Isn't the truly self-made man also self-engendered? In his explorations of the mechanics of self-pleasuring and self-creation, Heinlein made Philip Roth look like a piker. In Heinlein's 1959 story 'All You Zombies—', a combination of time travel and a sex-change operation allows the protagonist to become his/her own mother and father. In *I Will Fear No Evil* (1970) a ninety-four-year-old billionaire first has his brain implanted in the body of a twenty-eight-year-old black woman and then has his frozen sperm impregnate that body. In *Time Enough for Love* the quintessential Heinlein hero Lazarus Long makes love to two of his own female twin clones (who are also his daughters).

Taken together, Heinlein's books in his right-wing phase hardly add up to a logical worldview. How do we reconcile the savage authoritarianism of *Starship Troopers* with the peace-and-love mysticism of *Stranger in a Strange Land*? For that matter, how do those two books jibe to the nearly anarchist libertarianism of *The Moon Is a Harsh Mistress*? On a more practical plain, how could Heinlein have called for both limited government and a NASA committed to colonizing space (surely a big government program if there ever was one)? TANSTAAFL went out the window when a space or military program caught Heinlein's fancy.

But all these books share one trait: they ignore the consequences of people's actions. *Starship Troopers* gives us war without PTSD and guilt over slaughter (the aliens are Bugs, so can be exterminated without remorse) just as *Stranger in a Strange Land* is a vision of sex without strings ('grokking' means never having to say sorry). In *To Sail Beyond the Sunset*, which celebrates a father having sex with his teenage daughters, Heinlein gave us incest without trauma.

Heinlein described some of his books as being 'Swiftian' in intent. Regrettably, Heinlein lacked the rhetorical control of the *Gulliver's Travels* author. If Heinlein had written 'A Modest Proposal' some of his readers would have set up a child-eating cult. Aside from a 1941 *Yellow Peril* novel, Heinlein had a strong record as a critic of racism. But in *Farnham's Freehold*, Heinlein wanted to use inversion to show the evils of ethnic oppression: he took a middle-class white family and, via a nuclear explosion, threw them into a future where Africans rule the earth and enslave whites. So far, so good. Yet Heinlein's Africans aren't just a master race, they also castrate white men, make white women their concubines and eat white children (white teenage girls being especially tasty). Preaching against racism, Heinlein resurrected some of the most horrific racial stereotypes imaginable. *Farnham's Freehold* is an anti-racist novel only a Klansman could love.

Heinlein did his best writing in the 1940s and 1950s in the long sequence of 'Future History' stories (collected in the 1967 omnibus volume *The Past Through Tomorrow*) as well as novels like *Double Star* (1956) and *Citizen of the Galaxy* (1957). These stories and books taught millions of readers to live in the future, an irreplaceable gift.

The novels Heinlein wrote from *Starship Troopers* till his death are all, with the exception of *The Moon Is a Harsh Mistress*, literary and intellectual failures. The problem with these books isn't political but literary. As Heinlein admitted, when he became upset he got more verbose. Spitting mad at a world that didn't listen to the wisdom of Barry Goldwater, Heinlein's late books are very wordy indeed.

It's hard to appreciate the full pathological depths of mansplaining unless you've read late-period Heinlein, an experience comparable to being trapped in an elevator for six hours with a boorish know-it-all offering his theories on economics, politics, sex, aesthetics, military strategy, investing and myriad other topics.

In Heinlein's late books, rugged individualism was pushed to its extreme limit, becoming first curdled selfishness and finally a narcissism as dense and all-absorbing as a black hole. In *The Cat Who Walked Through Walls* (1985) a character mocks famine relief, saying 'stupid people; they had earned their famine'. In the same spirit, Heinlein wondered if all his fellow citizens deserved to vote. Hell, for late-period Heinlein, was other people. No wonder he often speculated that there was no reality outside his own mind.

In his old age, Heinlein turned his back on the future. His novels became nostalgic, masturbatory fan-fiction where he resurrected characters from earlier books and linked them into a single tapestry of interconnected self-referential stories. Even when he wrote about the future it was in terms of the past. In *Time Enough for Love*, we're told that the spaceships that spread humanity across the stars are 'the covered wagons of the Galaxy'. Frontier America becomes the goal to aspire to, not the past we want to build on. In the same novel, Heinlein's alter ego Lazarus Long returns to the Kansas of the early 20th century (a 'happy' time, we're told) and sleeps with his mother. What a depressing fate for a novelist who once was a gateway to tomorrow: wallowing in self-absorbed, sentimental reveries.

A biographer with an analytical edge might have examined the role self-obsession and political extremism played in hampering Heinlein's late fiction. Patterson's hagiographic approach not only skirts the issue but simply gives us Heinlein's solipsism in a new form: this is a biography where there is no reality outside of Heinlein to challenge the man's ideas or actions.

New Republic, June 8, 2014*

* This piece was expanded and revised for its inclusion in this book.

PHILIP K. DICK VERSUS THE LITERARY CRITICS

When the novelist Philip K. Dick died in 1982, the influential literary theorist Fredric Jameson eulogized him as 'the Shakespeare of science fiction'. At the time of this encomium, Dick was hardly famous. The author of more than fifty books, he had an enthusiastic following among science fiction fans. But he was rarely read by anyone else.

These days, Dick is far better known. Vintage publishes his fiction in a uniform paperback edition. Hollywood filmmakers transform his stories of imaginary worlds and conspiratorial cartels into movies like *Screamers* and *Total Recall*. Meanwhile, academic critics laud him as a postmodernist visionary, a canny prophet of virtual reality, corporate espionage and the schizoid nature of identity in a digitized world. Indeed, beginning in the last years of his life and continuing to the present, these critics have played a key role in the canonization of Philip K. Dick.

But did Dick return the favour? Not exactly. To their considerable anguish, Dick's academic champions have had to contend with the revelation that their hero wrote letters to the Federal Bureau of Investigation denouncing them. In these letters, Dick claimed that Jameson and other literary theorists were agents of a KGB conspiracy to take over American science fiction. When he sent these messages, Dick was not in the best state of mind: he frequently heard voices and saw visions, often bathed in a mysterious pink light. Even so, the news of his surreptitious campaign against his academic admirers has left some of them deeply disturbed.

In his fiction, Dick had a genius for turning reality upside down and inside out, writing novels in which time runs backward or the Nazis win World War II. Yet the celebrated 'reality breakdowns' of Dick's novels seem normality itself compared with the bizarre, unsettling missives he sent to the authorities in Washington, D.C. The laureate of radical postmodernism was, it turns out, a stool pigeon.

Dick started selling Science Fiction stories as early as 1951, when he was 22, but he never wanted to be a genre writer. Gifted with a quicksilver imagination and lightning-fast typing fingers, he planned to earn a living churning out pulp stories until he could find a publisher for his realistic 'mainstream' novels. To his dismay, Dick discovered that though he could easily sell Science Fiction stories and novels, he could not secure a buyer for his earnest and grim tales of working-class life.

Dick received a paltry $1,500 shot for his Science Fiction novels, which he produced at a rate of four or five a year; typically they were published as cheap paperbacks, with titles such as *Dr Bloodmoney* (1965) and *Clans of the Alphane Moon* (1964). Considering the conditions under which the novels were written and published, it is amazing that Dick managed to find any sort of intelligent audience. Yet the best of these books—notably, *The Three Stigmata of Palmer Eldritch* (1965) and *Ubik* (1969)—presented intellectually ingenious and emotionally lacerating dislocations of reality. In *Ubik*, the hapless protagonist, Joe Chip, travels to Des Moines across a landscape of rapidly decaying objects that are moving backward in time: coins and elevators, cars and airplanes become old-fashioned versions of themselves. Drawing on Science Fiction conventions to dramatize life in the postmodern age, Dick regularly explored the world of mind-altering drugs and shifting realities. Not surprisingly, John Lennon was a fan.

Dick's fiction of the 1960s resonated not only with the counterculture but also with the New Left. Dick, who came of age in Bohemian Berkeley, infused his novels with a satiric radicalism. As he noted in his diary, 'I may not have been/am CP [Communist Party], but the basic Marxist sociological view of capitalism—negative—is there. Good.' Dick's political imagination is evident in his recurring focus on the world of work.

Unlike most science fiction heroes, his protagonists are ordinary working folks who struggle against corporate cartels. (The novelist John Sladek once wrote a parody of Dick's work titled 'Solar Shoe Salesman'.)

Given Dick's countercultural themes and politics, his work naturally attracted leftists such as Jameson, Peter Fitting of the University of Toronto and Richard Pinhas, a French critic who went on to form a punk band. Istvan Csicsery-Ronay, Jr., a professor of English at DePauw University, notes that many readers in the late 1960s and 1970s thought Dick was 'expressing ... sly critiques of capitalism and the American bourgeois world picture'. The Science Fiction novelist Thomas M. Disch praised Dick for writing 'self-consistent social allegories of a more-or-less Marxist bent'.

In 1975, the journal *Science Fiction Studies* devoted a special issue to Dick's work. The critics were exceedingly generous in their praise. Polish novelist Stanislaw Lem acclaimed Dick as the only American writer of Science Fiction with any merit, 'a visionary among charlatans'. Fitting lauded *Ubik* as a 'deconstruction of bourgeois science fiction'.

But could these critics trust Dick? Even before their paeans were published, Dick had begun writing a stream of letters to the FBI. In the earliest of these, written on October 28, 1972, he asserted, 'Several months ago I was approached by an individual who I have reason to believe belonged to a covert organization involving politics, illegal weapons, etc., who put great pressure on me to place coded information in future novels "to be read by the right people here and there", as he phrased it. I refused to do it.'

Dick went on to suggest that this mysterious organization (which he claimed was possibly run by neo-Nazis) had successfully recruited at least one Science Fiction writer, Thomas M. Disch. 'I stress the urgency of this,' he wrote, 'because within the last three days I have come across a well-distributed science fiction novel which contains in essence the vital material which this individual confronted me with as the basis of encoding. That novel is *Camp Concentration* by Thomas Disch.' (Disch's 1968 novel portrays a totalitarian future America where dissidents are rounded up by the government and subjected to mind-control experiments.)

Around the same time, Dick grew suspicious of Stanislaw Lem, who was starting to gain an English-speaking audience for his satiric science fiction. In November 1972, Lem had secured permission to have *Ubik* translated into Polish. Because of Cold War currency restrictions, Dick was unable to collect royalties from this translation. He blamed Lem for the situation, accusing the Polish novelist of embezzlement.

In February 1974, Dick first experienced his pink-light visions, which continued without interruption until his death. They revealed to him an entire cosmology. Sometimes he experienced the world as a persecuted Christian living in imperial Rome; at other times he felt he was receiving messages from some future superior intelligence, which he named VALIS (Vast Active Living Intelligence System).

Dick was never sure whether the pink light was the voice of God, a message from a space alien, or a drug-induced hallucination (among other possibilities he entertained). Yet despite the pink light's uncertain nature, he often acted under its direction. VALIS issued cryptic theological messages but also offered Dick practical advice on how to deal with his son Christopher's hernia.

The visions also expanded his conspiratorial fantasies, which became global in scope. In March 1974, he claimed to have received two mysterious pieces of mail: a fan letter from Estonia and an anonymous clipping from a communist newspaper. Under the guidance of the pink light, Dick concluded that these letters were part of an effort to put his loyalty to the test. Connecting the letters to his dispute with Lem, he wrote to the FBI asking for assistance against the communist conspiracy.

On May 1, 1974, Dick got a phone call from Peter Fitting, who had written an article slated to run in the special Philip K. Dick issue of *Science Fiction Studies*. Fitting, who was spending a sabbatical year in San Francisco, wanted to visit Dick and bring along Jameson, Richard Pinhas and Pinhas's wife, Agneta.

Writing to the FBI after this phone call, Dick connected 'the Fitting group' with Lem and 'the flurry of weird mail of a Soviet type'. He believed that this proposed visit was a prelude to a kidnapping plot: 'The Fitting group, including ... most especially the foreign national [Pinhas], of whom I am most greatly afraid, in case he is not French but from behind the Iron Curtain—in fact maybe a Soviet police agent who wants to talk to me direct, or is from Poland anyhow, representing Lem....'

Despite these fears, Dick received 'the Fitting group' on May 15. Again writing to the FBI, he provided a surprisingly genial picture of the visit: 'You will be glad to know that in fierce debate we routed the Peter Fitting group, which consisted of four people from four different countries. Their purpose in coming to see me was to get an endorsement from me, recorded on tape, of a Marxist interpretation of my writings. With them, besides a lot of good liquor and a pretty girl, they brought at least three complex Marxist philosophical theses on my novels, one of which they translated from the French aloud, onto tape, for me to agree with. I told them this French doctoral thesis was entirely wrong. We had then a one-hour furious polemical debate in three languages, plus assorted Greek and Latin technical terms, after which they accused my tastes of being "in favor of God" as well as "right-wing fascist propaganda" and then departed, leaving their liquor behind (they did take the girl with them, though).'

Fitting himself provides a slightly different account of the visit in a statement prefacing volume three of *The Selected Letters of Philip K. Dick*:

'It was a very pleasant day. Certainly, there was discussion and even disagreement about the "meaning" of his work, but I think it fair to say that none of us were concerned about receiving his imprimatur on our readings, or worried that our various interpretations did not agree with the author's conscious intentions. We ate and drank a fair amount; Dick flirted quite a bit with Agneta in a kind of pidgin German.... All in all, a wonderful and amusing day.'

Fearful of arousing suspicion among his imagined enemies, Dick strove to please them even as he denounced them to the FBI and denigrated what he called their 'weird Marxist talk'.

In letters written in late 1974, Dick combined all his various fears into one elaborate scheme. Lem, he imagined, was a KGB agent orchestrating a vast conspiracy that included such pawns as Jameson, Fitting, Darko Suvin (a Canada-based critic who then edited *Science Fiction Studies*) and Franz Rottensteiner (an Austrian who at that time was Lem's Western literary agent). 'What is involved here,' he wrote, 'is not that these persons are Marxists per se or even that Fitting, Rottensteiner and Suvin are foreign-based but that all of them without exception represent dedicated outlets in a chain of command from Stanislaw Lem in Krakow, Poland, himself a total Party functionary.... For an Iron Curtain Party group ... to gain monopoly positions of power from which they can control opinion through criticism and pedagogic essays is a threat to our whole field of science fiction and its free exchange of views and ideas.' In countering this communist conspiracy, Dick again feared for his life: he believed he was in danger of being kidnapped and brainwashed by Lem and company. (To add another layer of complexity to this convoluted story, it is not certain whether all these letters reached the FBI. His wife of the time claims that Dick would occasionally write these letters and drop them in a garbage bin, sure that they would reach the proper destination if the authorities really wanted to see them.)

While Dick was alive the targets of his letters to the FBI were not aware of his duplicity. (For its part, the FBI responded with a single noncommittal thank-you note, and does not seem to have acted further on his reports.) But even without the knowledge of Dick's letters to the FBI, his critical supporters became increasingly uncomfortable with the eccentricities of his private life. As Csicsery-Ronay notes, 'For the New Left critics, the whole Pink Beam episode was an embarrassment and they never talked about it. It was just another wacky, tawdry Dick thing.'

Dick's admirers first confronted the issue of his letters to the FBI in 1991, when the relevant volume of his selected letters was released. The earliest response, by Robert M. Philmus of Concordia University, was also the harshest. Writing in *Science Fiction Studies*, Philmus described Dick's actions against Lem as 'slander to an extent that is not only actionable but (legally as well as morally) indefensible.'

Today, Philmus explains that he was angry because Dick's letters hit close to home. 'This was not something that was remote to me,' he says. 'These letters involved the denunciation of friends and acquaintances.' Yet even Philmus acknowledges that certain mitigating historical and biographical factors relax one's initial outrage. In particular, Philmus believes that Dick's own previous experience with security services sheds light on Dick's actions.

As it turns out, long before Dick approached the FBI, the bureau had approached him. In 1953 or 1954, Dick and his second wife, Kleo, were repeatedly approached by two FBI agents, who hoped (but failed) to recruit the young Bohemian couple to spy on students at the University of Mexico. According to Dick's biographer Lawrence Sutin, these encounters had a 'lasting' impact and planted the seed for Dick's future anxieties about the national security state. (Not all these anxieties were unjustified, either. In 1958, a letter Dick wrote to a Soviet scientist was intercepted by the Central Intelligence Agency. Ten years later, Dick lent his name to an antiwar ad that ended up in his FBI file.)

Of all those named in Dick's letters, Disch has perhaps been the most forgiving. In an email interview, he stresses Dick's personal agony. 'At this point, early and mid-1970s,' Disch notes, Dick 'really was freaking out on drugs, almost the whole pharmacopoeia except heroin. The drugs didn't destroy his gift entirely, even at his nadir, but they did make it impossible for him to distinguish between self-interest and Poe's "Imp of the Perverse". He loved to make trouble: witness those letters to the FBI.... He'd follow the moment's inspiration, which would lead sometimes to only momentary mischief (the FBI, after all, didn't take him seriously, so far as I know), sometimes to an okay novel.'

Disch also believes that Dick was motivated partially by 'pure envy, disguised as paranoid fantasy'. In a letter to Disch, written the day after his

October 28, 1972, letter to the FBI, Dick extravagantly praised *Camp Concentration* as 'not only the finest science fiction novel I've ever read but now that I've realized that, I find myself reflecting that it is the finest novel as such.' Disch is 'flattered' that Dick felt so threatened by *Camp Concentration* that he had to denounce the novel to the government.

Yet even if Dick's critics forgive his treachery as delusional, can they justifiably canonize him as a great subversive novelist? As Csicsery-Ronay noted in a 1992 survey of the history of Dick's literary reputation, 'Dick's paranoid fantasy seems to retroactively undermine the whole point of the effort to apotheosize him as an icon of critical, anti-establishment SF. The historical situation is profoundly, unnervingly Dickian. Even as the earnest critics are trying to establish models of resistance and redemption, their hero is secretly undermining them. The idealism of the beatification essays is now riven with our knowledge that their object was a traitor.'

Certainly Peter Fitting's views of Dick's work have changed. In 1975, Fitting had celebrated Dick's fiction for its transgressive power. In his view, most science fiction novels—like most traditional 'realist' novels—are ideological constructs that mask the fundamental relations between social classes. They proffer a 'conception of reality which mystifies the actual reality of the capitalist mode of production and the resultant repression and alienation.' By contrast, he lauded Dick for 'carrying subjectivity to an extreme' and thus 'reminding us ... that "reality" is a mental construct which may be undermined at any time.'

But speaking about Dick now, Fitting says with wary sadness that 'there hasn't been anything really interesting written about him in the last decade.... People aren't so interested in him.... It is harder to find a radical vision in his work.' Fitting believes that far from intentionally subverting Science Fiction, Dick was often 'confused', which made his work seem more complicated than it actually was.

Dick was an erudite, widely read man. But nothing in his career prepared him to appreciate the methods and styles of contemporary literary criticism. In one interview, he complained that he 'read a lot of ... criticism in which [critics] see a lot of ideas which aren't there at all.' Dick may have misread his critics, but in his view, the critics misread him. His story about being asked to plant covert neo-Nazi messages in his books can be read as a paranoid fantasy about literary criticism, which involves not just finding meanings deeply hidden in the text but sometimes also inventing meanings.

Csicsery-Ronay believes that Dick 'felt intimidated by and vulnerable to the eggheads', so his letters to the FBI were an attempt 'to protect his work from the interference of strange academics'. This type of 'anti-academic feeling' is 'strong in the SF community,' claims Csicsery-Ronay, who is the current editor of *Science Fiction Studies*. And indeed, Disch speaks for many authors in the field when he writes that he disdains 'SF academics' as 'Lukács-style Continental ideologues, who worshipped [Dick]—but in turgid prose and missing half the jokes.'

In considering Dick's ill-fated relationship with his academic admirers, Disch writes, 'I worry more about academe than Dick. The work has stayed in print, it's widely read, and whether it will continue to seem relevant depends more on history than the work itself. That is, he will be worth reading so long as he seems uncannily prescient.'

Dick's portrayal of a media-saturated world where reality is lost among simulacra is just as timely as ever, so perhaps we should heed Disch's advice to return to Dick's splendid fiction and leave the sad life behind. Yet separating life and art is difficult with a character like Dick, whose own life and art pushed so hard at the boundaries of the normal. Philmus recently observed that in 1974 Dick 'entered the world of his fiction'. And as Dick himself wrote to Fitting in that same year, 'It seems to me that by subtle but real degrees the world has come to resemble a PKD novel; or, put another way, subjectively I sense my actual world as resembling the kind of typical universe which I used to merely create as fiction, and which I left, often happily, when I was done with writing.'

Lingua Franca, May/June 2001

STANISLAW LEM'S COMMUNICATION FAILURE

Like many creators of science fiction, the Polish writer Stanislaw Lem is fascinated by what will happen when humanity makes its 'first contact' with an intelligent alien life form. In novels such as *Solaris* (1961) and *His Master's Voice* (1968), Lem suggests that the greatest problem will be communication: If we do meet genuinely otherworldly beings, how will we possibly talk to them?

Many science fiction writers have tried to resolve this dilemma by imagining aliens simply as human beings with funny costumes or pointy ears. But Lem has tackled the problem with stories about creatures so strange that they baffle the understanding. In Lem's most famous novel, for example, scientists struggle for decades to communicate with an intelligent ocean that engulfs the planet Solaris. Repeated failure makes some of the scientists bitter and sullen, as if they'd been rejected by a haughty lover. Strangely, Lem's own relationship with his Western audience has long been marked by the same botched communication and wounded love.

Not that the 81-year-old writer, who lives in Krakow, would seem to have much to complain about. Lem's forty-odd books have been translated into forty languages, and global sales figures top 25 million. The 1972 film adaptation of *Solaris*, directed by Andrei Tarkovsky, was hailed at the time as the Soviet Union's answer to *2001: A Space Odyssey*. In November of 2002 Hollywood finally responded with its own version, directed by Steven Soderbergh and starring George Clooney.

His work has been embraced by a global audience, it has also aroused deep distrust. During the Cold War, Lem ran afoul of both the world's superpowers. In the '70s, Lem's natural allies, American sci-fi writers, turned on him. And today, this prickly Polish visionary insists that fans and critics alike have misinterpreted his work. After the release of the Soderbergh version of *Solaris*, Lem issued a statement announcing that while he had no intention of seeing the film, he was troubled by its emphasis on romance at the expense of deeper philosophical concerns. Had

Solaris merely been the story of love between a man and a woman, Lem wrote, he could have just called it *Love in Outer Space.*

In his 1968 memoir, *Highcastle*, Lem recalls his childhood in the Polish city of Lvov. A socially awkward only child, he compensated for his loneliness by studying popular science and constructing elaborate fantasy worlds, inspired in part by American movies, as well as by the fiction of Jules Verne and H. G. Wells.

After World War II, Lem resumed his medical education and started writing fiction on the side. In 1947, he began working for *Zycie Nauki* (*The Life of Science*), a monthly popular science magazine. He soon ran afoul of the authorities for writing essays mocking the bogus, government-approved theories of the Soviet geneticist T.D. Lysenko. Burned by this experience, Lem turned toward the relatively safe haven of science fiction. Along with the Russian writers Arkady and Boris Strugatsky and a legion of East European fantasists, Lem helped turn sci-fi into an allegorical dissident literature.

Solaris mixed standard sci-fi themes with philosophical questions and became Lem's breakthrough book. As Lem's hero, the psychologist Kris Kelvin, studies the ocean of Solaris, he encounters a woman who resembles Rheya, his wife—or lover, in many translations of the novel—who'd committed suicide a decade earlier. Kelvin isn't sure if the reborn Rheya is merely a hallucination, or if she's the product of an attempt (friendly or sinister) on the part of Solaris to make contact with him.

Among other things, *Solaris* is a veiled attack on Marxism and its claim to have replaced religious mystery with a science of human history. Solaristics, the systematic study of the planet's ocean, is said to be a rational pursuit—but it's really, Kelvin notes, just 'the space era's equivalent of religion: faith disguised as science.' He adds: 'Contact, the stated aim of Solaristics, is no less vague and obscure than the communion of the saints, or the second coming of the Messiah.'

Solaris became a literary sensation in Eastern Europe, although in the Soviet Union it was made available only in a bowdlerized version that omitted a chapter deemed too 'mystical'. Lem followed this novel with more conventional sci-fi books about space exploration, as well as with satirical attacks on the folly of the arms race, and many nonfiction books.

In his massive *Summa Technologiae* (1964), Lem presented himself as an ironic Aquinas of the space age, offering detailed speculations on how future technologies might mimic and augment biological processes, yet still leave humanity unable to fully understand itself.

Meanwhile, Lem's work was making its troubled journey to the West. *Solaris* first became available to English-language readers in 1970, in a shoddy version derived from a French translation. (Despite every effort by Lem himself, it's still the only English translation in print.) Lem also began contributing essays on English-language sci-fi to scholarly journals and fan magazines alike. These essays were often acerbic: while he admired the work of Philip K. Dick, Lem saw himself as the heir to Kafka and H.G. Wells, so he had little regard for those mere hacks who wrote commercial fiction for the pulps.

Tensions with his American colleagues came to a head in a bizarre international literary incident. In 1973, in an effort to promote 'international goodwill', the Science Fiction Writers of America (SFWA) conferred an honorary membership upon Lem, a distinction that had previously been given to only one other foreign writer, J.R.R. Tolkien.

But in 1975, the writer Philip José Farmer, whose sexually frank thrillers Lem had criticized, raised objections to Lem's honorary membership. Farmer's concerns were echoed by an addled Philip K. Dick, who was experiencing fits of paranoia at the time. Dick maintained that Lem had embezzled royalties from a Polish translation of Dick's 1969 novel *Ubik*.

'The honorary voting of Stanislaw Lem to membership is the sheep voting the wolf a place at the communal hearth,' Dick warned SFWA members in '75. 'They certainly must be licking their chops back in Krakow right now.'

These attacks might not have gone any further if Lem hadn't published yet another critical article on contemporary sci-fi, 'SF, or Phantasy Come to Grief'. The article itself was acidic, but its impact was amplified by yet another translation problem. In 1975, the *Atlas World Press Review* put out a dubious English-language version of the essay under the inflammatory title 'Looking down on Science Fiction: a Novelist's Choice for the World's Worst Writing'. In this version, Lem is made to describe American sci-fi as 'bad writing tacked together with wooden dialogue'. Although he did call American sci-fi 'kitsch', the other accusation appears to have been invented by the translators.

The perpetrators of the World's Worst Writing turned on Lem. One

SFWA member accused him of attacking American sci-fi writers at the prompting of his Communist masters. Other SFWA members questioned his ability to read English or suggested, falsely, that he was profiting from pirated editions of American books. In a straw vote taken in 1976, seventy percent of SFWA's voting members supported a resolution to revoke Lem's honorary membership.

Lem did have some American defenders. In an open letter to the journal *Science Fiction Studies* in 1977, Ursula K. Le Guin declared: 'The SFWA is not a powerful organization, nothing compared to the Soviet Writers Union, say; but when it uses the tactics of the Soviet Writers Union, I think there is cause for concern, and reasons for shame.'

Today, former SFWA president Jerry Pournelle insists that Lem's membership was revoked because of technicalities in the group's bylaws, not politics. But in his 1977 exchange with Le Guin, Pournelle described Lem as someone 'who finds a communist regime congenial' and 'embraces communist egalitarianism'. In 1983, a letter to the editor in *Omni Magazine* denounced Lem as 'the most boring writer in the world—and an avowed Communist'—even as Lem and his family were preparing to go into exile in Vienna. (They returned to Poland in 1988.) Despite the hostility of the American sci-fi community, mainstream writers such as John Updike and Anthony Burgess started praising Lem's books in prominent places.

But Lem himself had already begun to turn away from the genre toward a more inward-looking experimentalism reminiscent of Borges. *A Perfect Vacuum* (1971) offered fictional reviews of non-existent books, for example; and a follow-up volume, *Imaginary Magnitude* (1974), gathered together introductions to another set of imaginary books.

Unlike more orthodox and optimistic sci-fi writers, Lem emphasizes the paradoxes and problems that new knowledge will bring with it. For Lem, artificial intelligence entails artificial stupidity. As the narrator of *The Futurological Congress* (1971) puts it, 'A smart machine will first consider which is more worth its while: to perform the given task or, instead, to figure some way out of it.... And therefore we have the malingerants, fudgerators, and drudge-dodgers, not to mention the special phenomenon of simulimbecility or mimicretinism.'

Although Lem continues to write today, all of his work since 1987 has been non fiction, much of it elaborating on the ideas of *Summa Technologiae.*

Peter Swirski, a literature professor at the University of Alberta and editor of *A Stanislaw Lem Reader* (1997) is working on a project to translate this work into English, along with Lem's little-known early novels.

But is Lem fated to be misunderstood? In his tangled statement on Steven Soderbergh's movie, Lem writes: 'I have not seen the film ... hence I cannot say anything about the movie itself except for what the reviews reflect, albeit unclearly—like a distorted picture of one's face in ripply water. However, to my best knowledge, the book was not dedicated to erotic problems of people in outer space ... I shall allow myself to repeat that I only wanted to create a vision of human encounter with something that certainly exists ... but cannot be reduced to human concepts, images, or ideas.'

Whenever Lem speaks about science fiction, there is a tangible sense of sadness in his words, like a man discussing a long-dead passion. For all his achievements and honours, Lem knows from experience that even the most well-intentioned attempts at communication can end in farcical misunderstanding.

Boston Globe, Ideas, December 15, 2004

COMICS

LITTLE NEMO

In the beginning of the last century, a little boy named Nemo was haunted by recurring nightmares of a bizarre and unruly land where the conventions of everyday life were turned upside down. By day, the boy was firmly lodged in the respectable and decorous world of middle-class white America. His frumpy parents kept up appearances in a solidly genteel household, complete with a white picket fence on the outside and an African American maid toiling away in the kitchen. The family's regular rounds included hosting cousins and in-laws, going to church on Sundays, and making the occasional jaunt to the department stores—which were just starting to emerge as palaces of consumption.

Nighttime allowed Nemo, a shy 7-year-old whose hair became rumpled as he tossed and turned in bed, to escape into the fabulous and slightly sinister realm of Slumberland. Unlike the daytime republic governed by President Theodore Roosevelt, Slumberland was ruled over by King Morpheus, a Jove-like patriarch whose furrowed brow and Old Testament beard commanded respect. In the echoing hallways of Slumberland, Morpheus was constantly receiving curtsies and bows from courtiers draped in colourful attire that combined the fripperies of 18th-century Versailles with the colours of a circus. Slumberland even had slaves, a profession recently abolished in daytime America. There were other signs that Slumberland was hardly an ideal egalitarian society, including the rough treatment meted out to African 'jungle imps'.

These slaves and imps were among the more disturbing oddities that Nemo encountered during his nocturnal voyages. Slumberland also abounded with butterflies large enough to umbrella you during a rainstorm, a giant turkey that gobbled up houses for Thanksgiving, a glass princess who shattered if you kissed her too passionately, carriages that were pulled along by horse-sized rabbits and airships that could carry you to Mars.

Of course, once you got to Mars, as Nemo did in 1910, you might have noticed that the line between fantasy and reality was not so firm as you had first thought. The red planet turned out to be ruled by a ruthless capitalist who owned not just every square inch of property, but even the air. Polluted by industrial emissions, populated by genetically modified monstrosities, and papered over with gaudy ads, Mars was the ultimate corporate dystopia. The poor Martians had to pay for the privilege of breathing.

Like Jonathan Swift's Lemuel Gulliver or Lewis Carroll's Alice, Nemo was a sober and innocent soul who travelled to a bizarre fantasyland which on closer inspection turned out to be a parody of the home that was left behind. Yet there is a significant difference between Nemo and his distinguished literary ancestors. Gulliver and Alice gained a foothold in our imagination thanks primarily to the writerly skills of their authors (assisted in Carroll's case by some charming John Tenniel illustrations). Nemo, by contrast, was a comic strip character whose newsprint universe was constructed by the pen of a cartoonist, Winsor McCay.

As imaginative a fantasist as the United States ever produced, McCay created unique effects that could only work in the art form of comics. Take as an example the famous Sunday page that ran on July 26, 1908. The early panels show Nemo snuggled in bed and ready for sleep, wearing pink-striped pyjamas. Nemo is startled to find he's not alone, since he hears the voice of Flip, his flippant, cigar-chomping Slumberland companion. Before he can even adjust to Flip's presence, Nemo is amazed by the fact that the bed he's been sleeping on is starting to grow. Along the first squat row of four panels the legs of the bed slowly rise, taking Nemo and Flip closer and closer to the top of the page.

In the next tier, the panels have lengthened to accommodate the new size of the bed, which has decided to take Nemo and Flip outside. By now the bed is so big it has to crouch a little just to get outside the front door. As it struts across the streets of New York, the bed dwarfs all the startled onlookers, including a police officer and a horse that raises itself on its hind legs in fright. (The horse is a visual pun for the magical bed, whose motions have an equine gallop.) By now, Nemo and Flip are so high in the air they are level with the full moon that follows their progress from panel to panel. Bright yellow, the moon is a colourful counterpoint to the evening gloom of the outdoor scene.

In the third and final tier, the panels are as long as stilts, which is what the legs of the bed resemble. We no longer see Nemo and Flip in profile;

rather, they are charging towards us at full speed. Losing its steady serenity, the moon bounces up and down in sequence with the out-of-control bed. Finally the legs of the bed are entangled in a church steeple, causing Nemo and Flip to hurl downward. (A freethinker, McCay was perhaps making a subtle joke about how religion hinders the flight of the human imagination.)

In the final panel, squirrelled away at the bottom right-hand corner of the page, Nemo awakes to find he's fallen out of his actual bed. In colour and size, the bottom panel mirrors the opening shot of Nemo at the top left-hand corner of the page: it's the visual equivalent of a poet's ending of a sonnet with an echo of the opening word.

This little story of the walking bed can be described, with more or less skill, in words, yet as a work of art it can only have an impact as a comic strip. The blending of words and pictures, the sequencing of images to tell a story, the use of the page as a unit of attention, and the shifting of panel size to match the narrative: all of these are comic strip effects. A prose or film version of this story would have to be structured very differently, just as a comic book adaptation of a good movie or novel would inevitably involve a reinvention (not to say flattening) of the story.

A hybrid form that merges words and pictures to create a new visual language, comics have their own special rules. More than any artist before him, Winsor McCay intuitively grasped this fact and allowed it to govern his aesthetic. His early mastery of the special language of comics explains the pride of place that McCay enjoys in the current celebrations of narrative cartooning as a distinct cultural form. As comics enter museums and literary magazines, the form runs the risk of being categorized as a subspecies of either fine art or literature. Little Nemo reminds us that while comics borrow from both illustration and prose narrative, they also have unique properties worth exploring and celebrating.

Ten decades after Little Nemo was first summoned to Slumberland, McCay is at the centre of a storm of publishing and curatorial activity. In the fall of 2005, the Hammer Museum gave McCay his own room as part of an exhibit on 'Masters of American Comics'. The accompanying catalogue by Yale University Press strongly focuses on McCay, not only for chronological reasons but also because of his pervasive impact on all subsequent cartoonists. This same year, Abrams Books brought out a revised and expanded version of John Canemaker's biography *Winsor McCay: His*

Life and Art, which is far and away the most scholarly and intelligent biography ever written about an American cartoonist.

Two smaller presses, Checker and Fantagraphics, are busy reprinting McCay's lesser-known comic strips, black-and-white fantasies that lack *Little Nemo*'s renown but have their own rewards. Most important, Sunday Press Books has released a massive *Little Nemo* collection that for the first time reprints a sizable sample of the strip in the exact proportions that it enjoyed in its original newspaper run. Having roughly the same dimensions as a *New York Times* page, *Little Nemo in Slumberland: Splendid Sundays* allows readers, for the first time in nearly a century, to appreciate the full scope of McCay's art.

Amid this flurry of commemoration, the exact nature of McCay's achievement needs to be defined. He was neither the first nor the greatest cartoonist. In terms of priority, there were other popular comic strips before *Little Nemo*: notably *The Yellow Kid, Buster Brown* and *The Katzenjammer Kids*. These strips were filled with rambunctious young brats who wreaked havoc on the adult world. *Little Nemo in Slumberland* began, somewhat unpromisingly, as a genteel response to this tradition. It was meant to be closer to a respectable illustrated book than the rowdy free-for-alls of the other comic strips. Fortunately, McCay's imagination freed him from the strictures of his original prissy mandate to be the virtuous alternative to the four-colour bad boys. More important, McCay understood how to tell a story with pictures in a way that his predecessors didn't. While we now look at *The Katzenjammer Kids* only out of historical curiosity, numerous cartoonists are still exploring the storytelling techniques McCay invented.

As for McCay's comparative greatness, a strong claim can be made on his behalf, but it has to be weighed against the achievements of George Herriman, Charles M. Schulz, Robert Crumb, Art Spiegelman and Chris Ware. (These are perhaps the most accomplished of the fifteen 'masters' honoured in the recent Los Angeles exhibit and Yale catalogue.) None of these cartoonists is quite the draftsman that McCay was, but they are all much better writers, especially possessing the essential caricaturist's gift of creating pen-and-ink characters that have the spark of life in them. Herriman's *Krazy Kat*, Schulz's *Charlie Brown*, Crumb's *Fritz the Cat*, Spiegelman's *Vladek*, Ware's *Jimmy Corrigan*: these are all characters that almost seem like our friends, revealing ever greater depth the more time we spend with them. Nemo, by contrast, is a colder and more remote figure who speaks in a quaint and stilted tongue.

Yet it speaks to McCay's centrality that every subsequent major cartoonist has harvested from the fields he first tilled. Herriman's full-page *Krazy Kat* strips played with panel shapes and sizes, just as *Little Nemo* did, with the entire page having an ornamental and decorative loveliness that gives cohesiveness to the individual elements in each panel. The interplay between fantasy and reality in Schulz's *Peanuts* is a continuation of McCay's work, as are the more outrageous psychedelic effects found in Crumb's work. As for Spiegelman, his most recent full-page strips about the September 11 attacks take much of their imagery from McCay's fantasies of urban destruction. (A sample page of *Little Nemo* is included in the back of Spiegelman's most recent book, *In the Shadow of No Towers*.) Chris Ware's ceaseless experimentation with design and colour provides yet more evidence of McCay's inexhaustible inspiration.

In the history of comics, then, McCay was the great pathfinder, the early scout who marked the trails that others would follow. If not the greatest of cartoonists, he has a uniquely pivotal role in the history of the form. Thanks to these new books, we can gauge the heights that McCay scaled as well as the work other cartoonists have done in his wake.

Born in southern Ontario to a middling Scottish immigrant family in 1867, Winsor McCay spent his life balancing the competing claims of childhood fantasy and adult responsibility. The need to escape the mundane monotony of conventional social life was the great theme of his life. From an early age, his supreme passion was for drawing, pen and paper being his surest route to another world. In the stuffy schoolrooms of small-town Wisconsin, where he grew up, he often risked corporal punishment because he preferred drawing in his sketchbook to any of the lessons offered by his teachers.

His father, a practical-minded real estate agent, sent the young McCay to a business college in Ypsilanti, Michigan. Rather than learn stenography and accounting, McCay fulfilled the classic boy's dream of running away to join the circus. Cutting classes, he headed off to a dime museum in Detroit, where he drew caricatures for small change.

Inspired by the popularity of P.T. Barnum's New York extravaganza, dime museums were of course closer to the circus and the freak show than to any educational institution. Amid dog-faced boys, bearded ladies and carnival barkers, all plying their trade, McCay found his true calling: drawing for dollars.

Aside from taking private lessons from a moonlighting art professor, who taught him valuable lessons in perspective and composition, McCay was done with schooling. In truth, the dime museum was McCay's Harvard and Yale. Throughout his life he would draw upon images taken from the big top: acrobats and clowns, parades and processions, elephants and orangutans.

In 1891, McCay moved to Cincinnati, finding employment designing posters for yet another dime museum. He not only kept company with freaks but was displayed as a curiosity himself: the locals were awed by his ability to draw lightning-fast with machinelike precision. Among those who were impressed was Maude Lenore Dufour, a flirty 14-year-old. Although a decade her senior, McCay wooed Dufour, quickly convincing her to elope with him. The age difference between the two might have been less shocking in the late 19th century than now, but it is notable that they ran off together without parental approval. Once again, McCay gave evidence of his tropism toward youthful escape.

Later in the decade, after Maude gave birth to a son and daughter, the young bohemian artist had to transform himself into a respectable family man. Leaving the shifty world of the dime museum, he found more mainstream employment as a staff cartoonist and illustrator, first for the *Cincinnati Commercial Tribune* and then for the *Cincinnati Enquirer*. In an era before photographs were integrated into the news page, illustrators were on call to work as visual reporters. McCay was often sent to cover fires, court cases, lynchings, and baseball games as well as to dash off editorial cartoons spoofing local politicians.

Even as a newspaperman McCay found a way to nourish the taproots of his imagination. As part of his duties for the *Enquirer* he illustrated a series of Kipling-inspired childhood verses that went under the title *Tales of the Jungle Imp*, by Felix Fiddle. Mixing racial caricatures of African tribesmen with fairy-tale stories about how animals like the giraffe and whale acquired their characteristic traits, this series gave early evidence of McCay's skill as a children's illustrator. Possessing the languid decorative ease of late Victorian storybooks, these early works lacked the crackling narrative drive unique to comics. However lovely, they remain apprentice work.

Perhaps McCay's personal life contributed to his turn toward fairy tales. After the births of his son, Robert, and daughter, Marion, McCay subtly transferred his emotional loyalties away from his wife and toward his children. Robert McCay would inspire the look of *Little Nemo*, while Marion served as the prototype for the less famous comic strip character Hungry Henrietta, an emotionally sensitive child who is constantly badgered and browbeaten by capricious adults. McCay doted on his children (and later his grandchildren) while becoming distant and diffident toward his wife. One granddaughter recalls that the cartoonist 'was like a child himself of about eight to ten years old.' Even his physique contributed to the affinity McCay had with children: standing at five feet five inches and weighing 130 pounds, he was as lithe and slight as a small boy.

By 1903, McCay's skills as a cartoonist had developed enough to attract big-city eyes, earning him a lucrative staff job at the *New York Herald*. New York in those years was in the grip of a notorious newspaper war between Joseph Pulitzer and William Randolph Hearst (with many lesser media barons entering the fray). Cartoonists were prize weapons in the intense battle for readership, with comic strip artists receiving princely salaries for drawing the adventures of an endless succession of mischievous boys. (Pulitzer and Hearst, capricious and volatile, were themselves overgrown children, hence ideal spiritual fathers of the *Katzenjammer Kids* and other reckless urchins.)

Print technology had advanced to the point where colour reproductions now possessed a brilliancy previously reserved for expensive art books. Both Pulitzer and Hearst believed that newspapers didn't just exist to convey factual information: they had to be as gaudy as a circus poster in order to attract readers. They paid top dollar to engravers and cartoonists to liven up their pages. The visual splendours of this newspaper era can be seen in a gorgeous coffee-table book, *The World on Sunday: Graphic Art in Joseph Pulitzer's Newspapers* (1898–1911), lovingly assembled by Nicholson Baker and Margaret Brentano. As this book makes clear, Pulitzer didn't use pictures merely as illustration or decoration. Rather, visual images were a central tool for making the news come to life.

As the diminutive McCay entered New York, a city of towering skyscrapers and overbearing press lords, he must have felt like Nemo overwhelmed by his first sight of Slumberland. Fortunately, his talent made McCay a natural fit for this visually ambitious publishing world, and he quickly rose to the top ranks of American journalism. He created a host of comic strips for the *Herald*, the two most important being *Dreams of the Rarebit Fiend* (which debuted in 1904) and *Little Nemo* (which emerged the following year).

A black-and-white strip which ran in the daily newspaper, *Dreams of the Rarebit Fiend* was the adult precursor to *Little Nemo*. Each strip followed the same general plot: a dreamer would have some sort of nightmare related to his or her daytime life and wake up at the last panel, inevitably blaming the harsh vision on ill-digested cheese (the rarebit of the title). But the nightmares had decidedly mature content: a man mocks Darwin and then turns into a monkey; a woman receives a leather purse from a male admirer which turns into an alligator eager to consume her; a parson dies but rather than receiving his eternal reward is cast into the fires of hell; a missionary finds himself turned into a meal by some ungrateful African natives, who complain that 'old hard shell skinflints' are hard to eat.

Frequently tackling sexual and religious taboos, *Dreams of the Rarebit Fiend* confronted the quintessential post-Victorian theme of bourgeois hypocrisy. All it takes is some cheese and suddenly the unseemly underside of conventional social life becomes visible. Better written than *Little Nemo, Dreams of the Rarebit Fiend* is McCay's most biting and satirical work. (Good samplings of the strip can be found in Winsor McCay's *Daydreams and Nightmares* as well as in the multivolume *Winsor McCay: Early Works*. Unfortunately, the latter title is poorly edited and prints the strips as blurry images much smaller than their original size.)

Little Nemo took up the theme of nightmares but in a gentler fashion. Created for the Sunday comics section, which was primarily aimed at children, *Little Nemo* was much more visually intense than *Dreams of the Rarebit Fiend*. Working closely with the engravers at the *New York Herald*, McCay made each *Little Nemo* Sunday page a distinct work of art. Eschewing the gaudiness of other comic strips, *Little Nemo* used colours that were delicate and evocative. Each episode offered a startling new view of Slumberland, a land that Nemo first feared but later grew to cherish.

Thematically, *Little Nemo* is the opposite of *Dreams of the Rarebit Fiend*. It is not about the fears and lies of adulthood but is rather the story of a child who grows confident in his imaginative powers. In one moving sequence, Nemo uses a magic wand acquired in Slumberland to transform a slum into an earthly paradise. The wand was, of course, the fictional counterpart to McCay's magical pen, which also had the ability to conjure up a beautiful alternative reality to the ugliness he saw around him.

Created in the wake of the Chicago Columbian Exposition of 1893, *Little Nemo* was as much an architectural fantasy as a fairy tale. McCay delighted in creating pristine fictional palaces, rich in colonnades and endless hallways. Like a child playing in a sandlot, he also took pleasure in tearing down what he had so quickly created. The fertility of McCay's imagination is both daunting and troubling. His mind moved too quickly to linger over his own creations too long. His need to create a quick succession of fresh images gives his work the rushed unreality of dreams, and sometimes the insubstantiality of dreams as well.

McCay's most important innovation as an artist was his close attention to movement. Half a generation before McCay, the photographer Eadweard Muybridge had already revolutionized our sense of how bodies move through space with his time-lapse studies of horses. McCay never directly copied from photographs, relying instead on his remarkable eidetic memory, but he internalized the lessons of Muybridge. All of McCay's characters, from flying mosquitoes to scampering little boys to trotting horses, move with the fluency of life. Because comics are a succession of images, frozen when seen in isolation but moving as we read the page, McCay's attention to motion brought to the foreground the distinctive aesthetic of the art form.

McCay's reliance on memory as his chief storehouse of images is further evidence of his deep insight into the nature of comics. Chris Ware, a sharp theorist of art as well as a greatly talented cartoonist, has repeatedly argued that comics are memory-drawings rather than life-drawings. 'A cartoon is not an image taken from life,' Ware notes. 'A cartoon is taken from memory. You're trying to distill the memory of an experience, not the experience itself.' Unlike a painter or an illustrator working in front of a model, a cartoonist is drawing images in sequence that must possess narrative flow. Memories, which are fleeting images in a hazy sequence, are the closest cognitive parallel for how comics work. (Dreams, of course, are nighttime memories, sharing the sequential fuzziness of retrospective thought.)

The original run of *Dreams of the Rarebit Fiend* and *Little Nemo*, roughly from 1904 to 1913, marks the height of McCay's artistic life. Aside from doing a daily comic strip drawing, often a full page in size, McCay had energy enough to moonlight in two other successful careers, as a lecturer and animator. In those days, cartoonists enjoyed genuine celebrity status and were frequently called upon to draw in public. It was the era when live entertainment was still part of everyday life, whether in the form of vaudeville skits or lectures by Chautauqua elocutionists. As an increasingly prominent cartoonist, McCay received many requests to give chalk talks, public lectures in which he would use a blackboard to illustrate how cartoons are made. One of the stars of vaudeville, he shared the stage with W.C. Fields and Harry Houdini, among other celebrities.

McCay's gift for capturing motion gave him yet another prominent role in history as a pioneering animator. Working with a minimal staff in his spare time, McCay created spectacular films, including *Gertie the Dinosaur* (1914) and *The Sinking of the Lusitania* (1918). In their ability to create the illusion of lifelike movement, these films were unrivalled until the efforts of Walt Disney two decades later. Whereas Disney commanded an army of assistants working full-time in a major commercial enterprise, McCay's experiments were supported largely by his creative ambitions.

McCay was almost inhumanly productive. By one estimate he produced more than a million drawings in his life, almost all of them of a very high quality of draftsmanship, with a few possessing genius. Canemaker's biography, rich in intimate details gleaned from personal letters and documents as well as many interviews, makes clear that McCay's relentless productivity was partially fuelled by the need to escape from a troubled marriage. Attractive and younger than her husband, Maude McCay was the subject of courtroom dramas and newspaper gossip, with stories suggesting that she enticed other women's husbands to stray.

Ray Winsor Moniz, the cartoonist's grandson, astutely observes that his grandfather would often 'leave a group of people, excuse himself, and go upstairs to work. He avoided arguments that way with Maude. His concentration and losing himself in his drawings was almost weird. It was an obsession. [He] used it to get away from the family or a problem. He used it as a retreat as well as a love.'

This love of drawing made McCay one of the most celebrated popular artists of his day, but his success was also his undoing. In 1911, McCay was hired by William Randolph Hearst to be a staff cartoonist. McCay started earning an outlandishly large salary, peaking near $100,000 a year (putting him in league with movie stars and the most successful of athletes). Alas, this salary came at a high cost. After letting McCay work for a while on a relaunched version of *Little Nemo*, Hearst decided that so highly paid an artist belonged on the editorial page. McCay was placed under the thumb of editor Arthur Brisbane, who told the cartoonist: 'You're a serious artist, not a comic cartoonist. I want you to give up [Little Nemo] and draw serious cartoon pictures for my editorials.' Hearst further decreed that McCay should stop wasting his time on vaudeville because his 'dalliance with the stage interferes with [his] regular newspaper work'.

After a lifetime of dodging adult responsibilities in order to give freedom to his childlike imagination, McCay was finally trapped. Because he and his wife were extravagant and feckless spenders, he needed the hefty salary that only Hearst could provide. But in order to earn that salary, McCay had to give up the two activities that meant the most to him: drawing comic strips and basking in the glamour of the stage. McCay did get to revive *Little Nemo* briefly in the 1920s, but by that time his creative fires had gone out, extinguished perhaps by the drudgery of illustrating the pontifications of Arthur Brisbane. The platitudinous tenor of these editorials can be measured by the cartoons, technically proficient but dull, that McCay supplied as illustrations. Typically they contained such vapid titles as 'Thank Heaven for Progress', 'Here God Has Placed Us', 'Who Carries the Load? Woman', 'Beware of the Word "Easy"', 'Our Glorious Public School', 'The Dreadful Curse of Drugs', 'Death Is Kind and Necessary: It Wipes Off the Human Slate and Makes Way for New Ideas'. When McCay died in 1934, obituaries noted the passing of an editorial cartoonist. *Little Nemo* was only a dim memory.

Late in life, McCay noted, 'I have never been so happy as when I was drawing *Little Nemo*.' This statement takes on a melancholy edge when we consider that he didn't give up *Little Nemo*; it was taken away from him. The imaginative freedom celebrated in *Little Nemo* becomes all the more precious when we realize that it was only fleetingly enjoyed by McCay.

McCay's life and career were rife with contradictions. His emotional immaturity allowed him to create art rich in complexity and depth. A top-notch artist, he worked in the most ephemeral of mediums: the newspaper page and the vaudeville stage. (Rather as if Michelangelo were hired to create ice sculptures.) Popular and celebrated, neither he nor any of his contemporaries did much to preserve his best work, almost all of which has been scattered and lost. Librarians tended to have a sniffy attitude to newspapers run by ruffians like William Randolph Hearst and rarely preserved the best sources of McCay's work. (The scandal of old newspapers being destroyed and half-heartedly preserved on microfilm has been well documented by Nicholson Baker in an earlier book, *Double Fold: Libraries and the Assault on Paper*.)

Only decades after McCay's death did museums start to realize he had left an important artistic legacy. While scattered examples of his *Little Nemo* have been reprinted, the full body is still not available. Although the book *Little Nemo in Slumberland: So Many Splendid Sundays* does give some restitution. By showing us McCay's art almost exactly as it first appeared, only on more permanent paper, the book restores the original experience of being immersed in Slumberland. This is not a book to read; it's a book to inhabit. It allows you to spend days exploring the byways of McCay's imagination. Quite simply, this is the most beautiful book of comics ever published.

In sum, McCay suffered the paradoxical fate common to cartoonists: wealth and fame did little to secure his place in the cultural pantheon. McCay's career is emblematic not only of what comics are capable of at their best, but also of the constraints that almost all cartoonists work under. Until very recently, comics have been a commercial art form, with little of the autonomy granted to the fine arts. Even so great a cartoonist as McCay operated under the tyranny of the marketplace (this perhaps explains the satirical jabs he occasionally makes at corporate capitalism).

The struggle for artistic freedom in a commercially dominated form is the central story of comics in the 20th century. This story provides the narrative arc that governed the careers of the cartoonists who worked in McCay's wake, inspired by his beautiful art yet afraid to suffer his ultimate fate. The canon of artists celebrated by the 'Masters of American Comics' exhibition—which ran in cities like Los Angeles and New York from 2005 to 2007—provides a good road map for how cartoonists have tried to deal with the McCay dilemma of creating art amid the bazaar bustle of the market.

As the title makes clear, 'Masters of American Comics' is very much an exhibit with an agenda: it's an attempt to create a canon, a short list that neatly encompasses the best the medium has to offer. Aside from Winsor McCay, the masters list includes seven newspaper cartoonists: Lyonel

Feininger (although best known for his paintings, he did two short-lived expressionist strips, *The Kin-der-Kids* and *Wee Willie Winkie's World*), George Herriman (the creator of *Krazy Kat*), E.C. Segar (*Thimble Theatre* and *Popeye*), Frank King (*Gasoline Alley*), Chester Gould (*Dick Tracy*), Milton Caniff (*Terry and the Pirates, Steve Canyon*), and Charles M. Schulz (*Peanuts*). There are three comic book artists: Will Eisner (who created *The Spirit* in the 1940s and was instrumental in solidifying the graphic novel form in the late 1970s), Jack Kirby (who co-created Captain America with Joe Simon and the Fantastic Four, the Hulk, Thor and many other characters with Stan Lee), and Harvey Kurtzman (the mastermind behind *MAD* comics). There are also four living cartoonists, all of whom sprang from the tradition of the 1960s counterculture and have created a diverse body of work that is difficult to summarize: Robert Crumb (best known for his stories about *Mr. Natural* and *Fritz the Cat*), Art Spiegelman (author of the groundbreaking graphic memoir *Maus*), Gary Panter (*Jimbo in Purgatory*, a Dada adaptation of Dante), and Chris Ware (creator of the graphic novel *Jimmy Corrigan* and many other works).

As lists go, this is quite impressive. One might quibble about the choice of Feininger (whose strips are lovely but very few in number). He seems like a sop to art-world respectability. The rest are not only all major figures and formidable talents; they also serve as markers for larger historical movements: to pick some obvious examples, Frank King stands in for the sentimental soap opera strips of the 1920s; Milton Caniff for the slick illustrators and adventure artists of the 1930s; Jack Kirby for superhero comic books of the 1940s and later; Robert Crumb for the freewheeling '60s. The lack of women on the list can be blamed on the sexism that governed both newspaper bullpens and comic book sweatshops (although there could have been more acknowledgement of the current generation of groundbreaking female cartoonists, such as Lynda Barry and Carol Tyler).

Yet even with this impressive masters list, we see how compromised comics have been by commercial concerns. There is a clear distinction between artists of the first rank and talented craftsmen who never quite freed themselves from the expectations of their audience or employers. McCay, we've seen, was an artist for a few great years but a craftsman for most of his working life. Many cartoonists have had similarly split careers. But a few rough demarcations are possible. To my mind, the true artists on the list are McCay, Herriman, King, Segar, Schulz, Crumb, Spiegelman,

Panter and Ware. The rest all did work that has value but lacks the essential jolt of personal feeling that only art possesses. However gifted a Chester Gould or a Jack Kirby might have been—and both did visually overpowering work—still they relied so heavily on the clichés and tropes of pulp fiction that it is difficult to emotionally connect with their art at any deep level of feeling. By contrast, the most offhand doodle from Herriman's pen has the intimacy of a handwritten love letter.

Herriman, in fact, provides an object lesson for the freedoms that a cartoonist could enjoy even while working as a newspaper wage slave. In many ways, Herriman was McCay's lucky younger brother. Born a Louisiana 'mulatto' in 1880, Herriman entered the New York newspaper rat race at the turn of the century, a few years ahead of McCay. (Up north, Herriman was allowed to pass as white, a harder performance in his native state.) Like the creator of *Little Nemo*, Herriman ended up on Hearst's payroll. But to Herriman, 'the Chief' was an indulgent patron rather than an overbearing boss.

Herriman's oddball strip *Krazy Kat* was initially popular when it emerged in 1913 but lost its mass audience as it became ever more eccentric and esoteric. But Hearst both loved the strip and valued it as a prestige winner (since it won praise from writers like Gilbert Seldes and E.E. Cummings). So he ordered his newspapers to keep running the strip until Herriman's death in 1944. It was a rare case of an early-20th-century cartoonist being valued simply as an artist and not as a circulation builder. (Comic books, the plebian offspring of comic strips, were even more dismally restrictive: they were mass-produced in sweatshops by artists who had to produce hundreds of pages a year to simply eke out a modest living.)

In recent years, as new scholarship has investigated Herriman's life and his strips have been extensively reprinted, we can see that *Krazy Kat* was a deeply personal, even furtive and private, work. The themes of 'passing for white' and the fluidity of identity run throughout *Krazy Kat*, a strip about a black cat that loves a white mouse. Herriman was allowed to explore such themes because he enjoyed the liberty allowed to modern artists: since few understood his work, he could do as he pleased. More typically, the other first-rate comic strip artists also had the freedom granted to clowns. Avoiding the melodrama and bluster found in more earnest strips, artists like King, Segar and Schulz stayed in the realm of comedy, where they could speak with their own distinctive voices. King's comedy was low-key and wry, based on a melancholy sense of the toll taken by the passage of time. Segar, by contrast, was the uproarious spinner of tall tales, with *Popeye* as both a parody of two-fisted heroics and an exemplar of roughneck gallantry. In its peak years, Schulz's comedy was brassy and bitter, a closely observed vision of childhood cruelty tempered only by verbal wit. Compared to the range and intelligence of these humorous cartoonists, more 'serious' artists like Caniff and Kirby seem blunt, mechanical, and all too easily imitated.

It was only with the emergence of the counterculture in the 1960s that the idea of comics as art became more than an intermittent possibility. In keeping with the spirit of the times, Robert Crumb and his peers refused to work under the strictures of corporate culture, whether for mainstream newspapers or comic book publishers. Instead, they hooked up with the underground press, or started their own fly-by-night companies, in order to produce work that was personal and completely uncensored. Of course, many of the underground comics suffered from the flaws of hippie art: they offered many pages of self-indulgent fantasies of sexual freedom mixed with druggy incoherence and a preference for sensationalism and outrage over subtlety and delicacy. However, the undergrounds freed comics from the golden cage they had previously inhabited.

If McCay was the pivotal cartoonist of the first half of the 20th century, Crumb was the medium's second major watershed. A maladjusted child of the baby boom, Crumb rejected the tinny slickness of postwar America and immersed himself in the rich craft values of the early 20th century.

Thanks to his friendship with fellow record and comic book collectors, he was deeply steeped in the traditions of the past. '*Little Nemo* is one of my all time favorite strips,' the 19-year-old Crumb wrote to a friend. 'McCay was a genius!' His stylistic influences are virtually identical to the table of contents for the 'Masters of American Comics' catalogue: McCay, Herriman, Segar and Kurtzman. From these predecessors he synthesized a style that combined the rich density of earlier art with stories about contemporary life.

Fearless in exposing his deepest sexual fantasies for the world to see, Crumb inspired a generation of cartoonists to believe that comics could be a personal art. As Art Spiegelman once noted, Crumb was 'the most influential of the underground cartoonists' whose achievement was 'to re-invent comic books. His fantasies were not mass-produced, pre-adolescent superhero power fantasies, but rather pimply post-adolescent sex fantasies—the Dreams of an Acid Fiend—with at least one foot firmly planted in the real world.'

Spiegelman himself went through a 'Crumb phase' and then, as the best students do, found his own voice. Like Crumb, Spiegelman is deeply rooted in the history of his own art, possessing an almost professorial knowledge of the arcane history of comics. (It's worth pointing out that both men gained their erudition of comics lore from the late collector Woody Gelman, who more than anyone else preserved the art of Winsor McCay and brought it back into print.) Spiegelman's comics gain much of their density from this knowledge of comics history: even the seemingly diary-like art of *Maus* is actually rich with allusions to comics and other early 20th-century art forms, the very choice of cats and mice as lead characters being an homage to the anthropomorphic tradition of Herriman and his contemporaries.

In sum, the current wave of art comics can be seen as a reclamation project: it is an attempt to redeem the art of the past, much of which was produced under commercial duress, by preserving the best that was done and incorporating it into new work. Artists such as Crumb and Spiegelman are both deeply traditional and innovative. Traditional because they have internalized the craftwork of earlier artists, and innovative because they have found fresh stories to tell with their well-honed skills. As Spiegelman likes to say, the future of comics is in the past.

Or to put it another way, the spiritual children of Winsor McCay still have dreams to draw.

Virginia Quarterly Review, Spring 2006

FRANCOISE MOULY AT THE 'NEW YORKER'

Editing *The New Yorker* is a little like being a controlled demolitions expert. In both jobs, you are entrusted with valuable, long-standing structures and explosive material, and given the responsibility of ensuring that targets are properly selected and that explosions leave no collateral damage. This characterization may raise the eyebrows of anyone who automatically dismisses the weekly magazine as a bastion of upper-middle-class triviality, the home of tepid and watery poetry, cartoons bafflingly dependent on Manhattan coterie knowledge, short stories that obsessively focus on the minutiae of domestic life and mildly left-of-centre political and cultural commentary. The tradition of mocking *The New Yorker* for being safe and bourgeois has a long intellectual pedigree. In a 1937 essay in the *Partisan Review*, Dwight Macdonald lamented that the typical *New Yorker* writer 'has given up the struggle to make sense out of a world which daily grows more complicated. His stock of data is strictly limited to the inconsequential.' A decade later, another *Partisan Review* stalwart, Robert Warshow, pushed Macdonald's argument a step further by arguing that *The New Yorker* at its best provides the intelligent and cultured undergraduate with the most comfortable and least compromising attitude he can assume toward capitalist society without being forced into actual conflict. It rejects the vulgarity and inhumanity of the public world of politics and business and provincial morality, and sets up in opposition to this a private and pseudo-aristocratic world of good humour, intelligence and good taste.

Macdonald and Warshow were bracingly forthright critics, but they were only half-right in their assessment of *The New Yorker*'s banality. It is more accurate to say that *The New Yorker*, from its earliest days, has had a divided soul, being a prime example of the 'bourgeois-bohemian' sensibility that Wyndham Lewis first dissected in his 1917 novel, *Tarr* (many decades before David Brooks resurrected and vulgarized the concept in his 2000 essay 'Bobos in Paradise'). To pigeonhole *The New Yorker* as a comfy cultural consumer item for moneyed liberals—tempting as it is—ignores the magazine's long history of publishing abrasive and subversive works of art and reportage amid more wishy-washy fare.

From the start, *The New Yorker* has livened up its natural blandness with bohemian spice. In finding a tone for his magazine, founding editor Harold Ross turned to a surprising source: the radical publication *The Masses*, an anti-capitalist outlet known for printing innovative cartooning and satire. From the ranks of *The Masses*, Ross acquired the services of such erstwhile rabble-rousers as Max Eastman, Otto Soglow and Howard Brubaker. As cultural historian Kenneth Lynn once noted, 'Rebels had served as the research and development wing of American society, and in the 1920s a middle-class culture co-opted, at least in part, its counter culture. *The New Yorker* had no use for the revolutionary rhetoric of *The Masses*, but adopted the earlier magazine's idea of natural-sounding, one-line captions for cartoons.'

Later, Ross and his successor, William Shawn, would turn to *Partisan Review*, the brain trust of American Marxism and modernism, as a reliable supply-house of writers who could keep *The New Yorker* faithful to its bohemian roots. From the pages of *Partisan Review*, Ross and Shawn recruited cultural critics like James Baldwin, Mary McCarthy, Harold Rosenberg, Hannah Arendt, Pauline Kael and even Dwight Macdonald. (Warshow, too, was asked to write for *The New Yorker*, but tragically died too young to make it into the pages of the magazine he once excoriated.) These essayists enlivened the magazine by bringing to its pages a prickly intelligence and a willingness to go far outside the comfort zone of Upper East Side cocktail parties. When Baldwin articulated the rage of the Black Muslims, or Arendt interrogated the banality of Adolf Eichmann's evil, they were bringing readers troubling and necessary news. By demolishing some of the ground that *The New Yorker*'s readers had been complacently standing on, these revolutionary destroyers helped to preserve an institution that might have otherwise lost all relevance.

The career of Françoise Mouly, who has served as art editor for *The New Yorker* since 1993, provides a latter-day example of the magazine's habit of hiring in-house radicals. Mouly first came to prominence as the founder and co-editor, with her husband, Art Spiegelman, of *Raw*, the key publication of the alternative comics revival of the 1980s. In eleven issues from 1980 to 1991, Mouly and Spiegelman brought to the insular and proudly philistine world of comics the stringent values of avant-garde art, including the idea that comics could be as fruitful a field for formalist experimentation as modern painting. Aside from serializing Spiegelman's groundbreaking graphic memoir *Maus*, *Raw* also showcased the early work of an array of talents that have continued to dominate comics, illustration and graphic design, including Charles Burns, Drew Friedman, Kaz, Ben Katchor and Chris Ware. Politically, the gritty, punk-inflected imagery that dominated *Raw* stood as a rebuke to the dominant Reagan-era aesthetic of complacent visual nostalgia.

Mouly and Spiegelman were hired at *The New Yorker* in 1993 by Tina Brown, then at the start of her brief, contentious reign at the magazine. Brown herself was, if not exactly a radical (she hailed from the high-glitz world of *Vanity Fair*, after all), at least a provocateur, and she arrived with a mandate to revitalize the literary institution after her immediate predecessor Robert Gottlieb had failed to shake off the interminable torpor produced by William Shawn's editorial dotage of the 1970s and 1980s. There were worse places to start than the cover. Characteristic of his perverse late-life preference for producing a sleep-inducing publication, Shawn once said that he wanted *New Yorker* covers to provide a 'restful change' from the more eye-grabbing images offered by other magazines. As John Updike once noted, the tumultuous year 1968—a time of assassinations, street protests, and international turmoil—was marked by *New Yorker* covers that showed a world at peace with itself, of blooming trees and sleeping dogs, of students studying in libraries and voters lining up in docile multitudes at the democracy's gigantic voting booth [....] It is almost as if, during these troubled and contentious '60s and '70s, *The New Yorker* protested, on its covers, by means of withdrawal.

The magazine's covers, as Shawn himself explained, 'tend to be more aesthetic and the subject matter for the most part is New York City or the country around New York City. The suburbs, the countryside. Sometimes it's just a still life of flowers or plants. It's not supposed to be spectacular.'

Tina Brown wanted 'spectacular'. Prior to taking over *The New Yorker*, Brown made her mark on *Vanity Fair* by publishing a controversial cover featuring Annie Leibowitz's photograph of the naked Demi Moore holding her ballooning pregnant belly. One of her first commissions from the Spiegelman/Mouly team was a cover about ethnic tensions in New York, resulting in a much-argued-over 1993 Spiegelman illustration of a

Hasidic man kissing a black woman that managed to earn cries of consternation from both Jewish- and African-Americans. The Shawn era of decorative doldrums and 'restful change' was over, with the trees, flowers, dogs and voting booths going (mostly) into mothballs.

Mouly's new collection, *Blown Covers: New Yorker Covers You Were Never Meant to See*, documents the Brown era and beyond, and shows how she gave the public face of *The New Yorker* a makeover, turning out covers that are much livelier and more timely while also skirting the edge of good taste, and occasionally getting reined in by the magazine's governing code of propriety. What does a cultural agitator do when she's put in charge of the covers of a venerable publication, one that, in recent decades, has had a tropism towards stuffiness? One predictable innovation was recruiting a cohort of artists from *Raw*, including Burns, Richard McGuire, Robert Crumb and Jacques de Loustal. Eventually, Mouly also brought on a wider array of cartoonists from outside the *Raw* orbit, like Daniel Clowes, Adrian Tomine and Seth. These artists brought the inventiveness and élan of contemporary narrative cartooning to *The New Yorker*.

Thematically, Mouly made changes, too, commissioning covers that were much more topical. In 1998, during the height of the Monica Lewinsky scandal, a Spiegelman cover showed Clinton addressing a press conference where all the phallic microphones are pointed at his crotch. Immediately after September 11, another Spiegelman cover featured the black twin towers against an almost equally dark background, bringing together the shocked mourning produced by the event with an Ad Reinhardt–inspired modernist purity. In 2004, the Canadian artist Anita Kunz painted a cover showing oil wells spurting blood, giving new life to the anti-war cry 'no blood for oil'. In October 2004, on the eve of Bush's re-election, Mouly herself painted a cover showing the shadow of a tortured hooded prisoner of Abu Ghraib cutting across the American flag. Perhaps most controversial of all was Barry Blitt's brilliant July 21, 2008, cover, which illustrated 'the politics of fear' by bringing together all the racial anxieties that surrounded Barack Obama's campaign: a White House scene with Barack (dressed in Muslim garb) fist bumping Michelle (dressed as an urban guerrilla), with a photo of Osama bin Laden hanging over the fireplace. (Blitt, incidentally, emerges in *Blown Covers* as one of the stars of the Mouly-era *New Yorker*, a cartoonist possessed of a mind fertile in ideas and a sporty, jaunty line.)

Aside from such notorious and much-disputed covers, Mouly's book also shows us all the ideas that didn't get past the drawing board, the clever notions that were aborted when they turned out to be too outlandish or questionable in taste. Thus we get scenes of the Pope showing his undergarments in the manner of Marilyn Monroe standing above a blowing grate (Blitt again), Bush and Cheney lying beside each other in post-coital satisfaction and Uncle Sam shooting up oil in his arm like a junkie (both Spiegelman). These failed covers give us some idea of the subtle demarcations of taste that govern *The New Yorker*: Bush and Cheney in Brokeback Mountain poses are kosher, but actually naked in bed is too much. Gay couples who are well-scrubbed and upscale are fine, but Robert Crumb's grotty and stubbly version of gender bending was spiked. To put it another way, the magazine is gay-friendly but wary of queer culture, regardless of its sexual orientation.

Successful satire requires a form of double consciousness, with the artist being able to view the world as both an insider and an outsider, and one source of double consciousness can be the experience of immigration. It's notable that many of the key figures in *Blown Covers* are not native to the United States. Mouly was born in France, Spiegelman in Sweden, Brown in England, Steinberg in Romania, Kunz and Blitt in Canada.

Perhaps because of her immigrant status, Mouly has done much to open up the pages of *The New Yorker*—or the front cover, anyway—to difference. Her attention to race has been especially important for a magazine which, as Updike once observed, was so 'super-sensitive and race blind' in the '60s and '70s that the diversity of American urban life often showed up only in the coded form of Saul Steinberg's covers featuring jivey Mickey Mouse knockoffs. Especially towards the end of his run as editor, Shawn seemed to think that the best way to deal with racism was to avoid any mention of cultural difference whatsoever. To their credit, Brown and Mouly have made *The New Yorker* much more willing to portray ethnic diversity and confront racism (a policy that continues under Brown's successor, David Remnick).

But Mouly has not entirely abandoned the habit of addressing race through iconic appropriation. The late Steinberg, perhaps the greatest of all *New Yorker* artists, served as a mentor to Mouly when she was getting her sea legs as an editor.

Steinberg once praised a Spiegelman cover dealing with the 1999 police shooting of Amadou Diallo for being 'a picture of a picture'. (The cop in this cover looked like one of the good-natured but dimwitted junior officers in Chester Gould's *Dick Tracy*, while his targets were citizens in a carnival shooting gallery.)

The phrase 'a picture of a picture' could easily describe both Steinberg's aesthetic and Mouly's: these covers don't just deploy standard cartoon languages, they frequently play with iconic forms, finding new layers of meaning in such familiar avatars as Santa Claus, the Easter Bunny and Father Time. The trick behind a successful cover is not just to make fun of such tried-and-true icons but also to tap into their hidden symbolic meaning. To draw a crucified Easter Bunny, as Spiegelman once did, isn't just sacrilege for the sake of sacrilege, but a reminder of how bland holiday imagery glides over the sometimes brutal roots of religious celebrations.

It's easy enough to enjoy *Blown Covers* as a coffee-table entertainment. The covers, both the ones that made the grade and the almost-rans, are by turns witty, shocking, wry, and melancholy, as well as visually snappy and debonair. But the deeper value of *Blown Covers* is the insight it gives us into Mouly's editing process. Editing is a very difficult art to write about, being by its very nature invisible, and based on thousands of tacit, unstated backstage decisions. *Blown Covers* shows that every idea that makes the page requires an editorial environment where new concepts are constantly being generated. Since the rejection rate is high, this can be frustrating for artists, but Mouly gets around this problem in part by allowing her artists to go all out during the brainstorming sessions, so that even if the idea doesn't make the cover there is still the pleasure of daring to think of something new and fresh. The failed ideas are the necessary fertilizers of successful covers. *Blown Covers* is an essential book for anyone who wants to understand the art and politics of magazine art editing.

One possible objection to the book is the narrow focus on controversial covers, which gives this volume a tidy thematic unity but obscures the full range of covers Mouly has edited. I'd like to see a companion volume that gives us the best covers of the Mouly era, whether they sparked anger or not. (The 2000 volume *Covering the New Yorker* offers a good sample, but deserves updating.) Tina Brown remains the master of the outrageous cover, as witness the recent issue of *Newsweek* anointing Obama the first gay president. Mouly has a similar, but slightly different skill: she likes to provoke thought as well as outrage.

Curiously and unexpectedly, the most recurring emotion in the covers of the Mouly era is jitteriness, which is true even of the pre-9/11 covers. Animating these covers is a kind of civic anxiousness, a concern about the fate of the American experiment in self-governance. Yet Mouly rightly distinguishes between *New Yorker* covers and traditional political cartoons. The aim of political cartooning is often turned outward at an external foe, who is tamed by being caricatured. The covers Mouly chooses, by contrast, are inward-looking attempts to give shape and form to hitherto unstated fears: to make them not smaller but larger in our psyches.

The New Yorker, Warshow argued in 1947, was built on 'a delicate balance of insecurity and security' and could 'exploit its nervous distaste for modern society only so long as the distaste does not grow into fear.' What makes Mouly a great editor is that she has an unerring instinct for confronting—and confronting us with—the sources of her unease. As a result of her confidence, the covers of *The New Yorker* are often the most honest pages in the magazine. The visual explosives she's detonated have a real impact, wiping out the ground beneath our feet.

Los Angeles Review of Books, August 2, 2012

BEN KATCHOR'S URBAN POETRY

Ben Katchor deserves to become an adjective. His work is Katchorian and nothing else. Critics earn their bread by finding apt comparisons, but finding useful analogies for Katchor's work is an elusive task. The cartoonist is a bizarre melange of competing tendencies: his deft weaving of half-believable fantasies suggests Jorge Luis Borges, his street-level alertness to urban life recalls Jane Jacobs, his verbal dexterity at describing sensual experiences echoes Vladimir Nabokov and his political concern over branding and globalization evokes Naomi Klein.

But perhaps the most apt conclusion is that Katchor illustrates William Hazlitt's observation that it 'is easy to describe second-rate talents, because they fall into a class and enlist under a standard; but first-rate powers defy calculation or comparison, and can be defined only by themselves. They are *sui generis*, and make the class to which they belong.'

Brooklyn born, Katchor is an anomaly, a New Yorker who constantly experiences the city with the hyper-alert eyes of a visitor. For more than four decades now, he has crafted his own special genre of comic strips dealing with the history and architecture of an imaginary New York, created with the goal of helping us appreciate the real city whose sheer physical and informational density defies human comprehension.

Katchor is blessed and cursed with an inability to shut himself off from the sensory assault of his native city. This marks him off from many of his fellow New Yorkers, who have learned that living in one of the world's great capitals of sensory overkill requires the ability to tune out the ceaseless chorus of background noise and millions of jostling and sometimes abrasive fellow citizens. Katchor belongs to the line of modernist artists whose intense sensitivity to sensory experience was an outgrowth of their experience in bustling big cities. Just as Joyce had his Dublin, Proust his Paris, and Nabokov his St Petersburg, Katchor has his New York.

This urban focus also aligns him with the great tradition of cartooning about city life that runs from Honoré Daumier to Winsor McCay to

Steve Ditko to Chris Ware. Modern sequential cartooning came of age with the rise of the industrial city, with comics being a perfect art for deft-handed flaneurs to record street life. Rectangular panels, the very building block of the comics page, call to mind the more literal blocks that make up skyscrapers. When we peer into the panels of a comics page, the experience is not dissimilar to peeping in on neighbours in an adjoining apartment building.

Hand-Drying in America, Katchor's latest collection of cartoons, brings together more than one hundred and fifty of his recent stories dealing with the minutiae of urban life.

A story called 'The Office Building Demystified' offers a clear example of Katchor's method and concern. It opens with a woman complaining about the facelessness of the modern office building, where 'there's no way of knowing what goes on inside.'

This lamentation sets up the cue for one of Katchor's patented explainer characters—here, as elsewhere, a dumpy, stooped, middle-aged man—to offer the lowdown on what we're missing: 'Within six months of occupancy, however anonymous the building's facade, the business affairs of each tenant begin to leave their mark—it's just a matter of knowing what to look for.' In a succession of panels that offer a skewed street-side view of the city, we're given examples: 'Here you can see a palpable greasy sheen of the lower floors of this building which houses the corporate headquarters of the Palsy Group: A national distributor of processed sandwich meats.... The cracked concrete surface of an uninviting public plaza announces the presence of a failing software firm.'

On a literal level, this urban exegesis is absurd, but as a series of playful theories it functions like one of Rudyard Kipling's Just So stories, taking something real and forcing us to look at it more closely by giving it a fanciful history. Katchor loves to zoom in on the everyday objects that we easily ignore: washroom hand dryers, the riot-gates that protect downtown stores, the folding chairs in a bingo hall.

Katchor is the poet of the mundane, the bard of the grubby, the lyricist of the half-seen world. As befits his focus on the ignored, his art rejects the goal of illustrational realism and instead is deliberately asymmetrical, often showing his people and places from unusual angles, as if the viewer were perched like a bird or had the upward glance of a small child. Because his great subject is perception and misperception, what we see and what we miss, Katchor has fashioned a foggy style that forces us to constantly decipher his images, which exist in ironic tension with his text.

Critics have often mistakenly labelled Katchor a nostalgist who conjures up a half-remembered New York. In fact, he is a satirical fantasist who is imagining an alternative New York in order to sharpen our awareness of the actual city. Or, more simply, he's a supremely Katchorian artist.

The Globe and Mail, March 9, 2013

CHRIS WARE'S 'BUILDING STORIES'

All of us are boxed in. This sentence can be taken as a figurative description of the way life traps us in social roles that are difficult to escape but it also happens to be literally true. We are born in boxes, live in boxes and die in boxes: hospitals, incubators, apartment buildings, houses, schools, offices, elevators, cubicles, prisons, shopping malls, big box stores, nursing homes, caskets, urns. Western architecture has never strayed far from its roots in Euclidean geometry, so the drama of our existence is played out on boxy stages defined by straight lines, right angles, squares, cubes, rectangles and other sharp-edged forms.

Architecture is not usually thought of as a narrative art form. But buildings exist in time as well as space. They are constructed at a particular moment, they weather a sometimes hostile environment, they age and need repair, and unless they are looked after they become ramshackle and ultimately fall apart or are demolished.

One way of defining the genius of Chris Ware is to say that he fuses the disparate forms of comics and architecture, using his nonparallel skills of visual storytelling to show how the buildings we construct are not just empty containers but influence us as much as we shape them.

This marriage of comics and architecture might sound surprising but it has a long history, which Ware, deeply knowledgeable about the past, knows well. The modern skyscraper emerged at the same time as modern narrative cartooning in the middle of the 19th century, although both forms had prehistories that extend further into the past. The classic Sunday-newspaper comic strip, with many panels on the page laid out on a grid has obvious parallels with tall many-windowed office buildings, a fact that pioneering cartoonists like Winsor McCay played with when they drew stories that used the New York skyline not just as a backdrop but as a virtual character. The drawing board of a cartoonist is not unlike the drafting table of an architect. And in both drawing comics and imagining homes, you work with grids, rectangles and cubes and need to have mastered perspective.

When I visited Ware in Chicago a few years ago to work with him on the *Walt and Skeezix* series reprinting the comic strip *Gasoline Alley*, I was struck by the depth of his architectural knowledge. Part of our research took us to the home of the long-dead cartoonist Frank King. Working from old photographs and his sharp visual memory, Ware was able to quickly notice all the changes that had been made to the house over the decades. Ware and our mutual friend Tim Samuelson, a leading expert on the architect Louis Sullivan, gave me a tour of Chicago, an astonishing experience because they seemed to have ready access, faster and more reliable than an Internet search engine, to salient information about virtually every significant building in the city.

Ware is a kind of non-religious animist. For him animals and physical objects, no less than people, have histories and biographies, and deserve the loving, reviving, liturgical attention that only art can provide. Ware's new graphic novel *Building Stories* is an attempt to extend the range of sympathy in narrative fiction to include not just human subjects but also the animals and objects that we interact with.

When we first approach it, *Building Stories* is not a book but a box. Long, rectangular, cardboard and covered on the front with colourful iconic images, *Building Stories* could easily be mistaken for a Monopoly set or some other kind of board game. Supporting the board game analogy is the fact that on the back of the box there are instructions that purport to tell you 'everything you need to know to read the new graphic novel *Building Stories*' and detailing the contents we can expect to find inside: '14 distinctly discrete Books, Booklets, Magazines, Newspapers, and Pamphlets.'

Taken together, these fourteen printed objects make up a non-linear graphic novel but they vary greatly in size, shape and content. The smallest items are pamphlets and paper strips no larger than the instruction manuals that often come with ready-to-assemble furniture or new electronic devises. The largest are broadsheets that, like *The Globe and Mail* you have to fold open to read, focusing on one part of the page at a time.

Ware has broken up his story into fourteen smaller books in part to reinforce one of the major narrative themes of *Building Stories*, the fragmented nature of modern urban life. But the separate booklets are also, each of them, beautiful objects of their own with the narrative specifically tailored to the physical form that they are encompassed in. For example, the smallest pamphlet deals, delicately and movingly, with the small daily interactions between a mom and her daughter. One of the largest broadsheets deals with death, which is both big news and physically hard to handle.

The printed book, we're constantly told, is becoming obsolete in the face of online competition. Perhaps so, but Ware is a partisan of tangibility, the tactile world of objects that you can touch, including books and buildings. Although a small snippet of *Building Stories* originally appeared online, the total object that Ware has now created could only exist in our three-dimensional world. In telling his stories through beautiful printed objects, Ware is making a strong case for the continued centrality of the book as a form even in an age of easy access to digital 'content'. Form and content in Ware's work are never severed but always imaginatively working together, like two partners in a stunning dance number.

But to praise Ware simply for his art or formal inventiveness is to give short shrift to the power of his storytelling. There are several characters in *Building Stories*, one is a century-old Chicago apartment wistfully remembering better days, another is the aged landlady who owns the structure as well as a bee who gets temporarily trapped in a windowsill. But the central character of the graphic novel is an unnamed young woman who lives in the top floor of the building.

Through the course of most of the fourteen books, the shape and texture of this woman's life is depicted with such precision and such candidness that she becomes one of the great characters of contemporary fiction, as fully human and believable as an Alice Munro heroine.

John Updike once defined his ambition to give 'the mundane its beautiful due'. That's what Ware achieves in his biography of his nameless heroine. We learn about the childhood accident that left her with one leg, her first love, an unwanted pregnancy, her loneliness, her marriage, her joy in motherhood, her discouragement at having to sacrifice her artistic ambitions, her pain at the death of loved ones.

Historically comics have been among the most misogynist of all art forms, but with *Building Stories* Ware becomes one of the handful of male cartoonists who has created an authentically convincing female character (an achievement that is also fairly rare in male-written prose fiction). She might be boxed in by life and cornered in buildings that don't offer her much room for expression, but she remains resilient, observant and sharp-witted. To meet her, and to see the environment that formed her, is the chief pleasure of *Building Stories*.

The Globe and Mail, October 5, 2012

SETH'S IMAGINARY LIBRARIES

Spend half an hour wandering through the stacks of a decent-sized library and you'll quickly be overwhelmed by the crushing weight of the literary past. More books exist than even the hardiest reader could digest in a hundred lifetimes. Some are slim pamphlets, others hefty tomes, but when crammed together on the shelves they present a daunting challenge. 'Of the making of books there is no end,' a biblical proverb assures us. And if that was true in ancient times, how much heavier is the burden of textual matter in the age of print-on-demand?

Yet even as books proliferate with unabated abandon, there is a persistent tendency to want more, to be unsatisfied with what we already have and to want to recover what is irrevocably lost or fantasize about what could be. The impulse to dream up imaginary libraries is a strong one, recurringly shared by many writers in the overlapping traditions of satire and fantasy.

Towards the end of the Middle Ages anonymously-authored parodic liturgies and mock-Gospels started to pop up, filled with pointed jests aimed at clerical folly. These were the precursors to an episode in Rabelais's 16th-century masterpiece *Gargantua and Pantagruel*, where a giant wastes his time reading such nonce-books as *On the Art of Discreetly Farting in Company*, by Magister Noster Ortuinus, and Tartaretus: *On How to Defecate.*

In his 2006 study *The Library at Night*, Alberto Manguel argues that Rabelais's lengthy catalogue of make-believe tomes constitutes 'perhaps the first "imaginary library" in literature'. It shouldn't surprise us that Rabelais's bookish satire on scholastic nonsense appeared in the dewy dawn of the early-modern period, when ancient masterpieces were being rediscovered and fresh volumes mushroomed as never before in order to keep newly built printing presses busy. The Gutenberg era was in full swing and Rabelais was registering the appalling fallout.

Post-Rabelais, countless other satirists—Dryden, Swift and Pope spring to mind—took up the job of writing fiction-within-fiction, filling their books with fabricated poets and battling books, complete with pseudo-scholarly footnotes. Perhaps the culmination of this tradition is Borges's *The Library of Babel*, which can be read as a lucid nightmare where the world becomes a vast and stifling storehouse for books maintained by a decadent culture that has forgotten how to really read.

As against the sly jocularity of Rabelaisian satire, imaginary books fulfill a more wistful and fanciful role in fantastic literature. In trying to make the flesh of his readers itch and twitch, H.P. Lovecraft occasionally refrained from describing his tentacled monsters and simply gave the titles of the ghastly grimoires used to summon the Old Ones, most famously the Necronomicon. Lovecraft endowed his fictional Miskatonic University with a rich library of lurid volumes, possibly the inspiration for the library at Hogwarts in the *Harry Potter* series and many other concocted book collections.

The books and stories that only have a wraith-like half-life within another work of fiction can leave a surprisingly permanent stain on the memory. In otherwise mediocre Sherlock Holmes story, the great detective makes an aside about 'the giant rat of Sumatra, a story for which the world is not yet prepared'. This tossed-off remark is my favourite passage in the Holmesian canon. What on earth is the giant rat of Sumatra? Why is the world not ready to hear about it yet? When will we be prepared to hear about it? Arthur Conan Doyle was wise enough to refrain from answering these queries since the suggestive power of his few words is much more electrifying than any fully drawn out story could be. Alas, several pastichists have lacked Conan Doyle's wisdom and have tried, with a predictable lack of success, to delineate the rat's tale.

Hints and fragments, the great modernists have taught us, can leave a much stronger impression than a story where both detail and themes are explicitly laid out. Lord knows Conan Doyle was no modernist but with the happy accident of 'the giant rat of Sumatra' he hit upon the aesthetics of fragmentation and the partial glimpse, the scattered fossils that we can use to reconstruct the dinosaur, the shards of pottery that evoke an ancient civilization. Derek Walcott keenly described the aesthetics of fragmentation in these words: 'Break a vase, and the love that reassembles the fragments is stronger than that love which took its symmetry for granted when it was whole.' Much of modern art takes its passion from the idea that the world is a shattered vase which is impossible to repair except through an act of the imagination.

Making up non-existent books is a metaphor for creativity itself. Every earnest writer starts with the assumption that the world's libraries, no matter how overstuffed, are still insufficient, that there is a lacuna that needs to be filled by more books. What other honest motive is there for writing?

Imaginary comic books and libraries are a recurring feature of the recent stories of the cartoonist Seth, who turns out to be heir to the dual traditions of satire and fantasy that have made fictional books a central motif. Readers of *Canadian Notes & Queries* will of course remember that Seth gave us a tour of 'the crumbling, but once grand headquarters' of this magazine which supposedly exist 'in the trackless wastes beyond Emeryville' (*CNQ* 79). In the north wing of the CNQ building smoulders the burnt-out husk of the once grand archive. All that survives are a few scattered pages from 'the remains of section 741.5—cartoons, comics and graphic novels. Scores of graphic novels, each, an original Can-Lit adaptation. Each, the only copy in existence.' From this invaluable collection, all that could be rescued are 'some short passages … a few scenes' (*CNQ* 80). The north wing is thus a library of scraps and fragments.

The tragic tale of the north wing serves of course as the pretext for the 2-page comic adaptations of CanLit classics that run in every issue of *CNQ*. But the story also illustrates Seth's grounding in the aesthetics of fragmentation. A full-length graphic novel adaptation of Marian Engel's *Bear* could easily be plodding and wearisome. But if you have cartoonist Joe Ollmann illustrate a 2-page snippet from Engel's novel, which purports to be the sole surviving scrap of a larger work, then the reader is given a seedling that can germinate in the mind.

Seth's 2005 graphic novella, *Wimbldeon Green*, started off as a series of sketchbook spoofs on the often nutty world of comic book collecting but acquired an extra layer of parodic energy and historical resonance by the many made-up comic books that litter the story. Many of these comics seem simply absurd, for example Fatsy #7 (the 'infamous flatulence issue—most copies destroyed' and valued at $3,000 mint). Yet as these fancied comic books accumulate Seth is able to evoke the misty-eyed passion that collectors have for their oddball objects of desire. One of the highlights of the book is an extended reverie on 'Fine & Dandy'—an imaginary comic book series devoted to the hijinks of a pair of Laurel and Hardy–style hoboes. *Wimbledon Green*'s fervent advocacy of 'Fine &

Dandy' makes you want to read their adventures, transforming you into a participant in his collecting mania.

Seth's latest graphic novella, *The Great Northern Brotherhood of Canadian Cartoonists* (or *The G.N.B. Double C*), is in many ways a companion volume to *Wimbledon Green* and like the earlier book can be read as a pseudo-bibliographical enterprise, a catalogue of largely non-existent creations. The book's confessedly unreliable narrator offers a guided tour of the history of Canada's cartooning past, a survey of history that cunningly mixes fact and free-floating fancy. In Seth's crazy-quilt mixture of actuality and fantasy, actual cartoonists like Doug Wright and Chester Brown jostle against Yvette Mailloux (creator of a long-running anticlerical comic strip allegedly popular in Quebec) and Sam Middlesex (whose multi-volume, multi-generational graphic novel *roman fleuve* seems like an alternative-universe version of Hugh Hood's *The New Age/Le nouveau siècle*).

Perhaps the highlight of *The G.N.B. Double C* is the account of The Great Northern Archive, where the treasures of our national cartooning heritage are kept. Shaped like a cluster of igloos and built in the wake of the centennial patriotism of 1967, the Great Northern Archive is in an impossibly remote location. To get to it you have to take a train far north 'past towns with names nobody's heard of'. Then you go on a steamship, which takes you to the misnamed village of Green Valley, where a rickety school bus carries you to the archive during the summer. In the winter you have to rely on a dog sled. 'Needless to say, no one visits in wintertime,' we're told. 'During those months the librarian and her assistants are virtually prisoners of the north.'

The remoteness of this imaginary archive is a neat metaphor for the difficulty of acquiring historical knowledge, for the hard-won journey that is necessary if you want to gather up the fragmentary leavings of an earlier time. In the age of Ebay, AbeBooks, and YouTube, we may think that the whole historical past is only a few clicks away. But in point of fact, actually possessing information about the past will always take time and effort. If the past is a foreign country, it's one that requires an arduous journey to visit.

In real life, Seth is a collector, archivist and historian. The history of cartooning is largely uncultivated soil and to learn the lore of his craft Seth had to spend countless hours scouring through used bookstores and other dingy havens of antiquarian artefacts. The fruits of his excursions into the pop culture past are evident in the archival reprint projects he's worked on (*The Complete Peanuts, Doug Wright's Family* and the John Stanley Library) as well as his essays championing various half-forgotten cartoonists. The creation of the Doug Wright Award is another prong in Seth's engagement with comics history. Taken together, these activities have had a profound impact on how those of us who care about comics understand the evolution of the form.

But if the genuine flesh-and-blood Seth is constantly researching the history of comics, he has an imaginative alter ego who flares up in the pages of *Wimbledon Green* and *The G.N.B. Double C* (quite literally so: both books have characters who are carbon copies of the cartoonist). This Seth-doppelgänger is less interested in what happened in the past than what could have happened. The alternative-Seth is all about the pleasures of supposition, the joy of conjecture and the giddy delights of hypothesis. Just as the real Seth fills his library with actual books and comics, the shadow-Seth dreams of all the books and comics that never were but should have been.

Taken together, the real Seth and his shadow self have given us a rich addition to the literature of imaginary libraries, works that offer a distinctive combination of the snark of satire with the pensiveness of fantasy.

Canadian Notes & Queries, Winter 2012

ACKNOWLEDGEMENTS

Thanks first and foremost to the Porcupine's Quill. It's an honour to be published by one of my favourite presses, one that has published many fine writers. I'd especially like to thank my editor Carmine Starnino, who first conceived the idea for this collection and has been invaluable in helping assemble it, and Chandra Wohleber, who has done a superb job bringing order to an unruly manuscript.

I'm grateful to the publications where these pieces first appeared, not just for commissioning them but also for their careful editing: *The American Prospect,* the *National Post*, the *Globe and Mail, The Comics Journal, Canadian Notes & Queries, The Walrus, Toro,* the *Boston Globe, Toronto Life,* the *New Republic,* the *Virginia Quarterly Review,* and the *Los Angeles Review of Books.* Among the many editors I've worked with, I'm particularly grateful to Alex Star, Jennifer Schuessler, Sarah Kerr, Heidi Sopinka, Ted Genoways, Mark Pupo, Ryan Kearney, Jared Bland, Alex Good, Mark Medley and Evan Kindley.

The essay on Robert Heinlein had been considerably expanded from its first publication in the *New Republic.* Many of the other pieces have been more gently revised.

ABOUT THE AUTHOR

Jeet Heer is a cultural journalist and academic whose work has appeared in such publications as the *National Post, Slate.com,* the *Boston Globe, The Walrus* and *The Guardian*. He has co-edited eight books and been a contributing editor to another eight volumes; among them *A Comics Studies Reader*. With Chris Ware, he continues to edit the *Walt and Skeezix* series from *Drawn and Quarterly*. Heer is the recipient of a Fulbright Scholarship. He divides his time between Toronto and Regina.

ABOUT THE TYPE

The calligraphy on the cover of *Sweet Lechery* was drawn by noted Canadian cartoonist Seth, who also contributed the display type for the titling, the initials and the dingbats.

The text face is Junius, named for Franciscus Junius, a pioneer of Germanic philology who was born at Heidelberg in 1591. The letterforms were digitized in the early 1990s from the Pica Saxon used to print Georges Hickes' *Thesaurus* (Oxford: Sheldonian Theatre, 1703–1705). Junius is primarily designed for use by medievalists, and is readily available for download from the English Department at the University of Virginia. In this case we were attracted by the somewhat rough-hewn character of the letters as a complement to Seth's calligraphy.